CHILDREN OF WRATH:
POSSESSION, PROPHECY AND THE YOUNG
IN EARLY MODERN ENGLAND

For Dan

Children of Wrath:
Possession, Prophecy and the Young in Early Modern England

ANNA FRENCH
University of Liverpool, UK

ASHGATE

Published by
Ashgate Publishing Limited
Wey Court East
Union Road
Farnham
Surrey, GU9 7PT
England

Ashgate Publishing Company
110 Cherry Street
Suite 3-1
Burlington, VT 05401-3818
USA

www.ashgate.com

British Library Cataloguing in Publication Data
A catalogue record for this book is available from the British Library

The Library of Congress has cataloged the printed edition as follows:
French, Anna.
  Children of wrath : possession, prophecy and the young in early modern England / by Anna French.
    pages cm
  Includes bibliographical references and index.
  ISBN 978-1-4724-4367-0 (hardcover)—ISBN 978-1-4724-4368-7 (ebook)—ISBN 978-1-4724-4369-4 (ePub) 1. Christianity—Social aspects—England—History—16th century. 2. Children—Religious aspects—Christianity—History—16th century. 3. Children—England—Social conditions—16th century. 4. Dualism—Social aspects—England—History—16th century. 5. Demoniac possession—England—History—16th century. 6. Prophecy—Social aspects—England—History—16th century. 7. Prophecy—Christianity—History—16th century. 8. England—Religious life and customs. 9. England—Social conditions—16th century. I. Title.
  BR750.F73 2015
  305.230942'09031—dc23

2015017495

ISBN: 9781472443670 (hbk)
ISBN: 9781472443687 (ebk – PDF)
ISBN: 9781472443694 (ebk – ePUB)

Printed in the United Kingdom by Henry Ling Limited, at the Dorset Press, Dorchester, DT1 1HD

Contents

Acknowledgements

During a research seminar some years ago, it struck me somewhat suddenly that little had been written on the experience of early modern childhood. Borrowing for a moment from the early modern gardening metaphors that were used to describe the lives of early modern children, this seed of an idea grew over time and its fruition is this monograph. As with any significant piece of work, this book has been the result of a fair few years of research, and many people have helped and supported me along the way.

Children of Wrath began life as a doctoral project in the History Department at the University of Birmingham. The community of staff and postgraduates at Birmingham, both during my time as a postgraduate and now as an Honorary Fellow, have provided much support and inspiration, for which I am hugely grateful, and without which this work would not have been possible. Particular thanks go to members of that community, both past and present: Louise Campbell, Richard Cust, Matthew Edwards, Elaine Fulton, Sylvia Gill, Vicky Henshaw, Nick Lloyd, Becky Pickin, Jonathan Willis, Katie Wright and Neil Younger. Finally, Christopher Wickham has, in the years after we first met during my postgraduate studies at Birmingham, continued to provide enduring encouragement and support. I must strongly acknowledge, too, the generous support of the Arts and Humanities Research Council, who funded this project from the beginning; and also the wider early modern community, most especially members of the European Reformation Research Group, particularly Hannah Cleugh, Peter Marshall and Laura Sangha, whose collective conversation and supportive spirit have encouraged so many postgraduate and early career researchers.

This book was brought to completion during my time at the University of Gloucestershire, where I benefited from the encouragement of colleagues and friends. Most especially I would like to thank Rebecca Bailey, Charlotte Beyer, Melanie Ilic, Roy Jackson, Andrew Lincoln, Gordon McConville, Nigel McLoughlin, Rachel Reid, Arran Stibbe, Linda Wilson and David Webster. Without the support and friendship of these people, the completion of this book, and other projects, would have been so much more difficult. Thanks also go to the students I have taught at Gloucestershire, for their innovative ideas, creative thinking and enthusiasm for the early modern world. I would like to thank Tom Gray and Sadie Copley-May at Ashgate for bringing this book to completion, as well as Katharine Bartlett for proofreading the final text, and John Pollack and Tom Hensle at the Kislak Center for Special Collections, Rare Books and Manuscripts, University of Pennsylvania, for providing a perfectly fitting cover image for the book.

A few final and heartfelt thanks go to other individuals. Friends and family I would like to thank include Elizabeth and Paul Billinger, Joe French, Margaret and Trevor Hartland, Lucie Pannell and Lloyd Pietersen. Alec Ryrie, who first sparked my interest in early modern history as my tutor and PhD supervisor, has also continued not only to support me but provide unceasing assistance and advice, having faith in me even when my own waned at times. Thanks, too, go to my parents, Valerie and Paul French, for supporting me to go to university and to undertake my PhD, and especially to my Mom for reading so many drafts of my work, and for making me so many meals (and cakes) when I was writing. Finally, huge thanks must go to my partner Dan Hartland, for enduring support, proofreading endless drafts, for making many cups of tea and pieces of toast, and for having confidence both in me and in what I could achieve.

Chapter 1

Children of Wrath: An Introduction

Early modern children were not strangers to the diabolic. According to a pamphlet originally published in 1573, the young Alexander Nyndge once described to concerned onlookers how the Devil had appeared to him. He looked, said Edward Nyndge, the boy's brother and author of the pamphlet documenting the case, like 'the figure of a great red or fiery Dragon'; he and his legions were the 'Infernall Angels'; he was the 'Prince of Darknes' and an 'old Serpent', a mortal enemy 'which keepeth his Castle'.[1] According to the tract, the young Alexander engaged in conversation with this fiend, during which he became the mouthpiece of the spirit, thus speaking in a 'base sounding and hollow voice', whilst announcing that the invading demon had come for his soul.[2] In another similar case, Rachell Pynder, who later confessed to having feigned her demonic possession, was asked what Satan had looked like when he appeared to her. She answered that he resembled a 'man with a gray bearde, sometime lyke five Cattes, sometimes to Ravens and Crowes'.[3] Yet another child, Thomas Darling, also provided colourful descriptions of his encounters with the enemy, who in turn appeared to Darling in the form of 'greene Angels in the window' and as a green cat with eyes of fire.[4]

Such descriptions of the Devil were far from unusual in the sixteenth and seventeenth centuries, but what is interesting about these testimonies is that, according to the publications which contained them, and, one would presume, as far as their readers were concerned, these detailed descriptions were coming from the mouths of child witnesses. Their experience was not limited to the Devil's wiles, however. Children could also, although in English culture admittedly less commonly, bear witness to godly appearances, or at least godly messages. These episodes, too, were reported in print. One tale printed in 1614,

---

[1] Edward Nyndge, *A true and fearefvll vexation of one Alexander Nyndge being most horribly tormented with the deuill* (London, 1615) *STC* (2nd ed.) 18753, sigs. AIIr and AIIIv.

[2] Nyndge, *A true and fearefvll vexation*, sig. AIVr.

[3] John Chrysostom, *The disclosing of a late counterfeited possession by the deuyl in two maydens* (London, 1574) *STC* (2nd ed.) 3738, sig. BIIr.

[4] I.D., *The most wonderfull and true storie, of a certain witch named Alse Gooderige* (London, 1597) *STC* (2nd ed.) 6170.7, sig. A3r.

for instance, tells of how a 14-year-old girl returned from the dead, to describe visions of angels 'shining like the beames of the sun', and an old, grey-bearded man who guided her.[5]

The children of the early modern period have been long regarded as the socially silent. This youthful social demographic was a group which made up the majority of people living in early modern Europe (this despite the high infant and child death rate); perhaps unsurprisingly, then, it was a group which attracted a large amount of attention, both from those whose reforming zeal saw children as the future of Reformed Christendom, and those who saw them as a threat to good social order. Children did not, generally, write down their thoughts (and if they did, they did so usually as adult diary writers looking back on their early years). They did not generally have the authority to shape the worlds around them – they were the taught, the moulded, the disciplined and the silenced. Indeed, as we will consider in this introductory chapter, historians of the early modern period more widely, and early modern childhood more specifically, have tended in turn to accept this belief in the voiceless and often highly indecipherable nature of childhood during this period. These little people slip through our fingers in texts, pamphlets, religious treatises and plays; they are out of reach, nearly impossible for us to grasp. When children were written about in these forms of literature, it was from the perspective of adults and it is therefore extremely difficult for us to access or understand the 'real' experience of childhood – if, indeed, early modern perceptions of childhood allow us to use this word usefully at all.

As with all silences in history, however, a relative absence does not mean that children were not significant within early modern culture, that they were not thought about, or that they did not occupy the minds or imaginations of the communities within which they lived. It is by examining these reflections of the child in the glass of what source material does survive that we can begin to intuit the shapes of this significance. This book, then, is very much one about the early modern imagination, and the cultural spaces given to beliefs about and perceptions of early modern children. These cultural spaces might seem lurid or unusual; they might, as in the case of Nyndge, Pynder or Darling, involve experiences which post-modern readers of the sources find improbable, if not entirely impossible; yet the imaginings of early modern society can tell us a great deal about the children they encompassed. Indeed, as its title suggests, this book

---

[5]   T.I., *A miracle, of miracles* (London, 1614) *STC* (2nd ed.) 14068, sig. C2r; further accounts of this case were published in Eyriak Schlichtenberger, *A prophecie vttered by the daughter of an honest countrey man* (London, 1580) *STC* (2nd ed.) 21818 and Anon, *The wonderfull works of God* (London, 1641) *Wing* (2nd ed.) W3377.

will explore the role of children both in cases of demonic possession and godly prophecy, and will use these superficially conflicting stories, these contemporary reports of extreme experience, to answer a set of questions about precisely which cultural spaces were afforded to children: the ways in which they could be imagined, the positions of authority they could, in these cases, seem to fulfil, and the reactions or recriminations to which they might be subject. Also, and most interestingly, the cases of possessed and prophetic children reveal to us a central idea, or problematic paradox, which existed at the heart of early modern beliefs about children: the notion that they were at one and the same time believed to have the simultaneous potential to be close both to God and to the Devil. By looking at such sources, what may have been seen as unusual and unrepresentative episodes of childhood experience can become a window through which we can glimpse a rather broader anxiety about early modern childhood. In these cases, it is possible to perceive that early modern children were seen to be both innocent, through their lack of carnal sin and real understanding of adult temptation, but also sinful, due to their associated inability to yet comprehend, to understand or to know God. The change and uncertainty surrounding child salvation in Reformation and post-Reformation culture laid this tension bare, and it sat awkwardly at the heart of the child's experience of early modern religion and culture, and, in turn, was reflected in early modern society's interactions with and approaches to the young. This work will, then, consider the reasons for, and reactions to, this difficult, dualistic and paradoxical spiritual status – and in so doing, it is hoped, illuminate at least a little of that reputedly invisible figure, the early modern child.

Key Arguments

As the opening of this introductory chapter illustrates, the spiritual status of the early modern child was often confused and uncertain, and yet in the wake of the English Reformation it became an issue of urgent interest. In order to understand why, we must first explore questions surrounding early modern childhood. In the following chapters, the monograph will move on to consider the 'ideal' modes of childhood behaviour which were established in various advice books and manuals, and subsequently explore some of the extreme religious experiences in which children were documented: those of demonic possession and godly prophecy. As might be suggested by anyone critical of the relevance or continued study of, for example, the events surrounding the by now well-documented European witchtrials, we cannot assume too much, make too many generalisations about, or extrapolate too readily from, the 'extreme' events or aberrations of history. Indeed, the involvement of children in cases of demonic possession and godly prophecy were not typical childhood experiences, and do not form the majority of such cases. Nevertheless, they still undoubtedly provide us with a window through which to glimpse the world of early modern children, if not directly then reflected in the interpretations of the adult authors who recorded them. These cases reveal to us events in which children could gain or be granted some form of authority, and in which writers and publishers framed children in positions of spiritual agency. Through these events and writings we can see the troubled, dualistic nature of early modern perceptions of the young – who were, it emerges, seen to be vexingly close both to devilish temptations and to God's divine finger.

As with any aspects of childhood in the early modern period (or indeed, the pre-modern world in general), it is generally not possible fully to recreate or to understand what the *experience* of early modern childhood, or the early modern child, might have been. We 'witness' the words of children, indeed any dialogue with the figure of the child or any piece of information about their education or entertainment, through the writings and observations of adult authors – or, alternatively, through the diaries of adults reflecting in hindsight on their younger selves. Hence, our writings about children in the past will inevitably weave together sources which document children's experiences as told by adults – or even simple perceptions of children, again as recorded by adults. Nevertheless, these sources are still useful to us as historians seeking an interaction with the early modern child. Through the works to be considered in this book, we can begin to understand and unpick perceptions, stories and even imaginings of the cultural spaces in which ideas about childhood could exist, circulate and gain currency. As the historian and literary critic Marina Warner has written, the imaginary, the extreme, the exaggerated and even the fictional can reveal much about a society and its beliefs, its fears and aspirations.[6] So, then, we can approach with care but also confidence those cases of children in witchcraft and possession cases in which they are depicted, as we will see, as the innocent victims of a dark and magical evil. Equally, we can also usefully consider the children who were written about as child prophets – close to God, visitors of celestial destinations and communicators of godly messages. Each of these models represents cultural understandings of the positions and roles children *could* fulfil, and they therefore have much to tell us about early modern

---

[6]   Marina Warner, *No Go the Bogeyman, Scaring, Lulling, and Making Mock* (London: Chatto and Windus, 1998).

childhood, both in terms of the perceptions that revolved around children, but also the experiences of the children themselves. Perception is not wholly separate from experience – each can shape the other, both in the past and now. The ideas and constructions present in these texts, however unusual they may appear at first glance, are in fact more broadly applicable, and more generally relevant, than they might at first seem. Indeed, a child does not have to a be a godly prophet themselves in order to live in a society which reserves that potential place for them; they do not have to be possessed in order to experience a culture, or to help shape a culture, which expresses and guards against just that sort of anxiety.

This book will, then, in these ways consider some of the perceptions, roles and experiences to which children were subject in Reformation and post-Reformation England. This was a period in which the world people had grown used to was being torn apart and challenged in a range of ways and at a number of levels, and in which the very nature of what it meant to be a family was changed forever. Furthermore, and more particular to our purpose here, Protestant Reformers fundamentally altered perceptions of childhood, breaking with Catholic tradition through their reforms of the baptism ceremony. Reactions to the Church's attempts to reform baptism ranged from grief over the loss of the reassuring exorcism ritual to Puritan anger over the fact that the mainstream ceremony still included rituals they considered to be superstitious, such as making the sign of the cross over infants. Either way, the status of baptism and the spiritual status of children were now cast into doubt. No longer assured of their salvation or of the efficacy of baptism, Protestant children were viewed as sites of unusual and intense contention: they were seen as both frighteningly vulnerable to the Devil and also as potential vessels for heavenly and prophetic messages. These dualistic depictions of children will be the core focus of the book, and they were a direct result of the uncertainties unleashed by the theological ructions of the Protestant Reformation.

The difficulty experienced by early modern people in comprehending their world has stretched well into the twenty-first century. Beliefs in demonic possession and witchcraft, for example, have confounded and challenged historians for decades. Possession has attracted some recent attention from historians, but few have yet considered in detail why so many victims of demonic possession were young. This book will argue that part of the reason was the changing nature of beliefs about the spiritual status of children, and their consequent vulnerability to the Devil and malign spiritual forces. Beliefs about children – their vulnerability, their ability as 'innocents' to reflect and contain divine and demonic conflict in ways adults could not – contributed significantly to the manner in which these cases unravelled. Through their battles with the

Devil, as reported in the literature covering their cases, young demoniacs, with the help of adult bystanders and 'exorcists', helped to orchestrate their spiritual delivery and were thus presented as advocates for their faith. This fact, which saw these children become embroiled in several religious battles – often between Catholic and Puritan attempts to exorcise demons and thus to depict themselves as the 'true' faith – will be a topic explored both through a reassessment of the accounts themselves, and through a consideration of the tangled saga of John Darrell, Samuel Harsnett and the child demoniacs. Harsnett and Darrell engaged in a series of tract wars in the late sixteenth century, in which Harsnett, a controversial figure within the Church of England, accused Darrell of conducting a series of exorcisms 'in the fashion of vagabond players, that coast from Towne to Towne' with their 'pageant of Puppits'.

Much can be gained by contrasting these beliefs with the traditions surrounding what might at first glance seem to be the polar opposite to instances of demonic intrusion: those of child prophecy. In early modern culture, children were one of the most likely social groups to see prophetic visions or to speak godly prophecy. This book will argue that these cases are, in fact, very similar to the instances of demonic possession. Prophecy cases can reveal to us further ways in which children could, whether unconsciously or otherwise, 'perform' widely understood and culturally recognised forms of behaviour. Indeed, whether or not children were seen to be possessed or prophetic depended on their audience and the context in which their behaviour was interpreted. As contemporaries often reminded themselves, the Devil may indeed appear as an angel of light. The roles of children in such cases were tightly bound with ideas surrounding divine agency and retribution, with God using chosen children for instance to solve crimes or to bring justice upon those who had done wrong. Likewise, the documented 'monstrous births' of the period – instances of deformed infants born to uncomprehending mothers and communities – were interpreted alternately as signs of God's judgement or His wrath, casting children as the physical symbol of divine will on earth. Such cases and publications provide us with further evidence of the ways in which early modern society grappled with the difficulties and ambiguities surrounding child salvation (which can be seen to be part of the much wider spiritual anxiety of the period). These new ideas were framed and contextualised within more familiar and traditional tropes and beliefs, such as those which saw God as visibly active in the world, and then used to provide comfort and assurance, or simply as a form of spiritual explanation or edification.

In the spiritual imagination of the period, then, children were both close to God and adjacent to the Devil, and their role was indeed a confused and contradictory one, tangled up with Protestant and traditional complications alike. Nevertheless, in acting out the behaviours prescribed for and associated with this contradictory status, children were not necessarily the 'socially silent'. Even in their reported experiences and second-hand depictions, as presented to us in these cases of extreme religious occurrences, children are revealed to us as individuals who could gain or be granted the forms of spiritual authority which were required to orchestrate their delivery from demons or, alternatively, to utter godly prophecy. These texts show children to be acting with, and to be accepted as having, a form of soteriological agency, or at least soteriological assurance. These actions, and the activity permitted in this particular cultural space, helped imply to early modern spectators and audiences that a particular child's salvation, and by extension the potential for *any* child's salvation, was secure. In turn, this reveals to us a religious culture which reduced the efficacy of baptism, thus muddying and confusing the spiritual status of children. Yet it was also a culture which found alternative ways to assure themselves of the spiritual safety of their children – because it cared deeply, or understood that the faithful cared deeply, about the fate of its children's souls.

Relevant Historiographies

It is perhaps this question of the care adults did or did not feel for their children that we should move on to consider. The study of early modern childhood will inevitably draw on related historiographies concerning both children and early modern spirituality. A fair amount of work considering childhood and religion together has been put forward, yet there exists a level of disagreement surrounding the concepts of 'child' and 'childhood' in the past. As Diana Wood argued in the preface to a collection on 'Church and Childhood' in *Studies in Church History*, the relationship between ecclesiastical ideas and childhood throughout time 'is shot through with ambiguity'.[7] The subject is a contentious one, since as we have already seen children could be depicted with a certain duality: represented as both innocent creatures, vessels for the spirit, and paradoxically as fragile beings susceptible to sin and demonic temptation. It is a key purpose of this book to bring together an even broader range of historiographies in order to cast new light on these difficult questions and disparate source material: to draw on secondary literature that has examined early modern ideas surrounding childhood,

---

[7]   Diana Wood, in *Studies in Church History: The Church and Childhood*, no. 31 (1994) Preface.

Protestant education, popular culture, magic and witchcraft, prophecy and godly providence. Necessarily, given this attempt to simultaneously deal with themes of lived religious experience, Reformation theology, and the history of childhood, the historiographies on witchcraft and prophecy will be considered respectively in the chapters dedicated to those approaches and topics. This leaves the current chapter free to provide an overview of the historiographies related to the study of childhood more generally – both those that are longstanding and those that have recently posed new and interesting research questions for the field (and to which this book's own juxtapositions aim to contribute).

Many of the debates concerning the history of childhood are rooted in a hypothesis set in the 1960s, with the publication of Philippe Ariès's *Centuries of Childhood*. Ariès's research raised many unanswered questions, some of which are especially relevant here. Has childhood always been associated with innocence? Have parents always held high expectations for their children? Was parental love possible in a climate in which infant death rates were extremely high? Ariès's convictions surrounding the latter question, and his view that love towards children was something which developed as expectations for the young to live beyond infancy or early childhood increased, have led to his work and approach being heavily criticised. Indeed, Ariès attempted to chart the development of innocence over time, arguing that the concept of 'childhood', and the belief that the young should be protected from worldly corruption, was a view that developed in more recent centuries, as human society became 'modernised'.[8] These contentions are questionable: the experience of any given emotion is hard to prove in any past society, yet the sources and ideas to be considered in this work add further to the voices seeking to revise these theories. Love, grief and concern were possible within early modern society, although it was expressed in different ways.

More recent historiography has attempted to add further nuance (or, in some cases, completely revise) Ariès's ideas, favouring continuity over change with regard to patterns of kinship and parental love.[9] One of the most interesting contributions to this field is Hugh Cunningham's *Children and Childhood*. Growing out of an interest in the development of the family – an approach spearheaded by Ralph Houlbrooke and others – Cunningham follows the development of child–adult relations between the sixteenth and twentieth

---

8   Philippe Ariès, *Centuries of Childhood* (London: Penguin, 1960) esp. Chapter 5, 'From Immodesty to Innocence', pp. 98–124.

9   See especially, Ralph Houlbrooke, *The English Family, 1450–1700* (London: Longman, 1984); Hugh Cunningham, *Children and Childhood in Western Society Since 1500* (London: Longman, 1995).

centuries. In a similar stance to Ariès, Cunningham traces the evolution of a more modern, 'middle class ideology' concerning the child. This ideology associates children with a set of ideas about childhood, a time of life connected with concepts of innocence and dependence. Thus, the terms 'child' and 'childhood' become separated: the former referring to a physical state and age, the latter to a set of ideals related to life experience.[10]

Historians and anthropologists such as Keith Thomas and Clare Gittings have presented similar interpretations of the lives of the young during this period. They have argued that the high infant mortality rate, in communities so constantly plagued by death, led early modern societies to become emotionally immune to its impact. Such lines of argument have been particularly developed by the anthropologically influenced work of Gittings, *Death, Burial and the Individual*. According to Gittings, pre-modern societies, in which the concept of the individual was alien, were more adept at dealing with loss and grief, especially the loss of an infant or child, who was not necessarily expected to live beyond their first months or years. Unaccustomed to the notion of the individual, and the idea that a human being could be irreplaceable, such cultures did not experience loss in the same way as 'developed' societies.[11] According to such historical opinion, ignorance of the concept of 'individualism' had a direct impact upon the bond between parents and their children. Due to the risk of loss, parents were emotionally withdrawn from their offspring, and barely grieved the loss of an infant, failing to form an attachment to a lifetime so often fleeting.[12] Hence, she argues that the notion of parental love and expectation evolved over a period of time with the increasing chance of survival after birth.

Related to this line of argument, Keith Thomas's 'Age and Authority in Early Modern England' explored the relationship between age and authority in early modern England, focusing on how adults might have perceived, and what they might have felt about, the young. Thomas argues that early modern England, as a pre-modern society, did not value children as we do now. Expressing a position similar to the views of Cunningham and Gittings, Thomas contends that, due to

---

[10]   Cunningham, *Children and Childhood*, Introduction.

[11]   Clare Gittings, *Death, Burial and the Individual in Early Modern England* (London: Routledge, 1988).

[12]   See, Ariès, *Centuries of Childhood*, esp. Chapter 5; For counter opinions see David Cressy, *Birth, Marriage and Death: Ritual, Religion and the Life-Cycle in Tudor and Stuart England* (Oxford: Oxford University Press), p. 10; 'Far from being a paucity of emotional warmth in these families, I find their emotional lives to have been complex and intense, especially affected by grieving and loving'; Cunningham, *Children and Childhood*, p. 52; see also Houlbrooke, *The English Family*.

high child mortality, relationships with the young were inevitably emotionally limited and curtailed: society and families were prepared for loss of children on a large scale. Hence, children did not gain any form of authority or strong roles of their own. Childhood was seen as preparation for adulthood, which, if reached, was when life truly began. However, Thomas acknowledges a rare moment in which children did gain authority and social status: when they behaved as little adults. The figure of the precocious and knowledgeable child, an adult before his or her time, could, Thomas suggests, lend authority and unprecedented attention to children in early modern society.

It will already be clear to the reader that this book will challenge many of these assumptions. Recent historical works, this one included, do not accept the theory that early modern communities did not love or grieve the losses of their children. Indeed, the works of Will Coster, Paul Griffiths, Hannah Newton and Lucy Underwood, for example, have begun to revise this position, and to pose new questions about the lives of early modern children and youths.[13] Evidence explored throughout this book, however, will reveal that Thomas's argument about 'little adults' has some significant mileage. Children who behaved as 'little Puritans', with a spiritual knowledge to rival even the most theologically astute adults, were indeed able to acquire high levels of authority and notoriety – but so, too, were a range of other theologically precocious 'types', as evidenced in the cases of child possession and prophecy.[14] It has already been argued that the existence of this range of roles argues strongly for a more intense relationship with the child than the traditional historiographies might suggest.

The works of those such as Ariès, Gittings and Thomas, and all the associated ideas about modernity, are rooted in an anthropologically inspired approach driven by the desire to discover a linear progression from medieval to modern. In this way, when faced with the idiosyncrasies of contemporary evidence, they can appear somewhat awkward. As in other areas of inquiry, a perceived relationship between Protestantism and the concept of modernity can lead to teleological arguments, which often see the Reformation as a progressive step towards the Enlightenment. Viewing the sixteenth century through the lens of later change can distort rather than improve our understanding of a period

---

[13]   See for example, Will Coster, *Baptism and Spiritual Kinship in Early Modern England* (Farnham: Ashgate, 2002); Paul Griffiths, *Youth and Authority, Formative Experiences in England* (Oxford: Clarendon Press, 1996); Hannah Newton, *The Sick Child in Early Modern England* (Oxford: Oxford University Press, 2012); Lucy Underwood, *Childhood, Youth and Religious Dissent in Post Reformation England* (London: Palgrave, 2014).

[14]   Keith Thomas, 'Age and Authority in Early Modern England', in *Proceedings of the British Academy*, Volume LXII (1976).

which was in truth rather more complex. This work will therefore attempt to challenge such positions, arguing instead that families of the Reformation era did indeed love their children – and that early modern society spent a lot of time thinking about, and worrying about, the young. Although these affections were expressed in unfamiliar ways, they are clearly discernible. For example, this intense concern combined with the focus on particular Protestant teachings formed a distinctive genre of prescriptive literature concerning the virtues of godly parenting. The resulting 'manuals' for parents provide us with a relatively clear picture of ideals about family life during this period, as will be considered in the following chapter.

All of this places the current work in the company of other recent works on early modern childhood which have indeed sought to break away from the traditional ideas which presume a lack of emotional affection for early modern children. Coster has considered infancy and baptism, while Griffiths has explored early modern youth; the *Church History* volume on 'Church and Childhood' also put forward a significant set of exploratory articles which pointed in a series of fruitful directions. Even more recently, Newton's work on children, illness and death explores how the young may have experienced sickness and prepared, within their families, for death, and Underwood's work explores the experience of child dissenters in post-Reformation England.[15] Alec Ryrie's new and groundbreaking book *Being Protestant in Reformation Britain*, moreover, has explored childhood as part of the wider Protestant experience, and some of my own previous work has considered children in the contexts of demonic possession and household education.[16] Building on this emerging body of work, this book will show how great emphasis was placed on the words of children, and upon the origin of those words, whether demonic or divine – in turn placing significant import and authority on the young, this supposedly silent and dismissed part of the community.

Again, it is a core contention of this book that a single historiography is not sufficient to arrive at a full understanding of the often confounding accounts of early modern children and their activities. Aside from the historiography

[15] Coster, *Baptism and Spiritual Kinship*; Griffiths, *Youth and Authority*; Newton, *The Sick Child in Early Modern England*; Underwood, *Childhood, Youth and Religious Dissent*.

[16] Coster, *Baptism and Spiritual Kinship*; Griffiths, *Youth and Authority*; Wood (ed.) *Studies in Church History* 301–12; Newton, *The Sick Child in Early Modern England*; Alec Ryrie, *Being Protestant in Reformation Britain* (Oxford: Oxford University Press, 2013); Anna French, 'Possession, Puritanism and Prophecy: Child Demoniacs and English Reformed Culture', *Reformation*, 13, (2008); Anna French, 'Raising Christian Children in Early Modern England: Salvation, Education and the Family', *Theology*, Vol. 116 (2) (2013).

surrounding childhood, then, this work will also draw on ideas and theories relating to Protestant religion as a 'lived experience'. Traditionally, early modern scholarship has tended to focus on questions of religious and theological change. Early modern research is now beginning to draw together theological and social explorations, to consider questions about how early modern religion was experienced by followers within their daily lives. Such works, including Susan Karant-Nunn's studies on emotion, as well as Leif Dixon and Arnold Hunt's explorations of predestinarianism, have begun to challenge the notion that early modern spirituality, especially the religious stripe branded as 'Puritanism', was simply a form of harsh or strict dogma that led adherents and followers into dark feelings of melancholy.[17] Rather, these recent works suggest that Protestantism, at its various levels of intensity, was pastorally focused and able to negotiate the emotional experiences of its adherents. This process of exchange can be seen at work in the anxieties around both prophecy and possession. The book will therefore draw on and contribute to such enquiries, looking at the ways in which the lived experiences of children were reported and reflected in accounts of extreme religious episodes, such as possession and prophecy, as well as the reaction of adults to these occurrences and the process of shared religious negotiation between adult and child, authorities and adherents.

The book will in this way look from various perspectives at how early modern authors represented children in the possession and prophecy texts. It will argue that children featured more prominently than we may have assumed in the lived experience of early modern religion, and even became objects of spiritual fame and notoriety. Most significantly, despite the fact that early modern theology taught society about the inherent sinfulness of children, and that Protestant authorities as well as Puritan ministers adopted strict forms of religious education for the young, in practice the religious experiences of children were negotiated, explicated and wondered at, with the help and commitment of adults. Far from simply being seen and not heard, or routinely cast into the rigid mould of the sinful child in need of education, children were instead listened to, guided, instructed and encouraged in their religious life and experiences.

---

[17]   See Susan Karant-Nunn's *The Reformation of Ritual: An Interpretation of Early Modern Germany* (Abingdon: Routledge, 1997) and *The Reformation of Feeling: Shaping the Religious Emotions in Early Modern Germany* (Oxford: Oxford University Press, 2010); Leif Dixon's *Practical Predestinarians in England, c. 1590–1640* (Surrey: Ashgate, 2014) and Arnold Hunt's *The Art of Hearing; English Preachers and Their Audiences, 1590–1640* (Cambridge: Cambridge University Press, 2010) esp. chapter 7.

Age and Innocence: Defining Childhood

Key themes throughout this work are those of age and innocence: when childhood was seen to begin and end, and how innocence related to age and childhood. It is, of course, difficult to judge when childhood begins and ends in any given society. Indeed, the term 'childhood' itself is anachronistic for the early modern world, in which it was not used, and in which even the concept which lies behind the word may not have been widely understood or comprehended – although, as this work argues, early modern society did have a definite understanding of children as 'other'. But, the time in which a person was deemed a child depended on a wide set of circumstances and conditions, and, as will be argued, did not necessarily relate to numerical age. Indeed, early modern society was not one in which numerical age was as important a marker as it is today. Frequently, in source material, age is given as an approximate: a child was judged to be around a certain age. Childhood depended upon things such as social position, and might last longer for those in more wealthy families. It could also depend on gender. It does seem that female childhood lasted longer than that of males, ending when women left the parental home in order to marry. The boundary between child and adult could also depend on physical size and capability – indeed, cases of prophecy and possession see children behaving in both recognisably young and yet simultaneously precociously adult ways. Through an analysis of these cases, then, we might be able to further our understanding of the early modern vision of childhood. It will emerge that, for early modern society, the definition of a child was more varied than today – and that it revolved around stage (both physical and spiritual) as much as, if not more than, it did around age.

During the early modern period, the idea of innocence, and how such a state related to infants and children, was ambiguous and fraught with tension. In terms of traditional Catholic culture, children were born evil, and were not able to gain salvation unless they had been baptised. Protestant culture altered this perception, stating instead that elect children, although born in sin, were saved by the choice of God, and that baptism could not impart grace or salvation. However, such ideas were not clear cut, and although society had been, officially at least, cleansed of Catholicism, traditional forms of piety and patterns sometimes remained. Hence, the spiritual status of children was complicated. Humanist beliefs, especially those surrounding innocence and education, also had a part to play in determining the moral status of the child. Protestant culture held that children were born in sin, whilst humanist belief told that they were born morally blank. Both Protestant and humanist thinkers recommended education, but for different reasons – to either to help to tame the inherent sin, or to write upon the blank. Whichever approach was given more emphasis, the implication was that an individual was a child until they had been sufficiently schooled regarding the ideal behaviours of adulthood. This book is in part concerned with how aberrant behaviours were folded into this process – and how the child was seen to be an active, rather than a passive, participant in it and in the spiritual community around them.

Structure

Following this initial introductory section, the book contains five further chapters which develop these ideas about early modern children, possession and prophecy, and the experience of living as a Protestant child in early modern England. The chapters also consider further themes throughout, including an examination of beliefs surrounding child salvation, education and 'popular' perceptions of the young. In order to set the stage for this investigation, Chapter 2, 'Children of Unbelief: The Inheritance from Adam', explores the ways in which early modern perspectives of childhood shifted during and after the Protestant Reformation, as well as changing beliefs about original sin and child salvation. Victory over the Devil was no longer to be won at the font – children, like all members of humanity, were left at the mercy of God's predestined plan. Children therefore had to live with both their original and actual sin, and it was up to God to decide whether a child was to be saved. Taken to its logical conclusion, Protestant predestinarianism meant that infants, even with the baptismal blessing, could be amongst the damned. Debates between various 'stripes' of Protestant believers served to further deepen such uncertainty. Thus the status of baptism and the spiritual status of children were cast into doubt and led to much anxiety. This chapter draws on the Sarum Rite and editions of the Protestant baptism ceremony printed in the *Books of Common Prayer*, as well as family advice manuals and instructive literature, in order to examine this change in Protestant perceptions of the young.

Chapters 3 and 4 move on from this vexed background to look at the involvement of children in cases of demonic possession. Firstly, 'Children of Wrath? Children in Cases of Demonic Possession' explores some examples of possession cases involving children, for example Alexander Nyndge, who as we saw at the opening of this chapter, battled with the Devil through a series of violent bodily contortions and even spoke in the voice of a demon, much to the shock of bystanders. The chapter explores the behaviours of children in such cases, and the authority they were given. Whether this authority was bestowed by author and text, or whether there was significant truth in these cases we will never know, yet it remains interesting that children were depicted in such a way, and these implications will be teased out in the chapter itself. Indeed, Chapter 4, 'Darrell, Harsnett and the Child Demoniacs', looks at how these stories, or cases, were played out on a wider social and religious spectrum, in particular the debate and pamphlet warfare that broke out between Samuel Harsnett and John Darrell in the late sixteenth and early seventeenth centuries. It is useful here to consider how these cases were influenced by changing attitudes to and beliefs about child spirituality during this period, and therefore what they can reveal both about such attitudes and perceptions, as well as their impact upon children and the anxieties which society felt about their spiritual status.

Chapter 5, 'Children of God: Cases of Child Prophecy', explores the involvement of children in cases of divine prophecy. It considers some of the instances in which children became the mouthpieces of 'divine' purposes, for example the case of William Withers, who attracted the attention of his local community as well as the press when he began to deliver prophetic warnings against the sin that was being committed by those living in sixteenth-century Suffolk. As this fifth chapter argues, one of the reasons for the 'excitement' occasioned by Withers's pronouncements was a belief in the potentially close proximity between children and God. As the chapter shows, the other side of the coin – the concomitant element of the early modern anxiety around child spirituality and the apparent dichotomy at the heart of the salvation of the young – were those cases in which children were depicted not as hosts for demons, but as chosen messengers for the word of God. These godly children, too, were not necessarily silent within early modern religious culture, and, as in the cases of demonic possession, they could become figures of spiritual authority and notoriety. Indeed, the similarities between the two typologies are so clear as to suggest a deep interaction and inter-relation: that key to all these cases, and to early modern perceptions of and concern for children alike, was an intense anxiety about God's judgement.

Finally, then, Chapter 6, 'Sin, Providence, and the Judgement of Children', furthers the concepts of child notoriety and authority by considering the relationship between children, prophecy, sin and judgement. This chapter explores prophecy cases in which the young were seen to be seeking retribution and justice for crimes committed against either themselves or God. The chapter uses crime narratives involving children, as well as early modern reports of 'monstrous births', to unpick the connections between such literature and early modern beliefs about, and anxieties surrounding, child salvation. It will be shown that, as in the case of the demoniac 'actors', prophetic children could be depicted as vessels of God's judgement, both as symbols of providence but also by speaking the word of God, or providing divine knowledge.

Throughout each of the chapters, particular issues of historiography and primary source material will be addressed and dealt with, in an attempt to not only bring together primary materials on the appearances of children in cases of extreme religious occurrence, such as possession and prophecy, but also to draw together and usefully synthesise historiographies that may usually be considered in isolation. These primary materials and historiographies include those that explore and represent ideas about childhood and child studies, early modern religious belief and Reformation thought, possession, prophecy and education. Finally, some conclusions will be made, with a particular focus on signposts for further study of the fascinating intersection between child, early modern spirituality, Protestant salvation and a community's approach to its youngest and most vulnerable members.

Chapter 2

Children of Unbelief:
The Inheritance from Adam

There is no man so fierce or wild,
But gentle may be made;
If patient eare he doe apply
To nurtures honest trade.[1]

This book is primarily concerned with the notion, or ideas surrounding the notion, of the early modern young as 'children of wrath', or, children who were perceived to be tainted by sin. As considered in the previous chapter, many questions abound from the core belief that children in this period held a difficult and slippery spiritual status. They were sometimes viewed as spiritually innocent and close to God, due to their lack of actual or committed sin, and at other moments seen as tainted with evil and demonic influences, due to the sinful and bloody nature of their conception and their birth. This was the perceived utility of the baptism ceremony – to wash away this perception of sin. Yet, in this period, the Reformation had significantly reduced the power and potency of this ceremony, viewing it as a 'washing' or a 'symbol', rather than the moment when God, through the minister, tore the Devil out of the child. Post Reformation, official theology told that children may be damned, if not chosen to be included amongst the elect, even if they had been baptised. Similarly, the opposite was also true – those who had not been baptised may be saved. What did all these questions mean for perceptions of, and experiences of, early modern childhood? Indeed, we have already seen that there was much potential for confusion and liminality in the body, or person, of the child. This book is concerned with those moments of uncertainty, the ways in which children were interpreted to be both innocent and depraved – and what contemporaries made of that difficulty. We will certainly deal with cases in which children behaved unusually at both ends of this contested spectrum – but first, perhaps, we should look at how authorised

---

[1]   Anon, *The office of Christian parents shewing how children are to be gouerned throughout all ages and times of their life* (Cambridge, 1616) *STC* (2nd ed.) 3180, p. 12.

texts, which sought to offer practical support, imagined children. We will also consider in this chapter the idealised advice these manuals offered, which sought to ensure that children of concerned and godly readers were not overly afflicted by the soteriological storm that swirled around their offspring's spiritual status. In this chapter, then, we will consider how official church teaching and doctrinally influenced family advice manuals and instruction books dealt with these thorny questions, which had real and inescapable consequences in the daily lives of children and their parents.

Closely related to the idea of baptism were concepts of the original sin inherited from Adam. John Donne told in a christening sermon that, 'for Adam's fault six thousand year agoe, I should be condemned now, because that fault is naturally in me ... I find it in the Scriptures ... we are born children of wrath, and therefore must be borne againe'.[2] Hence, all mankind, including those newly born and free from actual sin, or even from the thought of sin, were inherently evil and corrupted. Such a belief was derived from Christian doctrine, which states that all humankind is tainted by the original sin of Adam. According to Genesis 3, Adam fell to the temptation of the Devil, and brought sin and evil into Paradise. Augustine of Hippo thus spoke of man's utter wretchedness and complete disobedience, and the Protestant reformers eagerly took up this particular of his banners. Through the sin of Eve and transgression of Adam, all future mankind would inherit a sinful nature and the threat of eternal death. Though humankind had the potential to be spiritual, it had become driven by carnal desires, forsaking eternal life unless it could be freed by God's grace.[3]

Both early modern Protestant and Catholic doctrines incorporated this belief. Catholic devotion provided a pathway for mankind to navigate a way through sin to ultimate salvation, through good works and frequent acts of penitence, revolving around the seven sacraments. Reformed Protestant doctrine, on the other hand, further developed Augustine's notions of original sin and regarded salvation as a predestined mystery, derived from the inscrutable will of God, and was more pessimistic about the base nature of man. Jean Calvin wrote 'from the corruption that descended from Adam into all his posterity ... original sin is the depravity and corruption of our nature'.[4] The sin of Adam was seen to have

---

[2]   John Donne, (ed.) George R. Potter and Evelyn M. Simpson, *The Sermons of John Donne, Vol. 5* (Berkeley and Los Angeles: University of California Press, 1959) p. 101.

[3]   St Augustine, *Concerning the City of God against the Pagans*, trans. Henry Bettenson (London: Penguin, 1984) esp. pp. 569–75.

[4]   Jean Calvin, *Institutes of the Christian Religion*, vol. 2, (ed.) John Baillie, John T. McNiell, Henry P. Van Dusen (London: SMC Press, 1961) p. 1310.

ushered in the 'works of the flesh', the evils of the world, the flesh and the Devil – and its malign influence was not eradicated by baptism.[5]

Seventeenth-century writer Henry Ainsworth was not unusual in his conviction that 'all infants for their native sin, and all man for their actuall sinnes deserve damnation'.[6] Thus, while infants were seen to have possessed some form of primeval sin, and were deserving of damnation, if they reached adulthood they would be further tainted by actual sin; such was the state of total depravity. As Calvin wrote, 'even infants bear their condemnation with them from their mother's womb; for though they have not yet brought forth the fruits of their own iniquity, they have the seed enclosed within themselves'.[7] Indeed, for Reformed Protestantism, humankind was defined by the extent to which every one of its aspects had been invaded and degraded by the capacity, indeed the fertility, for evil – and infants were no different.

The fear that the physical world and flesh belonged to the conspiring enemy Satan was a common one during this period. As one tract warned, 'al the bloud within thy veines is corrupted, thy hart bloud is becom most filty poison, and thou art becom most ugly, deformed like the divell'.[8] Indeed, depicting the physical and spiritual worlds as dualistically opposed entities, one ruled by God, the other by the Devil, was a common conceit. The image of the battle between the depraved flesh and the soul owed much to the writings of Augustine, who clearly emphasised the shameful state of the flesh: 'the body is subordinate ... by reason of its inferior nature'.[9] According to Christian doctrine, God had created Satan in order to punish the depraved, in a sense to dispose of the spiritually void. As Henry Ainsworth argued, God 'delivereth evill doers to Satan to be their deluder, their tormenter'.[10] Thus, it was to be something of a comfort to remember that the Devil, although a dangerous enemy, could never stray from God's purpose or command. However, in practice, beliefs surrounding the Devil seemed to break free from such official constraints, and many contemporaries emphasised the dangers of the conspiring enemy, as both equal and opposite to God. The Zurich cleric, Heinrich Bullinger, warned that 'the devil, the author of sin, of uncleanness, and of death ... reigneth in the world, the prince doubtless

---

[5]   Calvin, *Institutes of the Christian Religion*, p. 1310.

[6]   Henry Ainsworth, *A Censure upon a dialogue of the Anabaptists* (London: 1651) *Wing* A813, sig. E3v.

[7]   Calvin, *Institutes*, p. 1310.

[8]   Dorothy Leigh, *The Mothers Blessing, Or the godly counsaile of a gentle-woman not long since deceased* (London, 1616) *STC* (2nd ed.) 15402. pp. 251–2.

[9]   St Augustine, *Concerning the City of God against the Pagans*, p. 586.

[10]   Ainsworth, *A Seasonable*, sig. E3v.

of the kingdom of darkness'.[11] In this way, the sin of Adam had, many implied, given the Devil much power over the world, thus introducing mankind to sin and death through damnation. As one pamphlet warned, 'The Divell hath [the] power of death ... he is the authour of it, by his malitious nature he brought it into the worlde: for God made it not, nor hath anie delight in it'.[12] Hence, all earthly creatures were to fear devilish temptation and pollution. Furthermore, and significant to this book, such a belief was extended onto the young. As one familial manual advised, mothers were to ensure that their children prayed to God each day, 'humble our selves at His foot', further urging them to 'call earnestly for the helpe of God to overcome the world for us, and to strengthen us by his power against the divell, the world and our owne frailty, and wicked fleshy lusts'.[13]

Perceptions of infancy were further influenced by their close proximity to perceptions of the nature of women, as females were known for their fleshly, carnal wants. Such beliefs are clearly evident in a sermon by Protestant cleric Sampson Price, 'what is hee which is borne of a woman that hee should be righteous?'[14] The Church and religious writers shaped the language which governed thinking about reproduction and childbirth, a stage of the lifecycle that was closely entwined with notions of women's sin, shame and bodily weakness. Such perceptions of danger and punishment were rooted in the biblical judgement; 'vnto the woman he said, I wil greatly increase thy sorowes, & thy conceptions, In sorowe shalt thou bring forthe children and thy desire shal be subject to thine hous-band, and he shal rule ouer thee'.[15] As John Donne argued during a christening sermon, 'a greater subjection lies upon her, then upon the Man'. This was due to her initial 'transgression towards her husband', which bore characteristic signs of the 'false and treacherous' nature of woman.[16] Thus, due to the stain of original sin, women were to suffer in childbirth, a liminal stage associated with looming danger, sickness and possible death.

Social historians have considered the social impact and the statistical evidence surrounding issues of childbirth and infancy. Indeed, modern demographic estimates of infant survival do reveal a fairly grim picture; during

---

[11]   Heinrich Bullinger, *The Decades of Henry Bullinger, The Fourth Decade, The Parker Society*, (ed.) Thomas Harding (Cambridge: Cambridge University Press, 1851) p. 281.

[12]   John Merbecke, *A booke of notes and common places* (London: 1581) *STC* (2nd ed.) 17299. p. 294.

[13]   Leigh, *The Mothers Blessing* (1616) pp. 75–6.

[14]   Sampson Price, *The Two Twins of Birth and Death* (1624) *STC* (2nd ed) 20334, p. 12.

[15]   Genesis 3: 16. Here and subsequently, italic letters have been added by the author (usually an 'n'). This is when, for example, the original source says something like 'childrē' or 'thē', or says 'ỹ' instead of 'ye'.

[16]   Donne, *The Sermons of John Donne*, p. 113.

the Elizabethan period approximately 2 per cent of babies died during their first day of life, 5 per cent within their first week, 8 or 9 per cent within a month, and 12 or 13 per cent would not survive beyond their first year, figures which worsened during the later seventeenth century.[17] In his demographic essay on the fate of women during this period, Roger Schofield has estimated that 9.3 women per 1,000 births (less than 1 per cent) would die. Most women had an average of six or seven pregnancies in her lifetime, thus a 6 to 7 per cent risk of dying in childbed, though the situation was more severe in London, due to generally poor demographic conditions.[18]

Whilst the statistics have been considered and quoted, it is also important to acknowledge the spiritual aspect of such lifecycle occurrences. This book will attempt to put some of this spiritual fervour back onto the bones of the historiography surrounding childhood and lifecycle. Indeed, women understandably feared the perils of labour. This fear is reflected in the tract written by the godly Jacobean Elizabeth Jocelin, who looked on her pregnancy in 1622 as a sentence of doom. In her work *The Mothers Legacie to her Unborn Child* she prepares for the likelihood of her own death by setting out instructions for the raising and spiritual nurturing of her children, thus providing a model of faith and fortitude for expectant mothers.[19] Birth was dangerous for both mother and the newly born child – and this danger was seen as both physical and spiritual. Eve's legacy was a lifecycle stage through which most women, and all new-born children, would pass. Contemporary writers commonly reflected upon the distressing passage of birth and infancy, as the words of Sampson Price reveal: 'we have a time to be borne, and as a man that hath passed over a dangerous bridge if hee turne bake quaketh to remember the danger he was in; so ... we looke backe upon the danger we escaped till our birth, and in it'.[20] Further, children were 'inflamed by hell, clouded with darkness and [often] passing as a shadowe', thus implying that the earthly lifetime of many newly born children was a fleeting one.[21]

---

[17]   Cressy, *Birth, Marriage and Death*, p. 117.

[18]   Roger Schofield, 'Did the Mothers Really Die? Three Centuries of Maternal Mortality in "The World we have Lost"', in Lloyd Bonfield, Richard M. Smith, and Keith Wrightson (eds), *The World We Have Gained: Histories of Population and Social Structure* (Oxford: Blackwell, 1986) pp. 231–60.

[19]   Elizabeth Jocelin, *The mothers legacie to her unborne childe* (London, 1635) *STC* (2nd ed.) 14625.7; also see a similar work concerning motherhood and spiritual preparation, Leigh, *The Mothers Blessing.*

[20]   Price, *The two twins of birth and death*, p. 12.

[21]   Price, *The two twins of birth and death*, p. 12.

The spiritual state of the child was not only seen to be polluted by its obviously female-dominated nature, but also by the carnal act of conception itself. Such a perception was, again, rooted in Augustinian notions surrounding the 'ferment of lust' and 'impure indulgences of vice'.[22] As the baptismal ceremony issued in the Elizabethan *Booke of Common Praier* stated 'all men be conceived and borne in synne', none could receive the kingdom of God 'except he be regenerate, and borne a newe of water and the holye gost'.[23] Furthermore, a sermon by Arthur Hildersham was just one of many to cite the fifty-first psalm, 'Behold I was borne ... in iniquity; and in sinne did my mother conceive me'.[24] Thus, the infant bore the heavy burden of both original and carnal sin.

Yet, paradoxically, childbirth also provided a means through which women could ultimately be saved. As a seventeenth-century tract by Dorothy Leigh argued, Mary's role in giving birth to Jesus saved mankind, urging mothers to appreciate, 'what a blessing God hath sent to us women ... for before, men might say: The woman beguiled me, and I did eate the poisoned fruit of disobedience, and I dye. But now man may say ... The woman brought me a saviour, and I feede of him by faith and live'.[25] Though women endured both physical torment and moral shame through pregnancy and childbirth, labour could also be seen as part of the human covenant with God. The Bible stressed the spiritual benefits of procreation, which could be seen as a positive aspect of marriage, a gift from God; 'the woman being deceived was in the transgression. Notwithstanding she shall be saved in childbearing, if they continue in faith and charity and holiness with sobriety'.[26] It was a Christian duty to nurture the future generation of Christians, and through such a role women could obtain, as David Cressy has written, 'sanctification, mercy and eternal comfort'.[27] Such an image was reflected by John Donne, when during a christening sermon he tells of how the joy of new birth can nourish and sanctify marital life, 'when God says ... "Let the waters be gathered into one place", and let all thy affections be setled upon one wife, then the earth and the waters become fruitfull, the God gives us a ... figure of the eternity of the joys of heaven, in the succession, and propagation of children here upon the earth'.[28]

---

[22]   Augustine, *Concerning the City of God*, p. 577.

[23]   *The booke of common praier* (London, 1559) sig. N3v.

[24]   Hildersham, *CLII Lectures vpon Psalme LI*, p. 275.

[25]   Dorothy Leigh, *The mothers blessing, Or the godly counsaile of a gentle-woman not long since deceased, left behind for her children* (London, 1627: Cf. first edition 1616) *STC* (2nd ed.) 15405, pp. 34–5.

[26]   I Timothy 2: 14–15.

[27]   Cressy, *Birth, Marriage and Death*, pp. 16–17.

[28]   Donne, *The Sermons of John Donne*, p. 116.

Hence, childbirth and infancy provided a means through which people could experience both the curse of Adam and the grace of Christ, becoming a microcosm of the history of humanity, encapsulating sin, punishment and redemption through Christ. Whilst regarded as a period of liminality and danger, new birth also enabled the people of the early modern era to be close to God, as well as to contemplate the possibility of salvation. This dual – and at first glance paradoxical – relationship between grace and sin will be seen again and again in the course of this monograph. Furthermore, the role of raising children was also seen to have important societal resonances in the early modern world. Whilst it would be overly simplistic to emphasise binary definitions between the 'public' and 'private' spheres, or even the male and female spheres, childbirth and child-raising were seen to have a direct impact upon the future of the commonwealth. Parents' role in childbirth and nurture was the linchpin in early modern society, educated and appropriately pious children provided future workers, subjects, parents and most importantly, future Christians.[29]

Protestant Doctrines of Salvation

> ... For the children being not yet born, neither having done any good or evil ...
> the purpose of God according to election might stand, not of works, but of him
> that calleth. (Rom 9:11)

Much of this book will be concerned with often contentious beliefs surrounding child-salvation. Indeed, as will be considered throughout this chapter, and indeed throughout the monograph, Protestant theories of predestination sat awkwardly next to perceptions of children and notions of childhood innocence and vulnerability: official beliefs in predestination, if taken to their logical conclusions, told that an infant or child who died (with or without baptism) could be damned. Yet, as will be argued, clerics, godly writers and Protestant polemicists took a more pastorally aware approach to ideas surrounding child salvation and child soteriology.

As we have already explored, the Reformation period saw a radical shift in prescribed beliefs within the Church, in particular those concerning soteriological doctrines. Such changes had a direct impact upon beliefs

---

[29] Cressy, *Birth, Marriage and Death*, p. 15, Cressy talks about childbirth as a 'private event with public significance, a domestic occurrence of which the commonwealth took note', such divisions between 'public' and 'private' may distort the nature of early modern society, and misinterpret the significance of the family as a commonwealth in small letter.

surrounding child salvation. The primary focus of Christian religion is to obtain redemption through Christ; to share the victory he is believed to have obtained over sin, death and evil. Both the Catholic and Protestant faiths, during this period, involved a complex mesh of ideas and images which centred on redemption achieved through death and resurrection. The traditional faith possessed many means through which an individual could help to secure eternal salvation, including seven official sacraments.[30] Indeed, Catholic worship involved a series of penitential rituals: ceremonies, worshipping of Saints, washings, cleansings and good works, designed to secure followers a place in Heaven.[31] The image of cleansing through Christ's blood, received at baptism and communion, was particularly important. Born sinful, the Catholic infant would receive complete cleansing and forgiveness at the font. Indeed, baptism was seen as the sure and only means through which to save the soul of a dying child. Throughout life Catholics would naturally commit a range of sins, for which, through sincere penance, they could repent and be forgiven. Hence, the pre-Reformation lifecycle was one of constant sin, repentance and forgiveness.

A further extension of this soteriological system was the belief that individuals could do penance, and thus be redeemed, for their worldly sins after death. Indeed, medieval Catholic doctrine told of Purgatory, a 'third place', where the majority of souls would be punished after death, before being released to the permanent destination of Heaven.[32] Such a belief system helped to retain a perceived relationship between the living and the dead, one of mutual responsibility in which the living could, through prayer and the purchasing of indulgences, effectively reduce the time in purgatory to be suffered by the deceased, a duty which would eventually be returned by those in Heaven.[33] Alongside Heaven, Hell and Purgatory, the Catholic afterlife also included *Limbus Patrum*, for souls of patriarchs who died before the incarnation, and

---

[30]　Alister McGrath, *Reformation Thought, an Introduction* (Cambridge: Blackwell Press, 1999) p. 87.

[31]　See Diarmaid MacCulloch, *The Later Reformation in England, 1547–1603* (London: Palgrave, 2001) pp. 1–7.

[32]　For surveys of medieval purgatory and the Reformation see esp. Peter Marshall, *Beliefs and the Dead in Reformation England* (Oxford University Press, 2002) Chapter 2; Eamon Duffy, *The Stripping of the Altars: Tradition Religion in England 1400–1580* (Yale University Press, 1992), Chapter 10.

[33]　Bruce Gordon and Peter Marshall (eds), *The Place of the Dead, Death and Remembrance in Late Medieval and Early Modern Europe* (Cambridge University Press, 2000) pp. 3–4; and Cressy, *Birth, Marriage and Death*, pp. 386–7.

Limbus Infantium, for the souls of infants who died without baptismal blessing.[34] In effect, this belief system fostered something of an economy of souls, through which the medieval Catholic Church retained the key to the afterlife, and thus ultimate sovereignty.

We have already briefly reviewed the principle ways in which the Protestant Reformers upset this consolatory apple cart, with significant repercussions for the ways in which children were received by their societies. The Protestant Reformation attempted to uproot the medieval belief system, on the grounds that one should not be able to control personal salvation. No longer were worldly actions, such as good works and prayers, seen to secure one's place in Heaven. Reformed religion told that salvation was only achieved by the exercise of faith and the inscrutable will of God. Good works during life had no efficacy, as far as salvation was concerned; baptism and communion were no longer seen to guarantee heavenly salvation to the participant, but were, officially at least, effective and spiritually beneficial means of grace.[35] Protestantism emphasised the overarching sovereignty of God, and humankind's total dependence on him; as one Protestant cleric grimly stated, 'No man must murmour against God's providence: It is not in the power of man to come into the world ... A divine hand ruleth all, everything hath its season, as a time ordained by God. The creature is governed by the Creator'.[36] Rooted as we have seen in the writings of Augustine, the Reformers stressed man's total depravity. Humankind could only be saved through faith, not earthly action. Hence, baptism no longer guaranteed infant salvation. Faith was imputed onto an undeserving mankind through God's grace; such grace was not given to all. Those who were predestined not to be faithful, Augustine had held, were not actively damned, but rather omitted from godly purpose. Calvin's decree of 'double predestination', however, held that God actively saved some, whilst damning others.[37]

God was believed in this system to predestine both those who were to be elected and saved, and those who were to be reprobate and damned. Protestant doctrine held that God predestined whether an individual was to be among the elect or reprobate before their birth. There was some debate as to at what point before birth – whether prior to the Fall or following it – but in either event no earthly intervention could alter the decision once made. Neither the elect nor the reprobate, however, were without sin – God's salvation of the few did not imply

---

[34] Peter Marshall, '"The map of God's word": geographies of the afterlife in Tudor and early Stuart England', in Gordon and Marshall (eds), *The Place of the Dead*, p. 112.

[35] Cressy, *Birth, Marriage and Death*, pp. 386–7.

[36] Price, *The two twins of birth and death*, p. 6.

[37] McGrath, *Reformation Thought, an Introduction*, pp. 124–5.

that original sin was less than universal. Therefore, newly born infants must be included amongst the damned, for the sin inherited through Adam affected all. As the anti-Anabaptist Henry Ainsworth wrote, if infants were not guilty of sin, 'then many (as all that dye infants) never fell in Adam, nor needed Christ's redemption'. Hence, to deny, as did the Anabaptist heretics, that children were born guilty with sin, was to deny the fall of mankind through Adam, as well as the importance of redemption through Christ. Original sin was simply one side of the redemptive coin: it was not possible to have one without the other, and that held significant implications for all, not least those who might once have had a reasonable expectation of having some control of their soul's destiny.

Here we will consider what impact such beliefs surrounding original sin had on perceptions of childhood. I will argue that Reformed belief was less black and white than strict theological readings would have us believe. Indeed, on a pastoral level at least, Reformed Protestant views surrounding salvation of children, and even the predestination of children's souls, were adapted and moulded to enable parents to cope with the potential loss of their young. As will be argued throughout this work, especially in the chapters on beliefs surrounding child prophecy, in this process of adaptation we can see traditional and well understood cultural tropes and ideas, such as those surrounding miracle stories or purgatory, re-used and reinterpreted to present and communicate new, Protestant ideas. These beliefs and adaptations, as will be considered, occurred on different parts of the social spectrum, and at various levels of intensity across it.

Indeed, changes in prescribed doctrine, through the removal of the direct association between baptism and salvation and the assertion of the mysterious decree of predestination, created much ambiguity surrounding child salvation. Despite this, Reformed religion provided a constructive and positive framework for raising the young – set out in a range of family advice manuals written by Protestant clerics. Within this framework, ideal models of behaviour were narrated for both parents and children. As this chapter will argue, such prescriptive roles formed a set of distinctly Protestant narratives of childhood. Such idealised narratives provide us with a glimpse of what kind of behaviour was expected of both parents and children, and also what kind of world these families inhabited. Of course, there were inevitably some significant (and interesting) gaps between what was prescribed and what happened in daily life, or between the advice manuals' visions of children and alternative cultural perceptions of childhood. There were also cultural aberrations, when we see children acting in, admittedly, extreme ways. Indeed, as was considered in the last chapter, although we cannot make generalist assumptions about extreme modes of behaviour, such as demonic possession, they can tell us about cultural tropes that existed, or the ways in which people were able to imagine children. In this chapter, we will focus in particular on prescribed ideals presented in family advice manuals and instruction books, which were often written by clerics to provide constructive, palatable and accessible advice to readers. But, as the remainder of the book will illustrate, at all points we must recall that the conceptions of children contained in these books were not the only ones on offer, and that they may have been knowingly working against some less authorised ones.

It would be fair to argue that familial literature and advice manuals were not being produced in an ideological vacuum. Rather, they reflect the anxieties felt in response to the ways in which people were raising children – from a clerical perspective. The advice manuals, the book-objects themselves, were most likely aimed at a more wealthy audience – but their ideas, written most often by Protestant clerics who took to the pulpit each Sunday, would have had wider applicability. The prescriptive and idealised information found in the manuals will provide a backdrop to the remainder of this monograph, of which the later chapters consider the pathological side of early modern childhood narratives – those of demonic possession and godly prophecy. Indeed, as we will see, early modern writers communicating ideas about children's roles in cases of possession and prophecy not only saw it as appropriate to describe children as 'miniature Puritans' or models of innocent yet vulnerable piety, but also as sites of spiritual ambiguity. Furthermore, there was a host of adult-type behaviour models available for children to potentially 'imitate' (or at least, adult roles into which they could be slotted by contemporary literature and its authors). Such stories reveal to us ways in which children from godly families were able to react and rebel against forms of strict spiritual education – but those strictures against which they were defined are worthy of study in and of themselves, both as reflections of the anxieties which authors assumed parents may feel, and as a demonstration.

Family advice literature reveals to us the idealised roles in which it was acceptable to cast children. The ways in which children were expected to show loyalty to their parents, and to the spiritual community at large, were numerous – but relatively uniform. To be a good child, a pious child, one had to behave like a small adult.[38] The correct child, as described within such texts, was the pious, adult-like figure: a Christian figure, who prayed, who read and who understood the word of God. Family advice literature depicted children in two most distinct roles: those of child as a sinner needing to be baptised and, even more significantly

---

[38] See discussion above, pp. 11–12, and Thomas, 'Age and Authority in Early Modern England'.

within Protestant texts, the child as scholar. Indeed, through scholarly activity and reading of the Bible both parents and their children, it was believed, could be reformed and saved. It is of considerable significance that even in ostensibly 'practical' domestic literature, the dichotomy between the untamed sinner and the committed student of Christ were clearly defined and routinely depicted: this vision of the child as walking a sort of spiritual tightrope lies beneath much of what family advice manuals had to say on the subject of child-rearing.

We will now briefly consider the particular characteristics of family advice manuals as a form of source material, before looking at the roles in which they cast children and the place, purpose and function of such forms of literature.[39]

Family Advice Manuals as Source Material

Family advice tracts and manuals were lengthy and doctrinally based works, which sought to provide a complete guide to the rearing of children, from birth right through to marriage and beyond. They also instructed readers how to find the perfect spouse, how to go about marriage, how to run a household and keep domestic servants, and sometimes even how to die gracefully. All such advice was issued on the understanding that a true Christian life was rooted in the basic principles of the Protestant faith. Hence, the manuals offered advice on 'howe ye shoulde bothe rule youre selfe and ordre your housholde' in order to establish that highly esteemed spiritual ideal, the 'housholde of faith'.[40] Understandably, then, these works had a lot to say about the raising of children.

Notably, such literature concentrated almost entirely, if not completely, on the religious education and *spiritual* wellbeing of children, rather than concerning itself with physical, medical or social concerns and particularities. It must be remembered that such evidence has a number of built-in biases for which historians need to make allowances. As well as the fact that material offering prescriptive advice will reveal more about the ideal than the reality,

---

[39]   For reading on family advice manuals, see Patrick Collinson's chapter 'The Protestant Family' in his *Birthpangs of Protestant England: Religious and Cultural Change in the Sixteenth and Seventeenth Centuries* (Basingstoke: Macmillan, 1988); Margo Todd, *Christian Humanism and the Puritan Social Order* (Cambridge: Cambridge University Press, 1987); Anthony Fletcher, 'Prescription and Practice: Protestantism and the Upbringing of Children, 1560–1700', in Diana Wood (ed.) *The Church and Childhood, Papers Read at the 1993 Summer Meeting and the 1994 Winter Meeting of the Ecclesiastical History Society* (Oxford: Blackwell, 1994).

[40]   Anon, *A glasse for householders* (London, 1542) *STC* (2nd ed.) 11917, A1r and A5r.

we must also keep in mind, of course, the authorship of such material. How typical the views presented in such familial literature were of late sixteenth and early seventeenth-century English society is debatable. Many of the tracts were produced anonymously, such as the *Office of Christian parents* of 1616, and the much earlier text *A glasse for householders*, of 1542, which provides an example of pre-Reformation (yet evangelical) ideas about child-rearing similar to later writings. Family advice manuals were not a new form of literature in post-Reformation England; they had existed before, in smaller numbers, and their ideas had been Protestantised by Reforming clerics.[41] Indeed, if we refer to Richard Whitford's 1530 text, *A werke for householders*, we can see a pre-Reformation example of clerical writers attempting to lay out ideal and prescriptive models of family behaviour. Whitford's text was more heavily structured around prayer and patterns of worship than later examples, which are more pastoral and more keenly directed at children and specific family circumstances. The post-Reformation authors who are known – the likes of William Perkins, William Gouge and Robert Cleaver – were notable, well published and seemingly well read figures.[42]

These men were significantly connected to godly movements within England. Robert Cleaver was a minister in Banbury, led by the influential John Dod, 'one of a handful of seventeenth-century puritan leaders with national standing'.[43] Cleaver wrote a number of works and sermons, covering subjects such as the proverbs and the Sabbath. His *A godly forme of household government* was published six times between 1598 and 1630.

Clergyman and author William Gouge, who was friends with influential Church of England movers such as Arthur Hildersham, published a fair number of works, both spiritually and politically motivated. Yet, his *Of Domesticall Duties*, published in 1622 and 1634, is the work for which he is most remembered. As the entry in the Oxford Dictionary of National Biography reads, the work was a: 'penetrating analysis of the godly household'. Gouge's pulpit was recognised

---

[41] See Anon, *A glasse for householders*; for an earlier, Catholic example of family advice, see Richard Whitford, *A werke for housholders* (London, 1530) *STC* (2nd ed.) 25425.

[42] See entries for these writers in the Oxford Dictionary of National Biography; Michael Jinkins, 'Perkins, William (1558–1602)', *Oxford Dictionary of National Biography*, Oxford University Press, 2004; online edn, May 2007 [http://www.oxforddnb.com/view/article/21973, accessed 27 Jan 2015]; Brett Usher, 'Gouge, William (1575–1653)', *Oxford Dictionary of National Biography*, Oxford University Press, 2004; online edn, Jan 2008 [http://www.oxforddnb.com/view/article/11133, accessed 27 Jan 2015].

[43] J. Fielding, 'Dod, John (1550–1645)', *Oxford Dictionary of National Biography*, Oxford University Press, 2004; online edn, Jan 2008 [http://www.oxforddnb.com/view/article/7729, accessed 27 Jan 2015].

as among the most popular and celebrated in London. From here he gave many sermons and lectures, which were attended by crowds of people. Hence, his theological ideas must have, on some level at least, been held in high repute by members of society at large.[44]

William Perkins, meanwhile, was also a well-connected and celebrated theologian, with Europe-wide fame, whose works were published extensively during the late sixteenth and seventeenth centuries. After a drunken youth, Perkins went on to become a Church of England clergyman, author and theologian. His brand of faith was similar to that of second generation Swiss Calvinists, such as Theodore Beza and Zacharias Ursinus. His work *Christian oeconomie, or, A short survey of the right manner of erecting and ordering a familie* was not the most significant of his works, published just once in 1609, but it still reveals the attempt of England's most notable Reformation-era theologian to lay out how early modern families were, ideally, to be ordered.

Dorothy Leigh, writer of the *Mothers Blessing,* although by no means a cleric, was nevertheless from godly stock.[45] Furthermore, her work was incredibly successful, being published in no less than 14 traceable editions between its first publication in 1616 and 1685. The text was written during her pregnancy, to be left behind for her sons, George, John and William, in the event of their mother's possible death. As Leigh wrote, 'I beeing troubled and wearied with feare, lest my children should not find the right way to heauen, thought with my selfe that I could doe no lesse for them, then euerie man will doe for his friend, which vvas to write them the right way, that I had truly obserued out of the written word of GOD ... '.[46] This illustrates godly families' desire to ensure that their children had the best possible chance of salvation, and that this would be at least in part achieved through proper instruction and education. The fact that Leigh's work was published so heavily reveals that the concerns she illustrates were likely to have been widespread, amongst the 'godly elite' at the very least.

Such Puritan persuasions do not necessarily signify outlandish opinions. The views belonging to the likes of Cleaver, Gouge, Leigh and Perkins, whilst perhaps more intense, were not necessarily far from the beliefs of the English nation. As has been argued, 'between 1560 and 1625 the doctrine of predestination was accepted without question by virtually all of the most

---

[44]   Usher, 'Gouge, William', *Oxford Dictionary of National Biography.*

[45]   For information on Leigh, see Sylvia Brown (ed.) *Women's Writing in Stuart England, The Mothers' Legacies of Dorothy Leigh, Elizabeth Joscelin and Elizabeth Richardson* (Stroud: Sutton Publishing, 1999).

[46]   Leigh, *The Mothers Blessing* (1616) sig. A2r–v.

influential clergymen in England, puritan and non-puritan alike'.[47] Perhaps their beliefs and views, whether thundered from the pulpit or written in published form, were representative of what was perceived to be going wrong within the English family, as the eyes of the spiritual perfectionist would have seen it. Yet, much like the lifestyle gurus of present-day society, just because they were perhaps somewhat purist in their views, does not mean that their advice was not followed, at least in part. Indeed, as we will see within this monograph, Reformed doctrine could be flexible, and was able to adapt itself to pastoral situations and the rhythms of the human life-cycle.

Baptism and Education

> For by reason of Adam's transgression, there is no man nor child but is naturally giuen to euil, and euill education doth make them ten times more euill. Therefore as young impes must be warily looked vnto in their planting, grafting, growing, and bearing of fruit, so are the children of youth: they doe most necessarily require verie great care, ouer-sight, and guiding, least they be vtterly spoyled, and come to confusion'.[48]

As part of God's purpose, Protestants also believed that it was humankind's correct vocation to nurture a future generation of Christians. Fundamentally, despite Protestant doctrine that asserted man's powerlessness to alter the decree of God by earthly action, much attention was given to the soteriological problems involved with securing child salvation. As mentioned above, the Christian life of a child was to begin at baptism. Despite fundamental changes in theology throughout the Reformation period, which downplayed the relationship between human ritual and salvation, baptism remained of huge importance to the life course of the infant. As a mid seventeenth-century catechism read, baptism was; '1. confessing original sinne, 2. beleeving God is there God and the God of their seed, 3. shewing the neede they have of Christ, so leaving the infant in the House of God; to grow up in his courts at the sole of Christ's feete'.[49] Baptism was, though not without exception or conflict, widely believed to be the most efficient way to safeguard the spiritual and physical wellbeing

---

[47]   Durston, Christopher, and Eales, Jacqueline, *The Culture of English Puritanism, 1560–1700* (Basingstoke, New York: Palgrave Macmillan, 1996) p. 7.

[48]   Anon, *The office of Christian parents*, p. 10.

[49]   Anon, *To Sions Virgins: or A Short Forme of Catechisme of the Doctrine of Baptisme* (London, 1644) *Wing* (2nd ed.) T1385, sig. A3v.

of children. Furthermore, it was the duty of Christian parents to ensure that infants received their baptism; as the anonymously written catechism further stated, 'the faith of the Parents carrieth the infants to the ordinance presenting it to the congregation'.[50]

Gouge spoke of 'parents ioynt care about their childrens Baptisme' as a 'dutie to be performed of parents to their children even in their infancy, and that is in regard of their spiritual good, which is this, Parents ought to procure that their children be rightly baptised in due season'.[51] Baptism signified the right children had to God's kingdom, and it was seen as 'euidence of that their right ... [and it] is parents duty to get them that euidence'.[52] As Gouge justified, 'Their conception and birth [was] in sinne', hence, 'Children drew contagion from their parents: therefore great reason it is that their parents should see them washed with the water of regeneration'.[53]

As well as a washing, it was believed that children would be comforted by their baptism, during their infancy and if they reached it, in later life. As Gouge wrote; 'The comfort which from the performance of this dutie will arise to Christian parents, yea and to the children themselves when they come to the age of vnderstanding. When parents behold the couenant of God surely sealed and confirmed to their children ... And it must needs also much comfort the childe when (being of vnderstanding) he shall know that from his infancy he hath carried the seal and pledge of his regeneration'. Finally, as Gouge also argued, baptism formed a core ritual of the Christian Church and society, 'the constant continued custome of the true catholicke Church, which ever since the Apostles time hath afforded the sacrament of baptisme to children'.[54] Hence, the image of children cleansed and comforted through baptism, their welcoming into the Christian community, was a powerful one.

Baptism formed the foundation of the correct Christian upbringing. Yet, due to a new scepticism surrounding the efficacy of baptism, which doubted the traditional and secured means of ensuring salvation for infants who died during early life, Protestant parents were directly faced with the problematic spiritual status of their infants and children, and the irresolvable issue of their salvation. As a result, much attention was given to instilling correct Christian values from the earliest days of a child's lifetime. Furthermore, clerical writers attempted to

---

[50]   Anon, *To Sions Virgins*, sig. A3v.

[51]   William Gouge, *Of Domesticall Duties, Eight Treatises* (London, 1622: Cf. first edition 1612) *STC* (2nd ed.) 12119, pp. 518–19.

[52]   Gouge, *Of Domesticall Duties*, p. 520.

[53]   Gouge, *Of Domesticall Duties*, pp. 520–21.

[54]   Gouge, *Of Domesticall Duties*, pp. 520–21.

persuade readers of the need to encourage such behavioural ideals in parents and their children: to make the godly parent and child depicted on the black and white print of the page into a pastoral reality. Hence, once baptism had been performed, the crucial means through which to shape your child for Heaven was to provide a good education, mainly through teaching the young to read.

Mid sixteenth-century writer John Merbeke, quoting the words of Swiss Reformer and friend to Calvin, Theodore Beza, wrote that children should be 'brought unto Christ, not onlie by baptisme, which is the seale of the kingdome of heaven, but also by godly education and bringing up'.[55] Similarly, familial tract writer Dorothy Leigh wrote 'stirre them vp to write' and encouraged parents to 'ensure that all your children, be they Males or Females, may in youth learne to reade the Bible in their owne mother tongue; for I know it is a greate helpe to true godlinesse'.[56] She continued to recommend that 'all your children may be tought to reade, beginning at foure yeares old or before, and let them learne till ten, in which time they are not able to do any good in the Commonwealth, but to learne how to serue God, their King & country by reading'.[57]

According to Leigh, the true written word of God was 'the pathway to all happinesse, and which will bring you to the chiefe Citty, new Ierusalem'.[58] Scholarly education was so important to Leigh that she advised no adult to accept the role of godparent unless he or she could ensure that the child 'shall be taught to reade, so soone as it can conueniently learne, and that it shall so continue till it can read the Bible'.[59] Hence, godly education was seen to be the key to a good life and potential salvation.

Furthermore, the notion that education and discipline would help to curb the inherently wild and evil nature of a child was a longstanding one. Traces of such opinion can be found in biblical passages, for example the Old Testament Proverb 'Foolishnes is bounde in the heart of a childe: but the rodde of correction shal drive it away from him'.[60] Much of this was tangled with beliefs surrounding original sin and the notion of humankind being born into sin, as has already been considered. Such perceptions were widespread throughout European Protestantism; a German sermon from the early sixteenth century claimed that 'just as a cat craves mice, a fox chickens, and a wolf cub sheep, so infant humans

---

[55] John Merbecke, *A booke of notes and common places* (London, 1581) STC (2nd ed.) 17299, p. 172.

[56] Leigh, *The Mothers Blessing* (1616) pp. 14 and 24.

[57] Leigh, *The Mothers Blessing* (1616) pp. 46–7.

[58] Leigh, *The Mothers Blessing* (1616) p. 15.

[59] Leigh, *The Mothers Blessing* (1616) pp. 25–6.

[60] Proverbs 22: 15.

are inclined in their hearts to adultery, fornication, impure desires, lewdness, idol worship, belief in magic, hostility, quarrelling, passion, anger, strife, dissension, factiousness, hatred, murder, drunkenness, gluttony, and more'.[61]

The belief in original sin and the perception that humans were born evil, gaining virtue through recourse to religion throughout life, is particularly apparent in analogies and metaphors comparing the education of the young and ignorant with horticultural images. The notion of cultivation, of shaping a child, was a common one, with a mixture of Protestant and humanist influences. Dorothy Leigh wrote, 'the nature of man is wholly corrupted with sinne, and is good for nothing: as the earth is fit to bring forth nothing but weedes, except it bee digged and dressed, and continually laboured and weeded'.[62] Hence, left to their own devices and nature, children would grow up badly. With care, however, young wills could be broken, and infant shoots could be trained to grow in the right direction.[63] During the early seventeenth century, a family advice manual, instructing the masters of households how to govern their children throughout all ages and stages, argued that:

> ... nothing is more fruitfull in vse, nor more goodly in sight, then a field well tilled and manured: so vnto Christian parents, which carefully and wisely traine vp their children and gouerne them, neglecting no dutie thereunto belonging; their children shall be a fruitfull field, a pleasant spectacle, ioyfull tidings, a comfortable remembrance, blessed of God, and honourable among men; in this life delightfull, in death hopefull, and in all occasions, healthfull, sweete, and praisefull.[64]

Indeed, the belief that the correctly ordered and well governed family was a natural part of the life-cycle, like tamed nature, a thing most fruitful and beneficial – in both life and death – was paramount within early modern society.

The parallels between notions of an educated mind and piety also stemmed, to an extent, from humanist influences. While Protestant literature revealed a concern for original sin, however, humanist scholars downplayed such factors. Dutch humanist Erasmus, often regarded as the voice of Christian humanism, was renowned for his emphasis on the importance of child education, his writings revealing opinions which were profoundly different from those preached and written about in Reformation England. He believed that nature had implanted in children the seeds of a desire for knowledge and a great capacity for memory.

---

[61]   Cunningham, *Children and Childhood*, p. 48.
[62]   Leigh, *The Mothers Blessing* (1616) pp. 80–81.
[63]   Cunningham, *Children and Childhood*, p. 48.
[64]   Anon, *The office of Christian parents*, p. 17.

Such a nature needed to be shaped: 'The child that nature has given you is nothing but a shapeless lump, but the material is still pliable, capable of assuming any form, and you must mould it that it takes on the best possible character. If you are negligent, you will rear an animal; but if you apply yourself, you will fashion, if I may use such a bold term, a godlike creature'.[65]

Erasmus compared a child to wax, to be moulded while soft. Whilst acknowledging a childish 'disposition to evil', he thought this was often much exaggerated, and it was mainly adults, 'who corrupt young minds with evil before we expose them to the good'.[66] Similarly, John Earle emphasised childhood innocence, writing in 1628, 'a child is a man in small letter, yet the best copy of Adam before he tasted of Eve or the apple ... his soul is yet a white paper unscribbled with observations of the world ... he knows no evil'.[67]

Hugh Cunningham has related such changes in mentality to modern views on childhood. He argues that the period of Renaissance and Reformation formed a stepping stone between traditional beliefs in original sin, and secularist developments during the eighteenth century. Such changes saw a decline in ideological views of children as innately evil, to secular ones, which saw childhood as a separate phase of life, where the 'individual' rights of the child became a growing priority.[68] Yet, although both Protestants and humanists valued education for children, I would not necessarily argue for an especially close or immediately progressive relationship between early modern child education and theories of modernity, as in reality the situation was much more thorny and complicated, often driven and tempered by religious and pastoral motivations.

Indeed, although both Protestants and humanist thinkers valued education, they did so for different reasons. Protestants saw education as a way to tame youthful rebellion and to instil ideas which would help to provide godly armour against temptation and the evil which was a natural part of a human race born in sin. Humanist thinkers, rather, believed that children were born blank, and that they could be shaped by whatever influences they were exposed to. Hence education would help to nurture children, and would write upon this blank.[69] Protestant education campaigns were not driven by ideas of the child as an 'individual' or with secularist aspirations, but rather with concern

---

[65] Cunningham, *Children and Childhood*, pp. 43–5.

[66] Cunningham, *Children and Childhood*, pp. 43–5.

[67] Cunningham, *Children and Childhood*, pp. 43–5.

[68] Cunningham, *Children and Childhood*, pp. 41, 61–2.

[69] For the intellectual nature of Reform, and the link between godliness and learning, see Alec Ryrie, *The Gospel and Henry VIII, Evangelicals in the Early English Reformation* (Cambridge: Cambridge University Press, 2003) pp. 157–69.

for child piety and ultimate salvation. Education was related to salvation, and was seen by godly writers as a means to an end, rather than as a virtue in itself, as espoused by humanist thinkers. Furthermore, it was parents' duty to provide such an education.

The Christian Duties of Parents and Children

> ... my little children, of whom I doe trauaile againe in birth, vntill Christ be formed in you ... [70]

According to the advice manuals, there was no human occupation or purpose more fundamental than that of the good parent. Contemporary literature acknowledged the purpose of marriage and parenthood as a godly ordained and biblically acknowledged aspect of Christian life: 'married folks ... whose marriage is for the procreation of children; who through Gods blessings hauing sonnes or daughters, are properly parents, according to Gods ordinance in the creation, whereof it is said, "Bring forth fruit, and multiply, and fill the earth (Gen. 1:18.)"'. [71] The duty of parents was to care for the physical and moral wellbeing of their children, and familial literature spoke with much compassion about how to care for the needs of the young. [72] As one tract explained;

> the office of the Parents is occupied in an honest care, a wise ouersight, and a constant guiding of their children vnto the ende ... The care is honest ... and for the comfort of their bodies and soules ... this must be done by a constant guiding: the eye, the hand, the tongue, and all that the parent doth, must be a guide to the child at all times, yea ... to direct and order him, that he grow and go forward, like an wholesome and kindly plant, spreading out his branches, and bringing forth much and goodly fruit in due season. [73]

When speaking about education, the role of parents went much beyond procreation and the basic necessities for survival. Rather, advice manuals and instructive forms of literature spoke of the godly-ordained role of parents, 'This name of Parents, is a name of dignitie, and of Soueraigne authoritie: a very

---

[70]   Leigh, *The Mothers Blessing* (1616) p. 11.

[71]   Anon, *The office of Christian parents*, pp. 1–2.

[72]   See Introduction, pp. 7–12 for summary of historiographical debates surrounding parental love.

[73]   Anon, *The office of Christian parents*, p. 9.

honourable dignitie it is to be head of the family, the fountain of the ofspring, and the ... cause of the childrens beeing'.[74] Furthermore:

> Some mens office is about stones, timber, mettall, and such like: some handle plants, hearbs, and flowers: some cattell, foules of the ayre, or fish of the sea: the physitian looketh to the health of the body, the Lawyer to the state of the lands or goods: but the Parent is put in trust with a more honourable charge, to gouerne the cheifest creature vnder heauen, to traine vp that which is called the generation of God ... Who can say their authoritie is light, and their dignitie small, and their charge of little value, to whome the king of heauen, the high and mightie God, committeth his sonnes and daughters to be ordered and gouerned all the dayes of their life?[75]

The role of the parent, then, was the most important occupation. Parents were charged with raising the next generation of Christians, and Protestant moralists were eager to encourage them to take such a role as seriously as any other profession. As mentioned earlier, infants and children were considered to be especially weak to the wiles and temptations of the Devil, due to the stain of original sin and their physical and spiritual weaknesses. Thus a fundamental part of parental duty involved safeguarding the spiritual, as well as physical, wellbeing of children. William Gouge advised 'pray for your children', and that such a duty 'must be performed before Parents have children ... and so soone as children are conceived, especially if they observe them to be quicke in the womb ... and againe when they are borne'.[76] Leigh prescribed a similar method for raising the young: during a child's months of infancy mothers were advised to 'blesse it ... when shee feeleth the bloud come from her heart to nourish it' when they were breastfeeding; later in life she should 'instruct it in the youth, and admonish it in the age, and pray for it continually'.[77]

The most natural gift from God, it was believed, was the love of a parent towards their child, and this was a theme commonly written about. The overwhelming nature of such emotions was often remarked upon, both praised for its joys, but also suspected for its ability to distract from God – interestingly, then, there is evidence here of a dichotomy of parenthood, as well as childhood. The natural love of parents was often seen to apply particularly to mothers, who were intimately involved with their young. As one manual stated, 'let no man blame a mother (who indeede brought forth her childe with much paine) ... she

---

74   Anon, *The office of Christian parents*, p. 9.
75   Anon, *The office of Christian parents*, p. 9.
76   Gouge, *Of Domesticall Duties*, p. 494.
77   Leigh, *The Mothers Blessing* (1616) p. 10.

[will] labour againe till Christ bee formed in them … since euery man knows, that the loue of a mother to her children, is hardly contained within the bounds of reason'.[78] Author of advice manual *Of Domesticall Duties*, Gouge, similarly wrote 'nourish, increase, and blow up this fire of loue'.[79] Gouge spoke of the powerful nature of the love of a parent for their child, '… if loue be in them, no paine, paines, cost, or care, will seeme too much. Herein appeareth the wise prouidence of God, who by nature hath so fast fixed loue in the hearts of parents, as if there be any in whom it aboundeth not, he is counted vnnaturall. If loue did not abound in parents, many children would be neglected and lost'.[80] However, he also warned against the evil of 'excesse doting' upon children; 'as they do who so unmeasurably love them, as they make reckoning of nothing in comparison of children'.[81] Such 'doting' could lead parents to forget God, 'Even God himselfe is lightly esteemed, his worship neglected, his Word transgressed … their owne soules forgotten thorow care of children'.[82]

Yet, parental love correctly applied would not lead to distraction or neglect of religion, but rather was to be seen as a beneficial part of godly purpose. A sermon by Hugh Latimer told of how the 'fatherly affection and love of parentes towards their children, is the good gift of God: And god hath planted the same in their hertes'. Such love was not without a worldly purpose, 'for the childrens sake: for it is an irkesome thyng to bryng up children … to kepe them, and waite upon them; and preserve them from all perill; if god had not planted such love in the parentes heartes … [it would be] impossible to doo so much for theim'.[83] Latimer acknowledged a further reason for love between parent and child, in its ability to illustrate, by some small means, the love of God for his people; 'An other cause is, wherfore god hath planted such love in the parentes hearts towards their children: that we might *lerne* by it, what affections he beareth towards us. For though the love of parentes towardes their children bee very great: yet the love of God towards us is greater'.[84] Thus, parental love could be seen as a microcosmic depiction of God's inscrutable scheme in its entirety.

It was the parents' duty to shape relationships within the family, between themselves and their children, and to lead by example. Parents would mould the

---

[78]   Leigh, *The Mothers Blessing* (1616) pp. 11–12.

[79]   Gouge, *Of Domesticall Duties*, p. 494.

[80]   Gouge, *Of Domesticall Duties*, p. 494.

[81]   Gouge, *Of Domesticall Duties*, p. 494.

[82]   Gouge, *Of Domesticall Duties*, p. 494.

[83]   Hugh Latimer, *27 sermons preached by the ryght reuerende father in God … maister Hugh Latimer* (London, 1562) *STC* (2nd ed.) 15276. sig. D3r–v.

[84]   Latimer, *27 sermons*, sig. D3r–v.

character and religious temper of their offspring; masters of families were to lead those under their care by good example, they must be 'diligent and carefull to reforme themselues, both inwardly and outwardly ... For as one candle cannot light an other, if it selfe be out'.[85] Parents, at the very least, hoped to see signs of election reflected in the moral and upright behaviour of a well raised family flock. Through their deeds, aspirations and moral stature, the child, it was seemingly believed (or at least, congregations were taught) could potentially inherit their spiritual worth and their eternal destination from their parental lineage; or at the very least, children with no spiritual guidance were very unlikely to receive God's salvation. Such a notion somewhat contradicts official Protestant predestinarianism, which told that each individual had to face God's fate alone; morality and judgment, it seems, could be seen to run in families. As *The office of Christian parents* phrased it: 'The iust man that walketh in his vprightnes is blessed, and blessed shall his children be after him: A good man shall giue inheritance to his childrens children: The childrens children shalbe a crowne to the Elders, and the Fathers a glorie to their children: The Children of Gods seruants shall continue, and their seed shall stand fast in thy sight'.[86] Such a statement was rooted in various biblical passages; from the Proverbs 'He that walketh in his integritie, is iuste: and blessed shal his children be after him'; and Psalm 102 'The children of thy servants shal continue, and their sede shal stand fast in thy sight'.[87]

Hence, writers often implied that faithful followers of Christ would be rewarded with likeminded offspring, as Gouge argued: 'Though God doe reserve in himeselfe a freedome to order his blessings as it pleaseth him, and to bestow them upon whom he will ... it is a very usuall course with him to extend his blessing to the children of the righteous'.[88] Such concepts were, then, pastorally neat, if not theologically sound, as they allowed clerics to comfort their parishioners, and to offer them hope and purpose. However, they also illustrate what kinds of theological gymnastics were occurring in Reformation England, and provide evidence of official Protestant theologies melting at the edges – due, I would argue, to the harshness of the doctrine of predestination to *child salvation* in particular. As considered in the Introduction, beliefs in predestination may have served as a comfort to some (as emphasised by recent historiography), on the deathbed for example, but for parents, who had the crucial job of raising the future generation of Christians, it was then important to offer them hope, to assure them that with hard work, compassion and

---

[85] Anon, *The office of Christian parents*, p. 11.

[86] Anon, *The office of Christian parents*, p. 17.

[87] Proverbs 20:7; Psalm 102:28.

[88] Gouge, *Of Domesticall Duties*, p. 510.

Protestant zeal, they could ensure their children's salvation. Not only this, such reassurances would also have provided comfort during the possible – and in early childhood especially the highly likely – event that a child might die. In the face of the religious uncertainties surrounding child salvation, which grew especially out of changes to the baptism ceremony, Protestant clerics and writers armed parents with a different set of tools: baptism might no longer offer the assurance of salvation, but godly parenting and providing a Protestant education would.

Understandably, the bond and sense of spiritual duty that seems to have existed between parents and children was not to be one sided. The texts, written by-and-large for heads of households and parents, may have focused more upon the role and duty of the parent: 'When God obligeth children by the fift precept, to honour Father and Mother, he doth by due equitie and answerable proportion, euen by the verie same commandement, tie the father and mother, to doe their office also to their children'.[89] At the same time, however, they also drew upon the other side of this coin: the parent–child relationship was to be a reciprocal one, especially as the child grew older. Hence, as parents' salvation depended upon how they raised their offspring, a child's salvation depended upon how they treated their elders. Children were warned, 'Of the authoritie of Salomon also speaketh, 'obey thy Father that begat thee', and the Apostle addeth, 'in all things': and this is established with such a sanction, that if the children doe not obey, 'they can looke for no peace or prosperitie'.[90] Further, even somewhat terrifyingly, God 'commaundeth the children to honour their parents, and directed Saloman to say, The eye that mocketh his Father, and despiseth the instruction of his Mother, let the rauens of the valley picke it out, and the yong eagles eate it (Prov. 30:17)'.[91]

The 'Little Church' and the Christian Commonwealth

> A Household is as it were a little Common-wealth, by the good Gouernment whereof, Gods glorie may be aduanced.[92]

The role of raising children was of fundamental importance, and was seen to be directly related to the future of the commonwealth. As can be seen from the reciprocal duties expected to be shared between child and parent, early modern

---

89   Anon, *The office of Christian parents*, p. 7.
90   Anon, *The office of Christian parents*, p. 8.
91   Anon, *The office of Christian parents*, pp. 7–8.
92   Robert Cleaver, *A godly forme of household* (London, 1603) STC (2nd ed.) 5385, p. 13.

society was an intermeshed one, in which the individual did not exist alone, but instead sat among an interconnected sea of faces – the faces of the family, the microcosm of society. The family was not a private institution, but rather one of public interest, whose workings were of interest to the Christian community in its entirety, and whose misgivings and misfortunes spilled out into the world beyond: 'And the manifold blessings in towne and citie, in ciuill and ecclesiasticall affaires, in tempestuous vprores, and bright-shining peace, and the comfort, ioy, and glorie that ariseth vnto Parents themselues, to their friends, to their countrie, and to honouring of the Gospel, do most manifestly declare, and as a loud trumpet soundeth foorth the wonderfull excellent benefit, which aboundantly floweth out of the well guiding and good ordering of children.'[93]

The idea of the 'Little Church', or the family, within the Protestant world, was directly related to Reformed theories concerning salvation. A godly family was a microcosm of God's church on earth, and his kingdom in heaven. As contemporary familial tracts argued, putting one's house in order was the first step towards establishing a truly Christian society. 'For such Householders, as pretend to bee great protestants, and sound professors of the Gospell, may long inough talke of discipline, and still complaine of the want of Church-gouernment; but all in vaine, and to no purpose, vnlesse they will begin this most necessarie discipline in reforming their owne houses.'[94] Families were the building blocks for a faithful and just world. As Cleaver's tract *A godly forme of household* illustrates, the notion of the 'little church' was doctrinally rooted. Quoting a passage from I Corinthians, Cleaver argued that the aim of every Protestant householder was to be ever so 'diligent and carefull in the trayning and bringing vp of his children and seruanutes, in the obedience and wayes of the Lorde', so that he may 'rightly deserue to haue ... a Church in his house'.[95]

During this period the relationship between the family, the little church and the Commonwealth was seen to be fundamental to social order. As Gouge argued, 'Oh if the head and seuerall members of a family would be perswaded euery of them to be conscionable in performing their owne particular duties, what a sweet society, and happy harmony would there be in houses? What excellent seminaries would families be to Church and Commonwealth? Necessary it is that order be first set in families: for ... good members of a family are like to make good members of Church and common-wealth'.[96] Indeed, the rearing of children in the home was seen to directly feed into the political and

---

[93] Anon, *The office of Christian parents*, p. 10.
[94] Cleaver, *A godly forme of household*, sigs. A2v–A3r.
[95] Quoting I. Cor. 16.19, Cleaver, *A godly forme of household*, sig. A3v.
[96] Gouge, *Of domesticall duties*, p. q12v.

religious ingenuity needed to face the hectic nature of 'public' life. As Perkins put it, some 'haue called the Familie, the first societie in nature, and the ground of all the rest. Some againe haue compared it to the Bee-hiue ... wherein are bred many Swarmes, which thence doe flie abroad into the world, to the raising and maintaining of other States'.[97] As Perkins continued 'Vpon this condition of the Familie, being the Seminarie of all other societies, it followeth, that the holie and righteous gouernment thereof, is a direct meane for the good ordering, both of Church and Common-wealth; yea that the lawes thereof being rightly informed and religiously obserued, are auaileable to prepare and dispose men to the keeping of order in other gouernements'.[98]

Furthermore, establishing a church in your house, according to the familial literature of the time, helped to pave the way to heaven. This could be seen as ironic, perhaps, in the face of a religious culture that was, supposedly, averse to anything tainted with Catholicism, of good deeds on earth, or of being able to steer one's soul along the path to eternal salvation, or even to plummet it towards damnation. Nevertheless, readers of family advice literature were encouraged to bring into the world 'children of God, and heires of the couenant' through worldly deed, actively 'promoting' the notion that education could lead to eternal salvation, whereas neglect of spiritual education would result in sure damnation.[99] Early examples of such Protestant household literature, such as *A glasse for householders*, produced before the main surges of Reformed opinion had shaken English religious beliefs to the core, could openly claim such a relationship. If heads of families were successful in establishing a 'household of faith' they would be 'sure to haue of God euerlasting lyfe for your rewarde' as well as reassuring readers that they would 'not to lacke suche thinges as are necessary for this presente lyfe'. It was far from surprising for the literature produced within a prominently Catholic culture to state that not only could you secure your own salvation, but also that of your offspring, 'you shall purchase a sure in-herytaunce for youre chyldren. For God neuer suffereth the sede of the iuste personne ....'[100]

However, it seems that such trends continued throughout the familial literature of the post-Reformation period, even within the works of the highly esteemed godly writers. Indeed, *The office of Christian parents*, published

---

[97]   William Perkins, *Christian oeconomie, or, A short survey of the right manner of erecting and ordering a familie according to the Scriptures* (London, 1609) *STC* (2nd ed.) 19677.3, sigs. A2v–A3r.

[98]   William Perkins, *Christian oeconomie*, sig. A3r.

[99]   Cleaver, *A godly forme of household*, sig. A3v.

[100]   Anon, *A glasse for householders*, sig. A7v.

anonymously in 1616, should have, presumably, known better than to claim that such earthly actions could influence the predestined decree of God. Nevertheless, it too argued that the 'true worshippe of God, and the right vnderstanding of many especiall morall duties' provided a 'means … to please God, and to obtain saluation'. The text did in fact check such an assertion with a doctrinally justified summary of predestination, 'The naturall man perceiues not the things of the Spirit of God; for they are foolishnesse to him, neither can he know them, because they are spiritually discerned'. (I Cor. 2:14) Adding, 'For the doctrine of Christians is the mysterie of God euen the Father, and of Christ, in whom are hid all the treasures of wisedome and knowledge'.[101] This reflected the contemporary notion that education and sound knowledge of the scriptures was fundamental, both to show outward signs of election, and ultimately to secure salvation.

Gouge in particular drew heavily on the intimate connection between correct family ordering and salvation. Indeed, his work speaks of salvation in the world hereafter, and signs of godly favour in this life. His *Of domesticall duties* goes to extraordinary lengths to hammer home to his readers the essential nature of spiritual nurturing: not only for acquiring salvation, but also in order to enjoy the fruits of this world. One of the work's chapters was entitled, most fittingly, 'Of appropriating prosperity and long-life to the obedience which children yeeld to their parents'.[102] According to Gouge, well educated and decently behaved children benefited both child and parent, by assuring, as far as was possible, both a comfortable and long life; 'Because a childes performing of his dutie to his parents is vnder God an especiall meanes that they doe well, and liue long (for as rebellious children make their parents with grief to come the sooner to their graues, so dutifull children make them to continue the longer in prosperity) the Lord in recompence promiseth to such a childe prosperity and long life'.[103] Hence, good behaviour resulted in longevity. In biblical terms, the relationship between worldly godliness and quality of life was, if read literally, established. In Paul's letter to the Ephesians, he states, 'Children obey your parents in the Lord: for this is right. Honour thy father and mother (which is the first commandement with prom*i*se) That it may be wel with thee, and thou maist liue long on earth'.[104] Gouge's work was in turn reinforced with such biblical justifications for good childhood upbringing, its benefits to both parents and children, and its direct implications upon quality of life on earth and salvation hereafter:

---

[101] Anon, *The office of Christian parents*, pp. 14–15.
[102] Gouge, *Of domesticall duties*, p. 145.
[103] Gouge, *Of domesticall duties*, p. 145.
[104] Ephesians 6: 1–3.

Children may further learne out of this promise, that in performing their dutie they doe good not only to their parents, but also to themselues: they procure their own welfare and long-life. What egregious fooles then are disobedient children: they regard neither God, their parents, nor themselues, but depriue themselues of their eternall happinesse, hinder their welfare, and shorten their daies.

Gouge based this extremely direct link between behaviour, worldly prosperity and ultimate salvation on passages taken from the Bible:

Fitly here-upon I may applie to vndutifull children these words of the Psalmist, 'Marke the obedient childe, for the end of him of peace: but the rebellious shall be destroyed: he shall be cut off ' (Psal. 37.37,38): and these of the wise-man, 'I know that it shall not be well with the disobedient, he shall not prolong his daies' (Eccl. 8.12, 13) : and these of the Prophet, 'say ye to the obedient child it shall be well with him, he shall eat the fruit of his doings, but woe to the transgressor, it shall be ill with him' (Isa. 3.10,11).[105]

Furthermore, Gouge's prognosis for the life and potential salvation of a disobedient and sinful child was an acutely negative one. He argued, quite simply, ' … when parents are too indulgent ouer their children, God doth punish the sinne both of parent and childe, by shortening the childes daies … ' (I Sam 2:34; II Sam. 18:14; I King. 2:25). Not only this, but the impact of the disobedient child reverberated far beyond the confines of the family; the worldly implications for children who were disobedient towards their parents were, to say the least, far reaching and, potentially socially devastating:

In that disobedience to parents, is a sinne that seldome goeth alone: for an vndutifull childe is commonly a verie lewd person many other waies. Considering the pronenesse of our nature to all sinne, it cannot be auoided but that they who in the beginning shake off the yoake of gouernment, should run headlong into all riot, loosenesse, and licentiousnesse: thus then sinne being added vnto sinne, it must needs bring mischiefe vpon mischiefe, till at length life be cut off.[106]

Indeed, the moral views advocated by writers of familial literature often veered towards the threatening. They were emotive narratives, saturated with emotive language, designed to influence English society and to encourage godly

---

[105] Gouge, *Of domesticall duties*, pp. 148–9.
[106] Gouge, *Of domesticall duties*, p. 146.

forms of behaviour. Badly brought up children, it was argued, were in earthly life a disgrace and discredit to their parents and a hindrance to both Church and commonwealth. Not only this, parents who failed to sufficiently indoctrinate their children were seen to be literally pushing their own offspring towards the gates of hell. As the *Office of Christian parents* argued; 'how vnseemely and dangerously they dishonour almightie God and what a way they open to the kingdome of Sathan, to sinne, to mischeife and miserie, by ill gouerning of their children'.[107] Similarly, Robert Cleaver was prone to threatening readers with descriptions of the Devil, and thus attempted to call an end to earthly injustice by frightening his audience with images of damnation-fire;

> ... in the extremitie of death, no one thing will bee more grieuous vnto the Parents and Householders, then (the Lord hauing giuen them the charge of so many soules to be furthered to saluation) that their owne tormented consciences shal presse them, in as much as they haue helped their children and seruants forward to their damnation; and so (which is more fearefull) they shall haue them spewing and foming out on their faces, continuall curses in hell, then accusing them for euer to be the murtherers of their soules, and cut-throats of their saluation.[108]

Hence, not only were these texts arguing that spiritual education could gently lead children towards their eternal salvation, but more extremely, that the neglect of such teachings could violently drive them towards eternal punishment.

Yet, their messages were not solely concerned with hellfire and damnation. These writers were, through their descriptions, providing parents and children with some form of agency; they were providing them with a choice: educate your children, and they will receive God's grace in both life and Heaven. Indeed, rather than teaching potentially difficult to comprehend Calvinist doctrines concerning the perils of double predestination, it would have been much more palatable, and also far more pastorally useful, to preach a doctrine of hope and salvation. Through linking good education and sound upbringing with godliness, Protestant leaders were, in theory at least, going some way to secure a form of social and familial regulation and control, as well as promoting a system in which parents and families could, by their very own doing, actively influence the eternal destination of both themselves and their children. They were, in a sense, producing idealised, or dualistic, narratives about the spiritual roles of parents and their offspring, which softened some of the harsher tenets of the

---

[107] Anon, *The office of Christian parents*, pp. 10–11.
[108] Cleaver, *A godly forme of household*, sigs. A4v.

Protestant faith. Surely, this must have, to some extent, inspired and encouraged many parents.

As was natural, parents wanted to ensure good for their children. Within a culture in which religion permeated the life course and events of most, if not all, people, part of this parental responsibility would have included securing child salvation. This desire to control, or to influence or know, the future – to have some hope of salvation, or to feel that as an individual you have some agency in knowing if you are to be saved, was a motivation familiar to the Catholic past. Whereas previous soteriologies had enabled Catholic worshippers to take part in a form of faith and worship which provided, through church attendance, prayer, confession and the baptism ceremony, some form of agency and comfort, the Protestant faith, officially, denied followers such assurances. The doctrine of predestination, as discussed in the introductory chapter, confronted followers with the realisation that their fate, and the fate of their offspring, was both mapped out by God and unknown to them, and yet, as recent historiography has sought to show, was still able to provide comfort to believers, through pastoral means. However, this work argues that it was more difficult to receive such comfort, if one was the parent of an infant, worrying about the salvation of their child's soul. Here we see family advice manuals, and continuing beliefs about the role and purpose of the baptismal blessing, providing some of that comfort – even though the theological beliefs underpinning them, most especially beliefs in predestination, do remain stoically intact.

Hence, this is not to question the Protestant credentials of these writers or their readers, but rather to emphasise the ways in which Protestant culture became skilled at communicating the new ideas in ways which could more easily be mapped onto the older understandings of the past. Despite the soteriological tensions of official doctrine, and the manner in which children had come to be seen both as vulnerable to both extremes of spiritual experience, these texts demonstrate the ways in which Reformation culture could imagine and adapt to more consolatory visions of children and child-rearing. New ideas, in a sense, were being presented in familiar forms, to ease the anxiety of parents and children alike. Indeed, this notion will be further developed when we look at alternative cultural visions of the young in future chapters.

This chapter has set out some of the prescribed methods for rearing children, as set out by clerics and spiritually motivated writers, to ensure that children might live good lives and that they could, at some stage, secure a place for themselves in Heaven. As has been shown, raising children was believed to be the most important occupation, and the core underpinning of Christian society. Baptised and well-reared children provided the foundation of Christian, and more specifically Reformed, society. However, as has been mentioned, such literature described how child-rearing and childhood *should* be. Indeed, much of the literature concerning children in the early modern period, as well as the relationship between Church and child, was concerned with prescriptive forms of behaviour. But, what happened when such modes and ideals were not adhered to? Or when the strict code for correct upbringing and indoctrination went so far that children began to react in a non-prescribed, pathological fashion? Or at least, when children, and cultural conceptions of children, took on more extreme or divergent forms? Certainly, children were unusually open to behaving both wickedly and beatifically.

As the following chapters will explore, alternative visions of early modern childhood abounded in literature which detailed cases of demonic possession and godly prophecy. Although, as considered in the previous chapter, there may potentially be difficulties involved when historians use cases of 'extreme' behaviour or examples of cultural occurrences which did not typify social 'norms', this does not render the consideration of the 'outer edges' of culture irrelevant. Indeed, what this work is concerned with is, in particular, the ways in which early modern society *imagined* their children – the cultural space that existed around children. Children were, most often, socially silent – yet, in texts concerning possession and prophecy, we hear their voices (even if they are imagined voices), and children take centre stage. Any historian interested in perceptions of and experiences of early modern children needs to include these ideas in their analysis. In the following chapters, then, we will explore the role of children in a range of popular tracts and pamphlets, in which they are not simply depicted as the passive infant at the baptismal font, or the keen scholar devoted to the gospels – but rather as positive agents in both the forming of their own identities and on a wider level of religious ideas and propaganda. We will consider how children, and ideas about the spiritual nature of children, formed narratives of childhood which were underpinned, complicated and contradicted by the sorts of official and temperate ideals depicted in the important-but-incomplete literatures of family advice. Hence, we will explore an alternative vision of the relationship between Church and Child, and the narratives and stories that enabled early modern society, in ways at times not so dissimilar to the authorised works of Perkins and his ilk and in others rather separate, to understand this sometimes fractious relationship – in which children are perceived as close to both the demonic and the divine.

Chapter 3

Children of Wrath?
Children in Cases of Demonic Possession

In 1573 a tract was published in London entitled *A booke declaring the fearful vexation of one Alexander Nyndge*, which detailed the possession case of a young boy from the county of Suffolk. During the January of that year, according to the pamphlet, the child suffered his first 'fit and vexacion'.[1] About seven o'clock during one winter evening, in front of his parents and brothers, Alexander's body began to swell, his eyes stared vacantly and his back began 'bendinge inward to his bellie'. Edward Nyndge, the child's brother and the author of the text, 'beyng bolder then other of the companye', immediately proclaimed that the child was demonically possessed and that the only course of action was for spectators, family and friends to pray to God for his safe deliverance, using the words of the Bible to drive out the evil spirit.[2] According to the text, the child suffered greatly during his affliction, experiencing such symptoms as occasionally losing speech and the control of his body. The pamphlet tells of how the boy declared to his brother Edward that the possessing spirit was 'marueilous afraid of you therfore I praye you stande by mee'. Edward advised his younger brother to 'earnestlie repent thee of thy sinnes and praye to God for the forgeuenes of the same', declaring that he would give his life for him to be saved from the demonological afflictions; 'my life for thyne ... the Deuill can not hurt thee, no rather then hee should I will go to hell with thee'. The spirit then, the text tells, attacked Alexander even 'more cruelly'.[3]

The age of the boy is not given, yet the reader can assume that he was a fairly young child, who was able to be carried around the house and to places of safety by his brothers. The text describes how the child's father called on all their neighbours to come to the boy and to help to pray for his safe recovery. Alexander suffered 'symptoms' typical of demonic possession, including his

---

[1]   Edward Nyndge, *A booke declaringe the fearfull vexasion, of one Alexander Nyndge. Beynge most horriblye tormented wyth an euyll spirit In the yere 1573* (London: 1573) *STC* (2nd ed.) 18752.

[2]   Nyndge, *A booke declaringe the fearfull vexasion*, sig. A2r.

[3]   Nyndge, *A booke declaringe the fearfull vexasion*, sig. A2v.

body being transformed into different shapes, losing control of his speech and speaking in the tones and words of the Devil in a 'hollowe' voice. As the spectators, supposedly led by Edward Nyndge, who adopted the role of 'exorcist', aimed to draw the demon out of the child, the spirit responded by contorting the child's body into further unnatural shapes: '... the spirit tranceformed hym verye owglye agaynst his chest, swellynge vpwarde to his throte, pluckyng his bellye iuste to his backe'.[4]

Compared to other cases of child possession which reportedly occurred during this period, Edward Nyndge, self-professed exorcist, actually seems to have had a relatively easy time with this particular demon. The assaulting spirit only remained with the child for three days (a very short space of time for such afflictions) and proved to be fairly easy to persuade to depart. On the first day of Alexander's possession, Edward asked the demonic spirit to communicate with him through the child. With very little encouragement the spirit answered, in its 'hollowe voyce', 'I woll I woll I woll'.[5] Edward then asked the spirit why he had chosen to torment his brother, to which it replied quite simply, 'I come for his soule'. Not wanting to be defeated, Edward informed the spirit that the assembled family and friends had 'a warrant in the form of holy Scripture' and that those who did repent of their sins and turn to God had the hope of salvation. The spirit responded by declaring that, in that case, he would have the child's 'soule and body to'.[6] However, and most conveniently, the spirit decided to depart from the child in time for the family to have their dinner, even if it was served a little late. The child was tormented for a further two days, during which time the family called the local curate to aid his dispossession. They read passages of the Bible over the child, most notably Luke, chapter 8, in which Christ casts out demons. They interrogated the evil spirit, whispering prayers into the child's ears, forcing it to depart, which it eventually did, out of a window.[7]

The case of Alexander Nyndge, whether or not and to what extent the reported events were true, is useful to historians for a range of reasons. For the purpose of this book, it provides an invaluable window through which we can glimpse early modern perspectives of children, and most notably the role of children in instances of demonic possession, which will provide the subject of the following two chapters. This chapter will explore this relationship between children and possession, something not considered in detail by historians to

---

4   Nyndge, *A booke declaringe the fearfull vexasion*, sig. A3r.
5   Nyndge, *A booke declaringe the fearfull vexasion*, sig. A3r.
6   Nyndge, *A booke declaringe the fearfull vexasion*, sig. A3v.
7   Nyndge, *A booke declaringe the fearfull vexasion*, sig. A3v–B1v.

have researched this field.[8] According to early modern perceptions, children were vulnerable to satanic assaults. As the case of Nyndge reveals to us, their small bodies provided the perfect playgrounds for demons, who could run riot, gaining control of their bodies, speaking through them and lifting them off the ground (as happened in the Nydnge case). The perceived vulnerability of children to the most mortal enemy, and the portrayed attempts of adults to help them to negotiate this difficult terrain, provide us with an interesting angle along which to approach vexed early modern beliefs about child spirituality and child salvation. In particular, as considered in the previous chapters, the reason why the young were seen to be especially vulnerable to such demonic assaults was connected to changing beliefs about children and their relationship to salvation more widely. As previously considered, the Protestant Church fragmented and pulled apart previous ways children were believed to be able to navigate the road to salvation, raising questions over whether or not children were seen to be spiritually pure or demonically corrupted – and one of the ways in which this tension was reflected was in cases of demonic possession.

In the Nyndge case described here, as well as in other similar reported instances to be explored below, child possession became symbolic of the wider battle between God and the Devil: a battle played out over (and in) the bodies of these afflicted children. In the case of Alexander Nyndge's possession, his brother Edward and the curate verbally attacked the demon, informing it that the tormented child could turn to God to gain redemption and the hope of salvation, and reminding the demon that it did not have that hope. When the demon stated that it was the Devil's disciple they mocked it, stating that 'thou art not hys disciple, thou art onlye an instrument, and scourge to punish the wicked'.[9]

As well as representing the vulnerability of children to the Devil and rendering their struggles as a symbol of the battle between God and the devil for human souls, these cases are also implicitly dealing with another battle, and potentially a worldlier one. In such an environment, where exorcists did battle with the Devil, theatrically drawing demons from children, a spiritual battle began to take place, as Protestants (most usually Puritan ministers) and agents of Catholicism (often Jesuit ministers) fought over the young children, attempting to prove that they and their church had the power to pull the demons from the possessed.[10]

---

[8] See below, pp. 60–62, for a full consideration of some key historical works to have explored demonic possession.

[9] Nyndge, *A booke declaringe the fearfull vexasion*, sig. B1r.

[10] See Marion Gibson, *Possession, Puritanism and Print: Darrell, Harsnett, Shakespeare and the Elizabethan Exorcism Controversy*, (London: Pickering and Chatto, 2006) esp. Ch. 1.

This struggle between the various shades of the Christian faith which existed in England is evident in the case of Nyndge, when 'one of the company' called on the Virgin Mary to aid Alexander, for which Edward 'rebuked' the individual, accusing them of offending God.[11] Such occurrences are evidence of the battle between various groups of Protestants and also Catholics as seen within such cases, and often tracts report that both Protestant and Catholic exorcists made visits to such spiritually assailed children – this public and confessional aspect of these cases will be considered in Chapter 4. In this chapter, we will explore the relationship between children and possession, and the reasons for and effects of early modern perceptions of children's vulnerabilities to the Devil, by looking at a range of possession cases, as well as some of the historical works that have attempted to untangle this most knotty of subjects.

As if to emphasise the manner in which these cases were as much entries in a wider debate as records of any particular or specific event, the case of Alexander Nyndge's possession was in fact re-published more than 30 years later in 1616. In this publication the story was retold with the addition of more sensationalist details, including an extension to the period of Nyndge's affliction from a few days to over seven months. The text includes at its opening a lengthy account of the power and subtlety of the devil, before launching into the case and describing a range of horrifying symptoms not mentioned in the original pamphlet, including strange moments of laughing, crying and dancing (the latter an activity much frowned upon by Puritans – and true to this new 'godly' emphasis the mention of Catholics being at the bedside of the child is removed from this later publication).[12]

Indeed, in this second remaining published case of which we are aware, Alexander Nyndge's signs of demonic intrusion were particularly stark: 'the spirit ... racked the said Alexander in a ... cruell manner: for he did use such strange and idle kinds of gestures ... that he was suspected to be mad'. Spiritual intrusion could be witnessed most clearly by a 'swelling or uariable lumpe ... swiftly running up and downe between the flesh and the skin'. The child was thrown violently by his afflicting demon, being often thrown 'head-long upon the ground ... drawing then his lips away, gnashing with his teeth, wallowing and foming, and the Spirit would vexe him monstrously and transforme his body ... by many violences'.[13] According to the 1616 tract, Alexander also refused food so he seemed to 'pine away', as well as experiencing a 'noise of slapping' from within

---

[11]   Nyndge, *A booke declaringe the fearfull vexasion*, sig. B1r.

[12]   Edward Nyndge, *A true and fearefull vexation of one Alexander Nyndge being most horribly tormented with the deuill* (London: 1616) *STC* (2nd ed.) 18753.

[13]   Nyndge, *A booke declaringe the fearfull vexasion*, sig. A IIIv.

his body.[14] These kinds of symptoms, more embellished in the later text, became increasingly recognised symptoms of demonic possession, as publications citing cases of demonic intrusion were churned out of printing presses in the late sixteenth century and beyond. The later publication of the Nyndge case reveals to us what audiences expected from a 'good' and grisly case – and it also reveals to us the ways children were meant to 'perform' during such moments. Some children, it seems, did just that.

Indeed, this chapter will consider whether or not children were, through their demonically inflicted 'illnesses', seen to be 'acting out' certain culturally recognised discourses or transcripts, an argument recently put forward by Brian Levack.[15] The term 'hidden transcripts' was first coined by James C. Scott, in his work *Domination and the Arts of Resistance: Hidden Cultural Transcripts*, in which he puts forward the notion that those members of society who are repressed develop 'hidden cultural transcripts' through which they can subversively question their oppression, whether consciously or otherwise.[16] This chapter will argue that not only were children acting out a form of hidden cultural transcript, often unconsciously gaining a form of agency through their actions, but also that children's perceived spiritual vulnerability and their ability to reflect and contain divine and demonic conflict in ways adults could not contributed to the ways in which these cases unravelled and were understood by early modern society. We will now consider some of these possession cases, whether genuine, imagined or performed, in more detail, looking at the context in which they occurred, their interpretations in the relevant historiography, and ask what these instances of child possession can reveal to us, however authentic or fictional they may be, about perceptions of children, their spirituality and salvation.

However, before exploring the role of children in cases of demonic possession, we must first consider what exactly is meant by the word 'possession'; both in terms of the historiographical interpretations that surround it, and even more difficult, in order to ascertain what early modern contemporaries understood by it. Early modern witchcraft and demonic possession has been the subject of much scholarly enquiry. Social scientists, psychologists and literary theorists,

---

[14]   Nyndge, *A booke declaringe the fearfull vexasion*, sig. A3v.

[15]   Brian P. Levack, *The Devil Within: Possession and Exorcism in the Christian West* (New Haven and London: Yale University Press, 2013). See below, pp. 61–2, for a consideration of Levack's main arguments.

[16]   James C. Scott, *Domination and the Arts of Resistance: Hidden Transcripts* (New Haven, London: Yale University Press, 1990).

alongside historians, have had much to say about the documented evidence.[17] I do not wish to add to the existing debates surrounding witchcraft – why people were able to believe in witches, or what this tells us about the 'progress' or success of Protestantism in relation to traditional religion. Rather, I seek to provide a fresh perspective, to discuss the history of witchcraft and possession alongside the history of childhood, as the two areas have much to say to each other – a dialogue that has not, until now, been heard in much detail.

Understanding Early Modern Possession

> By warrant of ... doctrine, a question commonly mooved, may be resolued: whether the seruant and child of God, may be bewitched or not? Out of that which hath beene said, I answer, he may: and that is plaine by the word.[18]

People in early modern Europe lived, according to their own perceptions, amid a multi-faceted cosmos, consisting of interpenetrating physical and spiritual worlds. These worlds were influenced and ruled by both divine and demonic agencies. The physical earth, created and ruled over by God, was scrupulously

---

[17]   For a psychological exploration of witchcraft, see Roper, *Oedipus and the Devil, witchcraft, sexuality and religion in early modern Europe* (London and New York: Routledge, 1994, 1995 edn.); for a literary interpretation of possession, see Sydney Anglo, *The Damned Art: Essays in the Literature of Witchcraft* (London: Routledge and Kegan Paul, 1977) and Philip C. Almond, *Demonic possession and exorcism in early modern England : contemporary texts and their cultural contexts* (Cambridge: Cambridge University Press, 2004); for historical and sociological interpretations, the most authoritative texts include Stuart Clark, *Thinking with Demons* (Oxford and New York: Oxford University Press, 1997); James Sharpe, *Instruments of Darkness: Witchcraft in England 1550–1750* (London: Hamish Hamilton, 1996); for anthropologically inspired theory see Keith Thomas, *Religion and the Decline of Magic* (London: Penguin, 1971, 1991 edn); Allan Macfarlane, *Witchcraft in Tudor and Stuart England: A regional and comparative study* (London: Routledge, 1999 edn); for interpretations of early modern demonology and witchcraft see Norman Cohn, *Europe's Inner Demons: The demonization of Christians in medieval Christendom* (London: Pimlico, 1993) a revised form of the now disregarded assumption of 'witch craze', as *Europe's Inner Demons: an enquiry inspired by the great witch hunt* (London: Chatto, 1975); more recent work includes Darren Oldridge, *The Devil in Early Modern England* (Stroud: Sutton, 2000); the most recent historical works on witchcraft include Darren Oldridge (ed.) *The Witchcraft Reader* (London and New York: Routledge, 2002) and Lyndal Roper, *Witch Craze, Terror and Fantasy in Baroque Germany* (New Haven and London: Yale University Press, 2004).

[18]   Perkins, *A Discovrse of the damned art of witchcraft* (Cambridge, 1608) *STC* (2nd edn) 19697, p. 222.

observed for signs of His presence. The Protestant Church attacked the material nature and tangibility of traditional belief systems. They regarded miracles on earth with scorn and destroyed the system of spiritual intermediaries which encompassed the 'magical' powers surrounding the Mass and sacraments, the communion of Saints and other devotional images or objects, alongside so-called 'popish' superstitious practices, through and with which people regarded their world.[19] Yet, the early modern world continued to be one in which the spiritual, and the supernatural, were highly perceptible. The smallest of signs – a misshapen tree, a clap of thunder, a monstrous birth – were read as signs of godly, or celestial, presence, etched onto the physical world.[20] There existed strong beliefs surrounding omens of godly providence, or of demonic interference, alongside a less orthodox undercurrent of beliefs in chance and fortune. Ghosts wandered the earth, fairies could lure unsuspecting victims, demons could tempt, spirits could enter the human body.[21] Heaven existed above, the celestial realm of God in which He governed his angels and archangels; Hell existed below, ruled by Satan and his league of demons. As Protestant divine William Perkins understood the nature of God's celestial and earthly creation, God:

> exerciseth ... a speciall kingdome, partly of grace in the Church militant vpon earth, and partly of glorie ouer the Saints and Angels, members of the Church triumphant in heauen. Now in like manner the Deuill hath a kingdome ... the kingdome of darknes, whereof himselfe is the head and gouernour, for which cause he is tearmed 'the Prince of darknes'.[22]

There has been, over the past few years, a surge of interest in this aspect of early modern religiosity, in the vitality and adaptability of traditional beliefs, and their place within a distinctively Reformed theology.[23] Alexandra Walsham and

---

[19] For a concise and eloquent account of the destruction of the traditional Catholic belief system, see the introduction to MacCulloch's *The Later Reformation in England*.

[20] Alexandra Walsham explores in admirable detail the notion of Protestant providentialism, in which 'God's sovereignty extended from the most contemptible of His creatures to the celestial, from the basest creeping worm, tiniest gnat, and fly to the noblest angels in heaven'. See her *Providence in Early Modern England* (Oxford: Oxford University Press, 1999), for quote, see p. 10.

[21] See esp. Diane Purkiss, 'Sounds of Silence: Fairies and Incest in Scottish Witchcraft Stories', in Stuart Clark (ed.) *Languages of Witchcraft: Narrative, Ideology and Meaning in Early Modern Culture* (Hampshire and London: Macmillan, 2001).

[22] Perkins, *A Discovrse of the damned art of witchcraft*, p. 5.

[23] The historiography surrounding early modern folklore has been growing in recent years, for beliefs in ghosts see especially; John Newton's (ed.), *Early Modern Ghosts;*

Peter Marshall, for example, have written about the complexity of early modern belief systems, and the intermeshing of the celestial, heavenly, preternatural and earthly worlds.[24] As P.G. Maxwell-Stuart has written, 'each of these worlds was connected in some fashion to everything else, as though creation were a giant, intricate web streaming outwards from God who sat spider-like in the centre and governed the whole'.[25] Each world was interpenetrating; each could spill into the other, thus unbalancing the fragile composition of the natural and social orders. It was within this framework of belief and comprehension that demonic possession was perceived as a genuine phenomenon, and hence could be feared.

What, then, did early modern contemporaries mean by the term 'demonic possession'? In the early modern period, the notion of 'being possessed' was not a new phenomenon, far from it. The Bible contains many examples of individuals being possessed by malign spirits, and thus falling ill or being driven to extreme madness. Jesus cast out possessing spirits and 'legions' of demons;[26] in one case transforming a madman, who existed 'in the mountaines, and in the graues, and stroke him self with stones' into a clothed and orderly member of the community.[27] This gift of healing was passed on to Jesus' disciples. Hence,

---

Proceedings of the 'Early Modern Ghosts' conference held at St. John's College, Durham on 24th March 2001 (Durham: Centre for Seventeenth Century Studies, University of Durham, 2002), a collection of essays which provides both an introduction to the field, but also suggests many angles of possible future research; Peter Marshall, *Beliefs and the Dead in Reformation*; Bruce Gordon, 'Malevolent ghosts and ministering angels: apparitions and pastoral care in the Swiss Reformation', in his and Peter Marshall's (eds) *The Place of the Dead, Death and Remembrance in Late Medieval and Early Modern Europe* (Cambridge: Cambridge University Press, 2000). For fairy and ghost beliefs see Purkiss, 'Sounds of Silence: Fairies and Incest in Scottish Witchcraft Stories'; also Thomas, *Religion and the Decline of Magic*, esp. chapter 19 ; K.M. Briggs, *The Anatomy of Puck, An Examination of Fairy Beliefs among Shakespeare's Contemporaries and Successors* (London: Routledge and Kegan Paul, 1959). For beliefs about angels see Peter Marshall and Alexandra Walsham, *Angels in the Early Modern World* (Cambridge: Cambridge University Press, 2006) and Laura Sangha, *Angels and Belief in England 1480–1700* (London: Pickering and Chatto, 2012). Little substantial work has been undertaken on devil beliefs – for a basic account see Oldridge, *The Devil in Early Modern England*; religio-political interpretations can be found in Johnstone's *The Devil and Demonism in Early Modern England* (Cambridge: Cambridge University Press, 2006) and his 'The Protestant Devil: the Experience of Temptation in Early Modern England', *Journal of British Studies* 43, April 2004, 173–205.

[24]   See especially Marshall, *Beliefs and the Dead in Reformation England* and Walsham, *Providence in Early Modern England*.

[25]   P.G. Maxwell Stuart, *Satan's Conspiracy, Magic and Witchcraft in Sixteenth-Century Scotland* (East Lothian: Tuckwell Press, 2001), p. 1.

[26]   Matt 10: 1; Matt 10: 8; Mark 1: 23–6; Mark 5: 2–20; Mark 9: 25.

[27]   Mark 5:5.

the belief that demons or evil spirits could invade the physical body and cause actual bodily harm, sickness or mental illness was an established one with a biblical precedent; it was one associated with disorder and nakedness, alongside public shame and fear.[28] Furthermore, the successful exorcism of such demons was seen to form part of the ongoing battle between God and Satan, illustrating human history in its totality, as told in Revelation. As King and occasional demonological writer James I of England (James VI of Scotland) wrote in a 1603 edition of his *Daemonologie*, the Devil 'knows not all thinges future, but yet ... he knows parte, the Tragicall euent of this historie declares it'.[29] Through this ideological mire, Christians believed (then and now) that God would eventually prevail – thus culminating in true religious conversion and spiritual order. Such associations and patterns of behaviour were recorded throughout literature from the early modern period. Indeed, it was from such biblically derived precedence that early modern writers and clerics gained their authority or 'proves' – from which they derived a 'theological science' – theories through which they could view their world.

The image of the spiritual battle between God and Satan – demoniac, audience and exorcist, alongside eventual spiritual resolution or religious conversion – was echoed throughout numerous cases of possession during the early modern period. Descriptions of such phenomena formed part of a wider preoccupation with witchcraft. It is to this extraordinary 'witch-craze', rather than the cases of possession, that historical opinion has often turned. Indeed, European witchcraft cases in particular, with their demonic pacts and Sabbaths, have featured, in the words of James Sharpe, among history's 'best bits', to be taken out and reinterpreted every so often.[30] Between 1450 and 1750 around 40,000 people, most of whom were women, were executed throughout Europe as witches.[31] Furthermore, some of the most notable members of society were convinced of the reality of both witchcraft and the power of the Devil, as King James understood:

> Although man ... was made to the image of the Creator, yet through his fall hauing once lost it, it is but restored againe in a part by the grace onelie to the elect: so

---

[28]   Acts 19: 12–16.

[29]   James I, King of England, *Daemonologie* (Edinburgh, 1603) *STC* (2nd ed.) 14365, pp. 4–5.

[30]   Witchcraft as part of our 'cultural baggage', Sharpe, *Instruments of Darkness*, p. 5.

[31]   Sharpe, *The Bewitching of Anne Gunter, a Horrible and True Story of Deceptions, Witchcraft, Murder, and the King of England* (New York: Routledge, 1999, 2001 edn), p. 65.

all the rest falling away from God, are giuen ouer in the handes of the Deuill that enemy, to beare his Image.[32]

As a result the world was perceived to be plagued by followers of evil – charmers, magicians, astronomers and witches – the 'vnlawfull instruments'.[33] In the English cases witches were accused of 'maleficium', inflicting harm on others through magical and malign spiritual powers, usually acquired by a pact with the Devil. Witches were widely believed to be the Devil's very worst 'instruments' on earth, with whom he established a covenant, binding his followers to him in a perverse imitation of the Christian covenant with God, and administered his sacraments, 'seals of his promises' to those deluded individuals who had, supposedly, chosen to worship him. Through witches, argued prominent demonological writers, the Devil was able to establish his kingdom; in the words of Perkins 'God hath revealed his will to the Patriarchs, Prophets, and Apostles, by familiar conference, by dreames, by inspiration, by Trances: In the same maner, Sathan hath his Divinors, and soothsayers ... to whom he maketh knowne things to come, by familiar presence, by dreames, & c'.[34] Witchcraft and possession were thus seen as perversions of the true Christian Church, the Devil's religion on earth.

The crimes such witches were believed to have committed were, in themselves, illustrative of social and spiritual concerns of early modern society. These witches, often elderly women or social outcasts, were accused of causing death and harm to people, most often children; they interfered with human fertility, killed livestock, damaged crops and spoilt butter. They were thus perceived to be a threat to the fabric of society; they inflicted pain upon youth, interfered with foodstuffs necessary for nourishment and survival, and prevented procreation.[35] Thus, witches were perceived to be doing the Devil's work in human society.

Our supposedly 'enlightened' and modern society finds it difficult to comprehend the notions of demonic pacts, spiritually possessed children and feverish exorcisms – this is, perhaps, what makes witchcraft so interesting. Nevertheless, we can apply many modern and interpretive theoretical tools to the subject, in order to ascertain how and why this happened, in the hope

---

[32]   James I, *Daemonologie*, p. 6.

[33]   Ibid., p. 26.

[34]   See Perkins, *A Discovrse of the damned art of witchcraft*, sigs. IIIr–v and pp. 6–7.

[35]   Sharpe, *Instruments of Darkness*, pp. 5–6; and his *The Bewitching of Anne Gunter*, pp. 64–9; for the perverse relationship between witchcraft and fertility, see Roper, *Oedipus and the Devil*; see also her more recent work on the subject of witchcraft, *Witch Craze, Terror and Fantasy in Baroque Germany*, especially chapters 4 and 6.

that if we can unravel the cultural symbols behind this extraordinary historical phenomenon, we can gain a greater understanding of early modern mentalities. Indeed, this most intriguing aspect of history has an equally fascinating historiography attached to it. The historical 'danger' in examining belief systems so far removed from our own, is the temptation to explain or justify them according to modern assumptions. Indeed, the sensational claims made by early modern contemporaries seem to bear no reference to the 'real' world, hence it becomes easy to view such beliefs as irrational, barbaric and intensely persecuting. We can blame them, perhaps, on the social, religious and political upheaval prevalent at the time of the European Reformations. Yet, we need instead to approach early modern society, as far as we can, on its own terms – to perceive the different notions it had to understand reality. In such a system of belief, the Bible and religious stories, alongside a perceptible belief in the supernatural – both godly and demonic – constituted reality.

The perceived reality of demonic interference established a real interest in its character and significance. Actual demonic possession, the belief that a malign spirit could enter the physical body, was believed to be a direct symptom of witchcraft by maleficium. During the early modern period, extensive tracts and pamphlets were circulated which detailed lengthy accounts of the torments suffered by demoniacs, who in their agonies provided onlookers with the names of those who had supposedly afflicted them. On the European stage, cases of demonic possession and successful exorcism were used in both anti-Catholic and anti-Protestant propaganda; this was the case in France, for example, with Huguenots and Catholics competing for the monopoly of religious truth, both sides seeking to convince audiences of their God-given power over evil, as well as, conversely, accusing the other of forgery and ignorant superstition. In England, meanwhile, accounts of possession seem to point to occurrences that were perceived to be widespread and quite severe; in the 1590s the divine George Gifford said, rather sceptically, that 'There be examples in many places, and daylie it is seéne, that the deuill is driuen out of some possessed, that where he did vexe and torment men in their bodies, and in their cattle, they haue remedie against him'.[36] Indeed, such cases also fuelled inter-confessional conflicts and rivalries, as various 'degrees' of the Reformed battled over the credibility of such afflictions, as will be explored in greater depth in the following chapter. According to early modern clerics and writers, God had allowed this spiritual

---

[36] George Gifford, *A dialogue concerning witches and witchcraftes* (London, 1593) *STC* (2nd ed.) 11850, sig. F3v.

'underworld' to flourish, in order to separate the religiously depraved from those who would be saved, as Protestant divine William Perkins wrote:

> If any doe thinke it strange, that Satan should ... oppose himselfe to the kingdome of God, and maintaine his owne principalitie, by such vngodly arts and exercises; They must knowe that this and all other euills come to passe euen by the will of God ... to trie and prooue his people, whether they will cleaue to him and his word, or seeke vnto Satan and wicked spirits.[37]

This contemporary focus on possession as a phenomenon of importance emphasises its usefulness to students and scholars of the period interested in the spiritual debates and controversies of the day. However, in relation to historical works written on the subject of witchcraft, possession has received less attention. Furthermore, very little historical research has so far explored the prominent role of children within such cases.[38] It is worth exploring what literature there is in order both to understand our own comprehension of possession, but also why it continues to be partial. The most significant writings to have been produced on the subject of possession are those by Stuart Clark, Lyndal Roper and most recently by Brian Levack. The theories of these historians offer a useful intellectual framework for the rest of this chapter, so it is worth exploring their writing in some detail before considering the cases themselves – and also, having sketched out the incompleteness of the historiography, we can in turn use those cases to probe beyond this mapped terrain.

Clark's *Thinking with Demons* considers the relationship between possession and illness, both physical and mental. He warns against viewing the early modern demoniac as a patient, or as a victim of pre-modern misdiagnosis; against superimposing 'categories of modern psychiatry on to the early modern diagnosis of insanity to produce what may be called a psycho-pathology of possession'.[39] Indeed, possession could, to both past and present 'observers', be

---

[37]   Perkins, *A Discovrse of the damned art of witchcraft*, sigs. VIr–v.

[38]   There are two isolated, yet extremely significant articles written on the role of children within cases of possession. They tend, however, to focus on the themes of Protestant politics and family authority, rather than on ideological or cultural concerns; see Thomas Freeman, 'Demons, Deviance and Defiance: John Darrell and the Politics of Exorcism in late Elizabethan England', in Peter Lake and Michael Questier (eds) Conformity and Orthodoxy in the English Church, c. 1560–1660 (Woodbridge: Boydell Press, 2000); and Sharpe, 'Disruption in the Well-ordered Household: Age, Authority and Possessed Young People' in Paul Griffiths, Adam Fox and Steve Hindle (eds), *The Experience of Authority in Early Modern England* (London: Macmillan, 1996).

[39]   Clark, *Thinking with Demons*, pp. 391–2.

blamed on a variety of illnesses. We must not, he argues, attempt to explain away forms of behaviour that members of early modern society took for granted. Clark prefers a more anthropologically influenced approach that attempts to understand elements of past behaviour as part of a cultural language, which can be unravelled in order to understand early modern society, or its present-day pre-developed equivalents, by their own paradigms of thought.[40] Within this work, the view that early modern behaviour must be viewed on its own terms, without resorting to the opinion that contemporaries were guilty of making some form of judgmental error, will be, as far as is possible, adopted.

More recently, Brian Levack's 2013 publication *The Devil Within* has sought to provide both a comprehensive synthesis and detailed set of possible explanations for demonic possession as a phenomenon of the Christian tradition. Levack's work, although primarily focused on the Reformation period, considers Christ's expulsion of demons as detailed in the New Testament, following these ideas right through to beliefs in possession during the period of the Enlightenment, whilst attempting to explore potential reasons for these occurrences. Levack argues that there may have been medical explanations for many of these cases, which can potentially explain some of the symptoms described by the publications and court trials. He also alludes to psychological explanations for beliefs in possession, which would be, as with any psychological reading of an event in the past, dependent on the social and mental experiences and perceptions of those living in the early modern period – psychological frameworks, he argues, are always culturally specific. Indeed, Lyndal Roper, whose work we will turn to in just a moment, preceded Levack in her exploration of the psychological, and psychoanalytical, dimensions of the early modern witch trials and demonic possession.

Levack also has some useful things to say on the relationship between fraud and demonic possession, drawing on cases such as that of Anne Gunter and Harsnett's attacks on both Catholic and Protestant (or Puritan) exorcists. These ideas, also considered in the work of Clive Holmes, will be explored further in the following chapter, with a particular focus on the way these supposedly fraudulent cases can shine light on the experiences of and roles played by early modern children, who were, after all, some of the key 'actors' in these events. For Levack, deliberate fraud may have been an explanation in some of these cases, but he argued that it was not the *only* explanation. Fraud may have had a place to play, when, for example, the 'demoniac' and their families had experienced

---

[40] For Clark's views on anthropological theory see his *Thinking with Demons*, pp. 396–400.

some commonly recognised symptoms of demonic intrusion, and may then have exaggerated a further range of possessions signs. His argument is similar for medical explanations of possession, where he makes the point, quite rightly, that for early moderns, illnesses such as melancholy and epilepsy were believed to have been caused by the Devil anyway, so then going further to make a connection with demonic possession would not therefore have constituted a huge imaginative leap. He also suggests that medical explanations cannot wholly explain the phenomenon of possession, as symptoms and responses varied greatly between Catholic and Protestant cases.

Levack's main argument is centred on the notion of cultural performance, in which he sees all participants (demoniac, exorcist, family members and neighbours, clergy and physician) as actors in a culturally recognised 'drama' or 'performance'. These participants, whether unconsciously or otherwise, 'acted in the way that members of their religious communities expected them to act. These expectations, and therefore the scripts that demoniacs followed, were significantly different for Catholics and Protestants.'[41] Indeed, we will consider the role of children in these 'performances', both Protestant and Catholic in the following Chapter. This 'cultural performance' interpretation resonates with arguments made by historians such as Clark and Roper, yet Levack's text is the first to push such an interpretation as its primary explanation, which, he argues, accounts for the variation between Catholic and Protestant cases. The notion that early modern society, which believed that the Devil was a real entity, who could cause demons to enter the physical human body, led to people living at this time to believe, wholeheartedly, in the reality of demonic possession – and subsequently also to dupe their contemporaries into believing they were possessed on some occasions when they were not. Here we will go beyond these ideas, to consider how the young were able to tap into these shared belief systems, and were able to gain authority and agency as a result.

As mentioned, Lyndal Roper uses psychoanalytical theory to attempt to unpick some of the causes that may have been behind early modern beliefs in demonic possession. In particular, she emphasises the connection between early modern perceptions of the physical body and beliefs in spiritual possession. For this reason, her work on exorcism and the theology of the body will be drawn on within this chapter. Indeed, Roper's emphasis on the importance of how a culture imagines or understands the body is a significant one. Early modern theories of the body can reveal to us the interconnections between what was mental, physical or spiritual; thus highlighting the causal links between spiritual powers and

---

[41]   Levack, *The Devil Within*, p. 30.

physical or mental illness at this time. According to Roper the upheaval brought about by the European Reformations fundamentally altered the understanding of the relationship between the physical and the spiritual. Protestantism, she argues, more severely stressed the difference between the profane and the divine. The permission of clerical marriage led to the conviction that human flesh could not be pure or sacred; and divine forces, such as those previously comprehended, or even experienced, through the Mass and saintly intercession could no longer be believed to be present in physical hosts. Furthermore, the Protestant decree of predestination stressed man's utter sinfulness and distance from God. This theological shift, intensified further by confessional rivalry throughout Europe, dramatised and internalised questions surrounding the relationship between body and soul.[42]

However, despite such fundamental shifts in thought, expressions of religious truths still continued to be revealed through physical sensation: hence demonic possession. The demoniac and observers gained a key role in expressing, and taking part in, a form of spiritual authority. Indeed, the physicality and 'marvellous' nature of the possession cases, 'the wide open mouth, the distension of the tongue, and the hands outstretched to Heaven ... as if the body had itself become a kind of blank sheet, with horror written clearly upon it, transparent evidence of the devil's presence', made possession cases fundamentally significant to both contemporaries and historians.[43]

This chapter will develop some of the themes introduced here, focusing upon their relationship to the key issues of childhood: illness and nourishment; misbehaviour and story-telling; definitions of religious truth and authority, and finally what beliefs surrounding possession tell us about the nature and impact of the Reformation. Crucially, however, we must acknowledge that none of these works have sufficiently considered the potent interconnections between possession and child spirituality during the Reformation. The relationship between children and cases of demonic possession can reveal much to us about early modern perceptions of children, understandings of demonism and Protestantism, and also the nexus between these areas – and how it was here where much of the anxiety about child salvation came to be fought. As we have seen, child salvation was open to a high level of uncertainty due to changes to the baptism ceremony. Clark, Levack and Roper each accept that cultural change was a reason behind possession cases, but none quite reach the argument we will explore throughout the rest of this book: that changes to how the Church dealt

---

[42] Roper, *Oedipus and the Devil*, pp. 171–4.
[43] Roper, *Oedipus and the Devil*, p. 175.

with and protected children's souls (and how they did not) caused considerable concern in society at large, and cases of possession and prophecy alike became for contemporaries ways and means of investigating, dramatising and even understanding these tensions. Children's souls were at risk, and the Protestant Reformation did not pretend otherwise; for theological and pastoral purposes alike, however, the perils of childhood could not be ignored.

Sharpe and Roper certainly see some cases of demonic possession as part of the narrative of early modern youth, rather than childhood.[44] The behaviour of some of the demoniacs, particularly notorious female demoniacs such as Anne Gunter (who attracted the attention of Samuel Harsnett as well as King James I) was, they argue, overtly sexual.[45] Young females behaving in a manner which was seemingly explicit and entirely 'inappropriate' have been seen as part of the carnal and licentious stage of early modern youth. This argument carries much weight, yet I would argue that in examples of childhood demonic possession, as explored here, the role of the child is in fact an essential underpinning of the cases. Whilst these children were up to the age of thirteen, and therefore theoretically omitted from the sexualised role envisioned by Sharpe or Roper, their role as child remains fundamental. Indeed, these children were living at home, under the protection of their parents, and had not yet begun service or apprenticeships; as with the case of Nyndge explored above, reference is continually made to their small size, their dependence upon parents and family and their innocence. Whether or not they had actually reached the stage of youth, by early modern definitions, we can never really know; but what is significant is that the texts describing their cases do not reflect such a perception. It may be that early modern readers would have brought to the texts a complex weave of their own understandings and preconceptions that we cannot hope to understand. Yet, if youth was seen as an age of physical development and sexual enlightenment, then there are no traces of these traits in the texts here explored. Indeed, such signs of youthful 'corruption' may have significantly undermined what these children were actually saying. If youth was seen as a battle between good and evil, perhaps these children were on the cusp – they themselves becoming a battleground between the conflicting wills of the satanic and the sacred. What is also possible is that these children were in fact being prepared for youth, being instilled with godly and puritanical ideas; it may have been against such an education that they were reacting. However, it is my understanding that progression through the life-course revolved around

---

[44]   See Roper, *Oedipus and the Devil*, chapter 8; Sharpe, *The Bewitching of Anne Gunter*; Sharpe, 'Disruption in the well-ordered Household'.

[45]   Sharpe, *The Bewitching of Anne Gunter*.

acquiring a set of physical and mental attributes appropriate to each stage, and this development perhaps varied from individual to individual, and therefore cannot be as easily categorised as modern day perceptions of age stages. Physical and mental strength, appearance and virginity were all determining factors in the hazy transition between childhood and youth.[46]

The Body, Domestic Space and Demonic Possession

Returning to the original focus of this chapter, the involvement of children in cases of possession during the early modern period, we should ask how these overarching belief systems, and the historiographical theories explored above, relate to particular cases of possession. How does the general relate to the intimacy of the individual case, in which child, family and local community became embroiled with fears of witchcraft and evil? Furthermore, what can individual cases tell us about beliefs surrounding and attitudes towards the young at this time? The story of Alexander Nyndge's affliction mentioned above was far from unusual, and the later publication of the pamphlet, with its intensified sense of hysteria, was typical of the kinds of symptoms and forms of behaviour supposedly exhibited by the young and possessed. The recorded scandals, tracts and pamphlets detailing cases of possession documented a variety of horrifying signs, both physical and mental, characteristic of those possessed. One significant case was that of Thomas Darling, whose case involved the infamous exorcist John Darrell, and will be considered in detail in the following chapter.[47] Indeed, Darling, also known as the 'Boy of Burton', was dispossessed in 1596 by famous exorcist John Darrell, later imprisoned for his 'fraudulent' practices. As Samuel Harsnett, the fiercest of Darrell's critics wrote; 'pretence is made that he cast a Diuell out of a boy in Burton, called Thomas Darling, then about the age of fourteene yeares'.[48]

---

[46] An illustration of this fact is contained in the diaries of Thomas Goodwin, who first received the sacrament aged 14. However, when he later attempted to receive communion, he was thrown out of the church by the minister, due to his small 'stature'. See Thomas Goodwin, *The Works of Thomas Goodwin, Sometime President of Magdalene College, Oxford*, Vol. 2 (Edinburgh: James Nichol, 1861) pp ii–iii. For reading on the development of youth, see Griffiths, *Youth and Authority*, esp. chapter 1; also Alexandra Shepard, *Meanings of Manhood in Early Modern England* (Oxford: Oxford University Press, 2003) esp. pp. 21–9.

[47] See Chapter 2, above.

[48] Samuel Harsnett, *A discouery of the fraudulent practises of Iohn Darrel* (London, 1599) *STC* (2nd ed.) 12883, p. 2.

During Thomas Darling's fits, the child displayed certain extreme symptoms; he 'ran round on his hands and his feete, keeping a certaine compasse: after that striving and strugling with groning, he fel a vomiting'.[49] Similar to Nyndge's case (the latter publication of it at least) the boy gained an extraordinary level of physical strength. In the case of the Throckmorton children, meanwhile, in which five daughters of a Yorkshire gentleman became, seemingly, demonically possessed, ten-year-old daughter Jane:

> ... fell vpon ye sodaine into a strange kind of sicknes and distemperature of body, the manner whereof was as followeth ... as one in a great trance and swoune lay quietly as long: soone after she would begin to swell and heaue up her belly so as none was able to bend her, or keepe her downe.[50]

Hence, the body was acutely observed for signs of the Devil's presence; it seems that, through the bodies of these small children, Satan was believed to hold much power.

The seventeenth-century version of Alexander Nyndge's possession case saw details of such symptoms exaggerated from those found in the original 1573 publication. According to the 1616 text, the child gained both strength and a loss of physical control and demeanour, he would:

> ... gather himselfe on a round heape under his bedcloathes, and ... would bounce up a good height from the bed, and beat his head and other parts of his body against the ground, and bed-stead in such an earnest manner, that the beholders did feare that he would thereby haue spoiled himselfe, if they had not by strong restrained him.[51]

The power of malicious forces over children was also seemingly extended to ideas surrounding nourishment. Indeed, though not previously acknowledged by historians of witchcraft, throughout cases of possession, children were often reported to be refusing food. Alexander Nyndge was said to have 'refused all kinds of meat for a long space together, insomuch as he seemed to pine away'. Such a symptom of illness was again attributed to the malign nature of his inhabiting demon, deduced through the observing of a 'strange noise of slapping from

---

[49]   I.D., *The most wonderfull and true storie*, p. 3.

[50]   Anon, *The most strange and admirable discouerie of the three witches of Warboys* (London? 1593) STC (2nd ed.) 25019, sig. AIIIr.

[51]   Nyndge, *A true and fearefull vexation of one Alexander Nyndge*, sig. AIIIv.

within his body'.[52] Similarly, Thomas Darling was unable to ingest food without resulting illness; the child was frequently reported to be 'casting up what he had eaten at Dinner', often 'meat was prepared for him, but before he could take it, he was overthrowne into a cruell fit', after which Satan spoke directly to the child, bribing him for his worship.[53] Such symptoms reveal the significant strength the Devil and his demons were believed to hold over the bodies of the young and possessed; literally taking their bodies over, depriving them of nourishment and draining their physical strength. On one more extreme occasion the pamphlet detailing the case reads:

> ... about one a clock (seeming verie well) he received some meate. But Sathan shewed himselfe to be a right Sathan, even a sore enemie to the Childe, (envying the good of his bodie, when he saw himselfe unable to hurt his soule) did let his digesting of it (as manie times hee did) by casting him presently into divers fits.[54]

In the case of one of the Throckmorton children, the Devil supposedly prevented one of the children from eating; 'At dinner time it plaide with her, for sometimes shee hath merry fits, putting her hand besides her meate, and her meate besides her mouth, mocking her, and making her misse her mouth.'[55] Thus, contemporaries clearly drew a link between the power of the Devil over the child and the issue of nourishment. Interestingly, in the cases explored here, the refusal of food was considered a sign of demonic intrusion – whereas in the cases of the prophetic children to be explored in Chapters 5 and 6, lack of hunger and nourishment were considered to be signs of godliness. Indeed, such ambiguities surrounding perceptions of children again reveal the nature of children's complicated and fluid spiritual identities – but also hint at the emphasis on bodily and spiritual welfare and nourishment which lay at the heart of contemporary interest in, and anxiety about, these cases.

The state of possession was, perhaps, seen to be responsible for a range of what we would now call childhood illnesses. In an age when food was often scarce and infant and child mortality high, refusing food would have had dire consequences and implications. For those children both spiritually and physically plagued, Satan was a likely source of blame; he was seen to be targeting the young, the most vulnerable, by corrupting their ability to eat and to gain nourishment. Such a perversion of the natural order, in which the young

---

52   Nyndge, *A true and fearefull vexation of one Alexander Nyndge*, sig. AIIIv.
53   I.D., *The most wonderfull and true storie*, pp. 1 and 16.
54   I.D., *The most wonderfull and true storie*, p. 18.
55   Anon, *The most strange and admirable discouerie*, sig. BIIIr.

were seemingly prevented from growing strong and healthy, resonates with Lyndal Roper's model of witchcraft and maternity. Here midwives, suspected to be witches, were believed to be draining away the youth of babies in their care, perversely nourishing their own old bones, at the expense of those of the young.[56] Indeed, Roper notes how, during the Augsburg witch trials, bewitchment was often associated with illness relating to a mother and her young children; sorcery caused children to suffer strange aches and pains, headaches and visions.[57] The theme of nourishment also had spiritual and religious implications at this time; the nourishment of the body was closely entwined with the nourishment of the soul and the Eucharist. The Devil's ability to disrupt this pattern of order and nature was clearly feared and suspected.

Indeed, in a more extreme case from 1594, again associated with sixteenth-century exorcist John Darrell, the Starkie family – to be considered in more detail in the following chapter – supposedly witnessed the spiritual affliction of seven family members. The gentle and pious Lancashire family, as they were presented to readers, had, according to a tract documenting their case, experienced much hardship and grief surrounding the health and wellbeing of their offspring. Nicholas Starkie's 'gentlewoman' wife saw '4 of her children (though at their birth likely to liue) yet afterward [they] pined away in most strange maner'. Such circumstances were blamed upon an 'vnnatural vowe' made against the family by local 'Papistes'. Eventually, Mrs Starkie gave birth to two healthy children, a son and a daughter, until 'they came to 10 or 12 years of age', when 'they were possessed and vexed with evill spirites'. The daughter Anne was subsequently 'taken with a dumpishe heavie countenance, and with a certain fearful starting & pulling together of her bodie'. Their son John was similarly tormented, 'as he was reading of a booke, something gaue him such a thumpe in the necke, that he was suddenlie striken downe with a most horrible strike, and said that Satan had broken his necke, lying there pitifullie tormented for the space of two houres'.[58] Arguably, such a case has much to do with maternal capability and fear of childhood illness and subsequent death. Demonic possession and affliction by evil spirits was blamed for the infant deaths of the Starkie children, as well as for the later illnesses of those that survived. We can thus see that spiritual answers were sought for the physical weakness of children, living in an age when infant and child mortality was high, and when children were vulnerable to sudden

---

[56]   See Roper's chapter on 'Witchcraft and fantasy in early modern Germany' in her *Oedipus and the Devil*, pp. 199–225.

[57]   Roper, *Oedipus and the Devil*, esp. p. 199.

[58]   George More, *A true discourse concerning the certaine possession and dispossession of 7 persons in one familie in Lancashire* (Middelburg, 1600) *STC* (2nd ed.) 18070, pp. 11–15.

illness and death. Indeed, stories and tales surrounding the Devil and demonic possession helped families to come to terms with the otherwise inexplicable loss of their children.

The afflictions reportedly suffered by young demoniacs were believed to be spiritual as well as physical. Thomas Darling became fixated with visions, in which he appeared to lose control over his senses; being dominated instead with spiritual illusions. He repeatedly saw a 'greene Catte that troubled him', and suffered vivid and fearful dreams about the Devil, green angels and cats. During such fits 'he wold sodainly and amazedly open his eyes, staring and shriking most pitifully, clapping both of his hands upon his face, not being able to indure the sight of such fearfull objects as he beheld'.[59] Similarly, in other reported cases children appeared to be losing grip of the earthly world, to being increasingly dominated by spiritual, invisible forces. In the case of the Throckmorton children, the offending spirit or spirits seized and took over the bodily faculties of the victims, who were reportedly deprived of all their senses during their fits so that 'they could neither see, heare, not feele any bodie'. Elizabeth Throckmorton, the eldest of the daughters who were all aged between nine and fifteen, appeared to 'struggle and plunge betwixt life and death, being both dumbe, deafe and blinde, her eyes closed up'.[60] These children, like Alexander Nyndge in the first story we encountered in this chapter, were reported to have become periodically estranged from the physical world, and to instead engage in lengthy conversations with an invisible demon, or even the Devil himself. The fear was, for early modern people, that the minds and bodies of the young, which were not fully formed and in a dangerous phase of youthfulness characterised by religious naivety, were particularly vulnerable to demonic assaults. As considered in the previous chapters, in a religious culture in which Protestants were encouraged to continuously 'check' themselves for signs of godliness or election, especially those who were closer to the Puritan disposition, attacks of this nature by the Devil needed to be read scrupulously for signs of demonic agency, and for those children who 'performed' well, for signs of potential godliness and thus salvation.

Today we would perhaps speak of the imagination, or the illusionary, to explain such episodes; however, to the early modern mind what constituted reality, or indeed imagination or delusion, was far removed from our own conceptions. The 'imagination' or mind was perhaps viewed as the invisible part of a person, the soul, which could itself be open to malign forces and corruption,

---

[59]   I.D., *The most wonderfull and true storie*, p. 4.
[60]   Anon, *The most strange and admirable discouerie*, sig. BIIr.

satanic thoughts and temptations. Beliefs in the 'reality' of dark dreams, or the idea that the Devil could enter the human mind, luring and tempting an individual to commit sin, were commonly recorded at this time.[61] The mind or imagination was a gateway to both good and evil, and the battle for human salvation – the almost palpable whisperings and desires of both God and Satan – could take place within such mental space. This, in turn, leads again to problems of analysis and definition for the historian, particularly for one engaged, as I am in this book, in understanding something not just of possession but of the people who experienced, witnessed and wrote about it. The perplexing nature of witchcraft accusations derives, as Roper has argued, from their 'epistemological status'. The historian's profession is to deal with 'fact', to search for 'truth', reliability, credibility – what, then, do we do with documents and stories which detail occurrences that we do not believe to be fact, or reality? Accounts of possession and witchcraft are not products of realism and cannot be scrutinised with such methods. They are rather 'vivid, organized products of the mind'.[62] The early modern mindset was different from our contemporary understanding; it was one of interpenetrating worlds, in which the mind and the imagination themselves had powers of their own.

What, then, can we make of such information? Why were children so prominently featured throughout these cases of demonic possession? Was it simply because, as spiritually unformed and weak creatures, they were seen to be open vessels, vulnerable to spiritual intrusion, or to active imaginations? Were they, due to their tender years, believed to be easy prey to the enemy of true religion, the Devil? Or, were they, because of beliefs about the taint of original sin, seen to be unchallenged by a state of true adult faith or repentance, and therefore the most likely members of society to be tempted by sin and evil? It was possibly a combination of all these factors. As James Sharpe has written, in one of the only recent articles to attempt analysis of this historical problem, concern over the age hierarchy 'permeated' early modern life – such a fact is evident in the information we gain from witchcraft accusations and cases of demonic possession. One of the most familiar examples of an early modern 'witch-craze', that of Salem in Massachusetts in 1692, further brought to 'popular' attention by Arthur Miller's play *The Crucible*, saw a group of young girls and women at the centre of an accusative frenzy, in which over 200 'witches' were discovered. As James Sharpe has suggested for England, 'indictments on Home Circuit

---

[61]   See in particular Oldridge, *The Devil in Early Modern England*, esp. Chapter 3 on Protestant experiences of the Devil – night terrors, deathbed fears, visions and temptation.

[62]   Roper, *Oedipus and the Devil*, p. 202.

of the assizes between 1610 and 1659 reveal 192 accusations of witchcraft, in which the alleged witches were supposed to have killed or harmed sixty-one adults and forty-four children'. Yet, despite the attention that witchcraft, as an historical subject, has received, few have questioned the social context and factor of age. Alternative, and now familiar social dichotomies, such as wealth, gender, social status, even old age, have been drawn into the witchcraft equation, yet the dichotomy of youth and age not so.[63] This chapter, and this book more widely, will seek to redress this balance. It will consider what cases of childhood possession (and prophecy) can reveal to us about children's place in the early modern lifecycle. These cases provide us with a window, a rare one at that, through which to glimpse the world of the early modern child. Although these texts are inevitably distorted, twisted by author and printer, perhaps we can catch small fragments of children's voices and of their actions, their affiliations and their spiritual worlds. Even if these stories are not 'true', the examples of these children, their spiritual struggles, their biblical knowledge, were published – and they became motifs of child suffering, children fighting the Devil, children holding spiritual agency – and these images were powerful.

During this period, and to some extent even now, the young and especially adolescents were recognised as being in a difficult and tempestuous period of life. The young were perceived as 'wild, headstrong and passionate, ever seeking to shock by rioting, swearing or unbridled sensuality'.[64] Such evidence of sin, the taint of the Fall, made them easy prey to the Devil, and as a consequence the young were allowed no authority, spiritual or otherwise. With the benefit of hindsight, we could now, perhaps, explain the high number of children implicated within possession cases by the fact that children were more likely to manifest symptoms that invited such explanation. Children were more likely to misbehave, to have tantrums, and, due to their physical smallness and weakness, to become ill or be afflicted by feverish fits. Early modern contemporaries were by no means ignorant of this fact, and sceptical writers, for example men such as Reginald Scot and Samuel Harsnett, the latter of whom we shall see in the next chapter waging a treatise war against John Darrell's widely published exorcisms, suggested earthly reasons for the afflictions suffered by supposed demoniacs.[65]

---

[63]   Sharpe, 'Disruption in the Well-ordered Household', p. 188.

[64]   Susan Brigden, 'Youth and the English Reformation', reprinted from *Past and Present* (95) 1982 in Peter Marshall (ed.) *The Impact of the English Reformation 1500–1640* (London: Arnold, 1997).

[65]   See esp. Reginald Scot, *The discouerie of witchcraft* (London, 1622) STC (2nd ed.) 20334; Harsnett, *A discouery of the fraudulent practises of Iohn Darrel*; and John Darrell, *The replie of Iohn Darrell* (England? 1602) *STC* (2nd ed.) 6284. The highly notorious cases of

Indeed, one early seventeenth-century medical tract suggested a variety of alternative explanations, blaming 'Insensibilitie, when they doe not feele, being pricked with a pin, or burnt with fire' on 'the Palsie, the falling sicknesse ... and diuerse other diseases'. Whereas fits were attributed to 'head-aches, gowtes, Epilepsies ... and disease of the mother', what, the tract asks, have they 'to doe with the Diuell, or with the dispossessing of him'.[66]

It was perhaps the shocking physicality of such reported cases that was most significant to contemporary commentators. Details surrounding the lack of bodily control, the violent fits, contortions and hysterical shouting echoed throughout numerous possession tracts. Yet, such symptoms were most commonly attributed to spiritual affliction. Clearly early modern society did regard children as particularly spiritually weak, as one contemporary pamphlet read: 'It cannot be denied that children are in nature the children of wrath ... born in sinne with ... none being exempted from the infection of originall sinne'.[67] As Roper has argued, possession cases represent the ambiguous and complex relationship between the perceived body and soul, the physical world and spiritual world, at this time. Through these possession cases children were seen as a microscopic battleground for the macroscopic warfare between God and the Devil, between the spirit and the flesh. It is, then, precisely in the interconnectedness of the early modern mindset, and the difficult and precarious physical and spiritual status of the period's afflicted children, that we can begin to perceive what drove contemporaries to be so interested in possession cases, but also how the cases themselves were entries in, and influences upon, the much broader soteriological debates of the English Reformation.

Protestantism itself focused upon the divide between spirit and flesh. Through the Protestant decree of predestination and the denial of the sacred nature of worldly goods – the sacraments, saintly effigies or relics, priests and the holiness of virginity – bodily flesh was now seen as corrupted and utterly sin-soaked in the face of the Divine. It has been argued by those such as Lyndal Roper that such tensions surrounding the body and flesh, in both the Protestant and Catholic

---

John Darrell during the second half of the sixteenth century included the dispossession, whether pretended or not, of 'William Somers at Nottingham: of Thomas Darling, the boy of Burton ... and of Katherine Wright at Mansfield ... and of his dealings with one Mary Couper at Nottingham'. For an historical account of these cases see Freeman, 'Demons, Deviance and Defiance'.

[66]   Edward Jorden, *A briefe discovrse of disease called the suffocation of the mother* (London, 1603) *STC* (2nd ed.) 14790, sigs. AIIv–AIVr.

[67]   Hieronymus Magomastix, *The Strange vvitch of Greenvvich, (ghost, spirit or hobgoblin) haunting a wench* (London, 1650) *Wing* (2nd ed.) 55920, pp. 4–5.

Reformations, contributed to the intensity of witchcraft accusations and fears.[68] There is some distance in this line of argument. Indeed, when considering the nature of spiritual doubt and fear concerning salvation experienced by some children and adolescents, as explored throughout this book, one can see how such fears could be projected onto the body. Also, when thinking about our present-day assumptions surrounding late childhood and adolescence, one can further see how concern surrounding the body could be related to such cases. The licensed misbehaviour allowed by possession enabled children, especially those at the late stages of childhood, to escape social expectations concerning physical deportment; through writhing, screaming and even playing, these children perhaps sought reassurance and attention from their families and their communities. It also allowed them to escape the parameters of the Protestant religion – during their fits and seizures, and their conversations with the Devil, children could challenge the rules and expectations of, but also be sites of accommodation and negotiation with, the Reformed faith.

'Children of Disobedience':[69] Misbehaviour and Possession Cases

The formulaic nature of the symptoms of demonic possession considered above, which detailed the extraordinary strength, the screaming, writhing and unusual swellings, has already been noted. Due to the notoriety of a few famous cases, such as those surrounding the exorcist John Darrell, and the cheap pamphlets produced in light of such occurrences, as well as through religious and biblical education, it is most likely that early modern society knew what it was to be possessed. It was, therefore, entirely possible, and in fact documented within contemporary publications, for individuals, or indeed children, to be able to feign, or to use language contemporary to the period in question to 'counterfeign', their own possession. Some cases explicitly point to such an accusation. Here we are dealing with a source genre of a different kind – clearly early modern audiences accepted that, in some circumstances, possession would be forged – whether at the instigation of the 'demoniacs' family, as in the case of Anne Gunter, or whether by the 'victims' themselves, as possibly with William Perry and in the cases considered below. Such instances do not seem to have

---

[68]   Roper, *Oedipus and the Devil*, p. 173.
[69]   'The children of disobedience', taken from Perkins, *A Discovrse of the damned art of witchcraft*, p. 5.

detracted, however, from the plausibility or impact of cases that were believed to have been genuine.

As we have already seen, in the late sixteenth century the Throckmorton family found themselves tangled within the web of a witchcraft case, and as the central feature of at least one now traceable pamphlet, *The most strange and admirable discouerie of the three witches of Warboys*. The five Throckmorton daughters acted out, for what purpose we will never know, a perfect possession scenario. Due to their afflicting demon the daughters were excused from the usual norms of acceptable behaviour. Such exceptions included meal times. In the case of one daughter:

> ... for sometimes shee hath merry fits ... whereat shee would sometimes smile, and sometimes laugh exceedingly, and amongst many other things, this is worthy to be noted, that being in her fit she looked farre more sweetely and cheerfully than when shee is awake.[70]

Such exemptions also extended to educational and religious expectations:

> In the morning being the Sabbath day, she came down into the hall towards prayer time, and being asked whether she would [read prayers] she answered that she would do as they would have her. Then was she asked whether she could reade, she sayd that she could once, but she had almost forgotten now: then being asked further whether shee had prayed that day, shee made answere it would not suffer her: then whether shee vsed to pray at home, she answered that it would not give her so much time. When someone said to her that God understoode the inward sight and grones of the heart, as wel as the lowdest cries of the mouth; she sodainely fell into her fit being more strongly and strangely tormented than ever she was before.[71]

Furthermore, being demonically afflicted also excused the daughters from general social decorum, for when a visitor made move to pray, 'no sooner had he uttered the first word, but even at one instant of time all the children fell into their fits, with such terrible scriches ... so wonderfully tormented, as though they should have beene torne in peeces'.[72]

---

[70]   Anon, *The most strange and admirable discouerie*, sig. BIIIr.
[71]   Anon, *The most strange and admirable discouerie*, sig. BIIv–BIIIr.
[72]   Anon, *The most strange and admirable discouerie*, sig. BIIr.

Such instances of misbehaviour, due to the demonic illness that afflicted the girls, attracted not punishment, but rather indulgence and attention, as evidenced by the following line: 'Above all things she delighteth in play: she will picke out some one body to play with her at cardes, and but one only, not hearing, seeing or speaking to any other'.[73] Cases of possession did at times provide a licence for misbehaviour and the breaking down of accepted social boundaries.[74] This fact is nowhere more clearly shown than in the case of John Starkie, who during one of his fits behaved in something of an animalistic manner:

> being in bed he leapt out on a suddaine with such a terrible outcry, that amazed them all, being tossed and tumbled a long time, being exceedingly fierce and strong like a mad man, or rather like a madd dogge … snatching at and biting euery body that laide holde on him, not sparing in that fitt his owne mother: smiting furiously all that came neare him, hurling the bed staues at their heads, and throwing the pillowes into the fire.[75]

We could attempt to analyse the purposes of the Throckmorton daughters and the Starkie children. They could, perhaps, have been genuinely sick, have felt themselves abused in some way, or, referring back to the notion of hidden cultural transcripts mentioned above, at least have believed themselves to be demonically afflicted. Alternatively, they could have been manipulated into feigning their illness by elders, much like the case of Anne Gunter. However, it could also be suggested that the children were staging a form of religious and social rebellion, refusing to pray, to read or listen to scripture. Amongst this variety of possibilities, it is difficult for the historian to identify the 'truth' within cases of possession. The stories and accounts we read within such cases are distortions of events, distanced from us by the literary intentions of the pamphlet writer, and by the alien conventions and assumptions of an age far removed from our own. Very often historians conclude that we do not always need to search for the truth in such cases – regardless of how close such stories and accounts were to the reality of the events they depict, they can, to those interested in cultural frameworks, reveal much about contemporary belief systems and mentalities. However, in some cases the accusation of childish misbehaviour and feigning of

---

[73]   Anon, *The most strange and admirable discouerie*, sig. BIIv.

[74]   James Sharpe highlights the inappropriate behaviour exhibited by the young woman, Anne Gunter, in his *The Bewitching of Anne Gunter*. Also see his 'Disruption in the Well-ordered Household'.

[75]   More, *A true discourse concerning the certaine possession and dispossession of 7 persons in one familie in Lancashire*, pp. 15–16.

demonic possession has already been levied, thus providing a slightly different perspective. We will now turn to two of these cases.

One spectacular account of such a case was put to print in 1574. The tract, entitled *The disclosing of a late counterfeyted possession by the devyl in two maydens*, describes in some detail the misdemeanours of two seemingly wayward girls, Agnes Briggs and Rachell Pynder. Significantly, the criticism of the author was directed towards those who had initially diagnosed the symptoms of possession, alongside those who had proceeded to publish such transgressions; the 'wilful and indurate ignoraunce of suche as had the matter in handling, being as they professed themselves, godly men, plentifully adorned with fayth, and sent of God to disturbe the devill of possession'.[76] The pamphlet contains all the essential ingredients of a 'good' possession story with which we are becoming familiar, including bodily contortions and strange devilish voices; during Agnes's fits 'the lyppes moved with non suche moving as coulde pronounce the words uttered, the eyeledes moued, but not open, she had greate swellinge in hur throte, and aboute the gawes, and the voyse was somewhat bygger then the childs voyse'.[77] The child's exorcism contained the emblematic battle with the Devil, in which 'Saythan sayde he wold tare us all in pesses'.[78]

However, during the child's later confession, the young Agnes admitted that she had simulated the act of being possessed. Furthermore, she had gained such an idea from overhearing the mother of one Rachell Pynder, who had claimed that her daughter was possessed, so that 'she woulde swell, and heave her body marveylously, and that she dyd avoyde at her mouth, in her traunces, beare, a blacke stike threede, and a feather, which this examinant hearying, determined to practise the lyke'. Later that same night the girl, with a collection of materials gathered from her bed chamber, feigned her first affliction and on 'purpose shee fel into a traunce'.[79]

Such a devious and somewhat dramatic act required a fair level of imagination, as the child supposedly confessed, she 'pulled some of her heare from her head, which she had put in her mouth. And in her traunce shee cast the same out of her mouth'. Indeed, she did the same with 'a litle peece of lace', 'a crooked pynne' and 'two nayles'. She also delivered 'divers straunge countenaunces, feigning divers straunge voices, and noyses ... in a monstruous manner'.[80] One obvious question

---

[76] Chrysostom, St., *The disclosing of a late counterfeyted possession by the devyl in two maydens*, sig. AIIr.

[77] Chrysostom, *The disclosing of a late counterfeyted possession*, sig. AVIIr.

[78] Chrysostom, *The disclosing of a late counterfeyted possession*, sig. AIVv.

[79] Chrysostom, *The disclosing of a late counterfeyted possession*, sig. BIr.

[80] Chrysostom, *The disclosing of a late counterfeyted possession*, sig. BIr.

about this case arises: what about Agnes's similarly afflicted elder friend, Rachell Pynder? Indeed, she too confessed to her devious behaviour, having also feigned her own demonic illness. She also voided household items from her mouth, mainly feathers from her pillow and silk, admitting to sometimes filling 'hir mouth so full, that it woulde stoppe in hir throte'. In her trance she similarly 'feyned divers straunge and hollowe speaches within hir throate', though she would, unsurprisingly, refuse to speak in Dutch or Latin.[81] Again, such details provide us with a window, albeit a misted one, through which we can gain some idea as to how even the most extreme symptoms could be simulated. Possession was a common enough concept to be tolerably imitated; but despite this potential for fakery, it also remained a potent enough state of spiritual excitement still to be of keen interest – to the audience, and the demoniac herself.

Indeed, such evidence provides us with an extraordinarily rare glimpse into the mind and actions of mischievous children. While we can only guess at their purposes, perhaps an attempt to copy or impress each other or simply to gain attention, their confessions nevertheless reveal to us the formulaic nature of possession at this time, and the sphere of female gossip, narrative and conversation in which such concerns circulated. What is also most significant is that Agnes did not read herself how to feign such symptoms, but overheard from a neighbour what was involved. Similarly, Thomas Darling also overheard a conversation between elders which led him to diagnose his own demonic infliction. The confession of the two children signifies that the early modern readership was prepared to accept that feigned cases of possession would occur. Furthermore, some writers were keen to draw attention to cases which they believed to be, or they could 'prove' to be, forgeries – these writers included the likes of Harsnett, who believed that such cases were a discredit to religion, and that they wreaked of 'popish' superstition, a trait which he believed should not be displayed in Protestant circles.

It is perhaps understandable, due to the nature of childhood, and the context in which early modern children were raised, that the early years of life were believed to be especially vulnerable to the wiles and temptations of the demonic. As we have seen, children were believed to be tainted by the spot of their original sin. The nature of what we now perceive to be childhood exuberance and experimentation, the expression of their personal will, against the background of Protestant values, may have been taken as evidence of sinfulness and corruption, and thus a way open to the Devil. Children were seen to be impressionable and easy prey for Satan, they needed assistance and guidance to find their way to God.

---

[81] Chrysostom, *The disclosing of a late counterfeyted possession*, sig. BIr–v.

As some contemporaries understood the circumstances: 'I see also how soone these yong things, God leaving them to themselves, and to their strong soone budding corruptions, like soft waxe, take suddaine sathanicall impressions'.[82] Hence, it was the responsibility of both family and society at large to curb such wilfulness and corruption, as well as to aid those unfortunate enough to have experienced the threats and promises of Satan first hand.

The Devil needed to be driven from the young, and it was therefore advisable to 'resist him in the beginning, to quench his sparkes with prayers and teares in the first kindling, to crush his injected temptations, as yong serpents in the heads, and cocatrices in their shells'. For, 'give the Divell an inch, and hee will take an ell; sup of his broth, and eate of his roast meate, it being dangerous to give his waters the least passage, or to entertaine the least sparke of his hellish heates into a harbouring heart'. [83]

Conclusions

Therefore, a few words to conclude this third chapter: the formulaic nature of witchcraft and possession cases shaped spiritual anxieties about the vulnerability of children, the active agency of Satan in the world, and disorderly behaviours and beliefs. I do not argue that such cases were, in every instance, manipulated by demoniac, audience or author to become a form of dramatised fiction. It is most likely that individuals within society, especially spiritually and physically vulnerable children, could actually believe themselves to be possessed. In such cases both demoniacs and spectators were adhering to hidden cultural transcripts that were firmly rooted in contemporary belief systems concerning the power of the demonic in the world, as well as in fears about the spiritual status of children, caused in large part by Protestant soteriology, which uprooted traditional belief systems concerning the efficacy of baptism and the destination of children's souls after death. The role of the possession narrative, one of the core historical points throughout this chapter, whether 'created' by parents or children themselves, was not a process of deliberate or cynical manipulation, but was a form of cultural rhetoric, drawn on to fill gaps in knowledge or understanding, to enact some form of social protest or rebellion, or perhaps used as a creative tool by writers, to explain and make sense of such spiritual uncertainties. At times, however,

---

[82]   Magomastix, *The strange vvitch at Greenvvich* p. 7.
[83]   Magomastix, *The strange vvitch at Greenvvich*, pp. 6–7.

children were responsible for feigning their own possession and creating religious and social disorder.

Indeed, the role of children within such 'wonderfull and true' stories was not simply one of religious passivity or naivety. Most interestingly, such cases reveal to us the ability of the young to manipulate existing belief systems, and to adapt them to their own purposes. They also show how much attention and spiritual authority children were able to wrangle out of their local, and even national, communities. Furthermore, such cases, when discovered, do much to illustrate contemporary attitudes surrounding the young, their moral worth, and spiritual status. Without legitimate access to the pulpit or printing press, the views of women and children are largely obscured from our view. However, through such violent and perverse challenges to the correct social and religious order, we can gain some insight into the private religiosity of the socially quiet. Possession cases provide an unrivalled window into the religiosity of children at this time, both in terms of children's comprehension of and role within religious life, but also concerning social expectation surrounding the spirituality of children.

Such cases are instances in which Church and child, the Protestant religion and the young, came into some form of ideological conflict, or at least an awkward form of ideological compromise. Wherever the final conclusion of contemporaries lay, the mere circulation of such material, and the significant controversy and debate it caused, reveals that images and stories surrounding the early modern child, and perceptions of the relationship between Church and child, or spirit and child, had a great propaganda value. Most significantly, the conflict and debate such stories ignited forms an important part of the picture detailing how Protestant belief worked at various levels throughout the Reformed Church. Throughout cases of possession children were perceived, quite literally, to be a battleground between good and evil; an exaggerated form of the state of childhood more generally perhaps. This battleground was fraught with theological implications, and was therefore too important to be left merely to the 'popular' tracts which have been the basis of this chapter. Indeed, so certain were contemporary writers and thinkers that possession and children were of considerable importance to the broader controversies of the time that exorcism, demoniacs and salvation itself came to be fought over in a series of paper wars towards the end of the sixteenth century. We will now turn to those exchanges to understand a little more about the deep confessional disquiet of which possession can be seen as an emblem.

Chapter 4

Darrell, Harsnett and the
Child Demoniacs

In the previous chapter, we considered the nature of beliefs surrounding the personal body and domestic space in relation to children and possession cases. Such issues are very much related to perceptions of early modern interiority and personal or domestic culture. The naming of a 'witch', for example, was often tussled with and fought out within local communities. As we considered, children, alongside other 'victims' of witchcraft and black magic by *Maleficia*, fed upon and recycled local gossip and popular stereotypes about witches. Furthermore, when they became demonically possessed, children stepped beyond normal, or accepted, social boundaries – they thus broke the unspoken codes of authority and hierarchy, which structured homely and interior life. We will now turn to consider the wider implications of the roles of children within cases of demonic possession. Indeed, the child within the possession narrative did not simply occupy the world and minds of domestic or local culture. Rather, their spiritual plights and struggles also became integral to a much wider stage and audience.

Cases of possession can reveal to us aspects of early modern religious culture, in which children were temporarily granted iconic authority, through which they became the mouthpieces for certain strands of religious belief. Such a position allowed children not only to trespass social boundaries, or to temporarily defy social superiors and accepted authorities, but also, much more significantly, to gain power and authority of their own – whether or not this authority existed in reality or whether or not it was in actuality experienced by the children considered is not necessarily significant. Indeed, as considered in the Introduction to this work, the experiences of children and perceptions of children are inevitably linked to one degree or another, and what matters here is that the cultural space was created for children to be perceived and viewed in such ways. This power or authority we see children possess in these cases held wider, public interest, was both spiritual and political, and was derived from the popular perception that children were not simply vulnerable to demonic temptation, but were also acutely, and due to their youth and innocence, particularly, receptive to the Divine. Such a power was based upon a biblical precedent, concerning the chosen lambs of God, as will be considered in the following chapter, and thus contributed to a continuous dialogue of beliefs surrounding the spiritual receptiveness of the young, and the notion of childhood innocence.

As will be explored, two of the central figures to bring the role of child possession narratives to the fore, both to exploit their religio-political nature and to drag them into polemical realms, were John Darrell and Samuel Harsnett. John Darrell was a man of books and learning. The Nottingham-born Darrell had graduated from Queens' College, Cambridge, in 1579, before going on to study law at the Inns of Court in London. He was, in some circles, seen to be a man of excellent religious repute. He was a staunch Puritan, closely connected to influential members of the godly ministry, including the much published Arthur Hildersham, based in Ashby-de-la-Zouch. This made him, to the likes of the more 'moderate' voices of the 'official' Church of England such as Richard Bancroft and his then chaplain Samuel Harsnett, a Puritan dissenter of the most annoying sort.

Darrell, the self-professed exorcist and 'Devil-finder', would travel in the dark of the night, to the homes of the young and possessed. With a growing reputation, he would answer the pleas of their distressed parents, and with his coterie of followers he would diagnose the Devil's presence, before engaging in the task of drawing out demons, entering into dialogue with them and quashing them with Holy Scripture. Darrell's exorcising ministry began in 1586, when Katherine Wright was sent to him by a neighbour. After two attempts at healing her, Darrell was seemingly successful at curing the child. Not content with such a 'modest' victory, Darrell's exorcising style became increasingly elaborate and spectacular, and the demons he encountered, seemingly, increasingly ferocious. Darrell's ascent to significant fame was ignited in 1596, with his dispossession of Thomas Darling. Then in 1597, he exorcised no fewer than seven demoniacs in the Lancashire home of Nicholas Starkie.[1] If Darrell had not had such a keen

---

[1]   For details on the career of Darrell, see his *DNB* entry; Thomas S. Freeman, 'Darrell, John (*b. c.*1562, *d.* in or after 1607)', *Oxford Dictionary of National Biography*, Oxford University Press, 2004 [http://www.oxforddnb.com/view/article/7168, accessed 29 July 2014]. Also Harsnett, *A discouery of the fraudulent practises of one Iohn Darrel*, which includes a discussion of the Katherine Wright case; Darrell's encounters with Thomas Darling and the Starkie children are documented in I.D., *The most wonderfull and true storie* and More, *A true discourse concerning the certaine possession and dispossession of 7 persons in one familie in Lancashire*. See also Freeman's 'Demons, Deviance and Defiance'; for details on specific Darrell cases, see especially D.P. Walker, *Unclean Spirits, Possession and Exorcism in France and England in the late Sixteenth and early Seventeenth Centuries* (London: Scolar Press,

desire to extensively publish his 'mysterious' doings, then perhaps he might have been left well alone by the religious authorities. Yet, as it was, his polemical works attracted the attention of Bancroft and Harsnett, the latter of whom began an earnest campaign against exorcists of all types and extremes of religious persuasion. Indeed, Harsnett was vehement in his convictions, and was at times criticised for his extreme bluntness, evident for example in his disapproval of exorcists, in lines such as: 'peddling Exorcist of the rascal crue, who wandered like a chapman of small wares', with his ridiculous 'puppet-play' performance.[2] Darrell's professional demise came in 1598, when he became acquainted with William Sommers, a 21-year-old musician's apprentice from Nottingham. Sommers later confessed to the authorities that he had, with Darrell's instruction, feigned his demonic malady. This added grist to Harsnett's mill. He had long been aware of Darrell's fame and reputation, and he thus began a direct crusade against the exorcist and his allies. In his final work, Collinson argued that the actions of Darrell (and others like him) sparked the attention of Bancroft – not necessarily just because they involved the somewhat ominous dispossession of demons, but because of what they revealed about the nature of Puritanism itself. Collinson wrote:

> In a major provincial town like Nottingham, the interest [in possession] was so great that for a time the pulpit rang with nothing but the Devil, and the town was split into two. A little late in the day, Bancroft came to the realisation that this was where the truly revolutionary potential of Puritanism lay, and [tackling] this was his best chance of ultimately confuting it.[3]

This reveals how significant these cases could become, both religiously and politically. Most interesting to our purpose here is that children, and young people like Sommers, played significant roles in such cases.

1981) parts 3 and 4; and the introductions to individual case transcripts in Almond, *Demonic Possession and Exorcism in Early Modern England*, esp. chapters 4, 5 and 6. For recent work on the career of Darrell, see Marion Gibson, *Possession, Puritanism and Print* (London: Pickering and Chatto, 2006).

   [2]   F.W. Brownlow, *Shakespeare, Harsnett, and the Devils of Denham* (Newark: University of Delaware Press, 1993) p. 251, see also Clive Holmes, 'Witchcraft and Possession at the Accession of James I: the publication of Samuel Harsnett's "A Declaration of Egregious Popish Impostures"', in John Newton (ed.), *Witchcraft and the Act of 1604* (Leiden, Boston: Brill, 2008).

   [3]   Patrick Collinson, *Richard Bancroft and Elizabethan Puritanism* (Cambridge: Cambridge University Press, 2013) p. 149.

Bancroft's ally, Harsnett, in comparison to Darrell, was a man of the 'official', reformed English Church. His spiritual persuasions were marked by a more orthodox and restrained moderation. In 1597 the newly appointed Bishop of London, Richard Bancroft, made Harsnett one of his chaplains as well as making him vicar of Chigwell. During this time the two men formed a close friendship and alliance. In March 1598 Harsnett was involved in a commission condemning Darrell's 'hoax' exorcisms, before writing his notorious *A Discovery of the Fraudulent Practices of John Darel* in 1599. In 1603 he published a similar tract against the perceived evils of the exorcists, this time aimed at those of a Catholic persuasion, *A Declaration of Egregious Popish Impostures*. Indeed, Harsnett needed to maintain the impression of condemning both Puritans and Catholics to an equal degree. The focus of this tract was a series of 'spectacular' exorcisms conducted by Jesuit ministers in the house of a recusant gentleman, Sir George Peckham of Denham, Buckinghamshire. In 1604 Harsnett's efforts came to fruition with the passing of new legislation concerning witchcraft and exorcism. Canon 72 of the new Church Canons ruled that no minister, without special permission from the Bishop (which would rarely, if ever, be granted) was to attempt 'upon any pretence whatsoever, whether of possession or obsession, by fasting and prayer, to cast out any devil or devils'; thus, officially at least, driving possession out of the remit of the established Church.[4] Integral to Harsnett's argument was the notion that such miracles only occurred during biblical times, when Christ healed the sick by drawing spirits from them. In 1605 Harsnett also became involved with the feigned possession case of adolescent Anne Gunter, daughter of Brian Gunter of North Moreton, Berkshire.[5] Harsnett presented the demoniacs both as brainwashed victims and deceitful accomplices within possession cases. Hence, the children involved within such cases were not necessarily seen to be the beneficiaries of authority or religious notability. In the eyes of certain early modern sceptics they were nothing more than pawns, caught in a polemical warfare between various interpretations of religion.

---

[4]   Thomas, *Religion and the Decline of Magic*, p. 579.

[5]   For details on the life of Samuel Harsnett, see his entry in the *DNB*; Nicholas W.S. Cranfield, 'Harsnett, Samuel (*bap.* 1561, *d.* 1631)', *Oxford Dictionary of National Biography*, Oxford University Press, Sept 2004; online edn, Jan 2008 [http://www. oxforddnb.com/view/article/12466, accessed 29 July 2014] Also, see Harsnett, *Discouery* (1599) and his *A Declaration of egregious popish impostures* (London, 1603) *STC* (2nd edn.) 12880, also transcribed and reprinted in Brownlow, *Shakespeare, Harsnett, and the Devils of Denham*; see too Stephen Greenblatt, 'Shakespeare and the Exorcists' in *Shakespearean Negotiations* (Berkeley and Los Angeles, University of California Press, 1988), pp. 94–128; Clive Holmes, 'Witchcraft and Possession at the Accession of James I'. See too Sharpe, *The Bewitching of Anne Gunter.*

Indeed, as the Darrell–Harsnett battle can reveal, possession cases were an important area of political and religious negotiation. Cases of demonic possession were, in a sense, tools for propaganda and polemical persuasion. Those who could control possession, and thus who could control perceptions of demonic agency and religious or spiritual intervention or even providence on earth, held religious and spiritual authority, alongside, from a 'popular' perspective, potential political power. This is why the struggle over the cases of demonic possession, and more intimately, the struggle over the children involved in such cases, was so important to the key players, most especially Darrell and Harsnett. As Stephen Greenblatt has argued in an article on Harsnett's *Declaration of Egregious Popish Impostures*, such texts became weapons in the Church of England's state-supported attempt to wipe out 'pockets of rivalrous charisma'. Furthermore, to note Edward Shils's phrase, such religious charisma had 'awe-arousing centrality'. These dramatic instances of spiritual and demonic visitation and personification allowed the 'extraordinary' to come into direct contact with the ordinary, and thus allowed spectators and participators to touch 'vital sources of legitimacy, authority and sacredness'. Such intense spiritual contact was, in a sense, comforting, to the immediate participants, but also to the audience, upon whose awe such occurrences depended. This was then, a community of believers, centred around a small and sick child. Together, child and exorcist testified to the power of true faith, invoked the Devil, called upon God through prayer and fast, and in Catholic instances praised the Virgin, the Eucharist and the Pope.[6]

The opportunity for religious and political propaganda that the possession cases attracted has been the subject of a modest amount of historical enquiry, most of it centred around Harsnett's *Discovery* and anti-Catholic leanings. Stephen Greenblatt, F.W. Brownlow and more recently Clive Holmes have explored the religious and political value of the texts, rooting their arguments in the sphere of spiritual rivalry, in which varying definitions of the sacred fought over fragments of the possession stories, each attempting to imbue the narratives with their own interpretations of truth, drama and deception. Indeed, each spiritual camp, the Puritans at one extreme, the Catholics and Jesuit ministers at the other, and those Greenblatt and Brownlow have termed 'Anglicans' somewhere in between, struggled to obtain the final word in this unravelling drama.[7] It was, primarily,

---

[6]   Greenblatt, 'Shakespeare and the Exorcists', pp. 96–7. Shils's is quoted here also.

[7]   See Brownlow, *Shakespeare, Harsnett, and the Devils of Denham*; Holmes, 'Witchcraft and Possession at the Accession of James I'; Gibson, *Possession, Puritanism and Print*; Greenblatt, 'Shakespeare and the Exorcists', Greenblatt considered the text from a literary and new-historicist slant; he looked at the connection between Harsnett's tract and Shakespeare's *King Lear*, and explored what he saw to be Harsnett's attempt to 'de-mystify'

a struggle for authority and spiritual supremacy. However, the authority and power Darrell and Harsnett fought for, and the religio-political power their historians have sought to recreate, did not simply or truly belong to the exorcist or bishop: they belonged, most acutely and extraordinarily, to the child.

Indeed, the theme of authority – authority against age and social superiors and religious or spiritual authority – is central to the possession cases. As has been acknowledged, the possession narratives became heavily politicised, and as explored in the previous chapter, they allowed the young victims to break away from accepted age and social orders. Yet, the cases also allowed children to acquire a more iconic authority; not an authority which was simply derived from perversions against age, social or gender orders, but one that was seen to be ethereal and 'godly' in its essence. Before we turn again to the individual cases, it is first necessary to define the meaning of 'authority' as it was understood and silently perceived in early modern society. In their volume of essays on authority, Paul Griffiths, Adam Fox and Steve Hindle have argued that authority is, or was, 'the power or right to define and regulate the legitimate behaviour of others'. Furthermore, early modern society was:

> ... organised around a series of overlapping power struggles which sought to regulate and order the lives of people at every level. In the governing principles of rank, gender and age, the values of hierarchy and place were ordained and elaborated. The positions of rich and poor, men and women, the young and old were articulated and disseminated in an effort to make them seem natural and inevitable ... The order of things was always and everywhere rehearsed and reinforced.[8]

Similarly, in the same volume, James Sharpe, when writing about possession cases and 'disruption in the household' has spoken about 'numerous webs of authority', and the licence for misbehaviour becoming possessed, or believing oneself to be possessed, could allow, and he speaks of the temporary nature of this authority, which allowed the young and possessed to trespass age-defined social orders.[9]

---

the possession narratives, to draw the mystery out of them by relating the demonic farces to stage play. We will return to these ideas later.

[8]   Paul Griffiths, 'Introduction', in Paul Griffiths, Adam Fox and Steve Hindle (eds), *The Experience of Authority in Early Modern England* (London: Macmillan, 1996).

[9]   Sharpe, 'Disruption in the Well-Ordered Household: Age, Authority and Possessed Young People'.

However, the role of 'godly' or spiritual authority within these cases has not been considered. In the context of early modern understanding, these children were not simply seen to be misbehaving. They were not understood to be becoming temporarily obnoxious; to be reacting against the austere nature of a puritanical upbringing; or themselves becoming a personification for change and upheaval in the reforming world. Indeed, the restructuring of the church or the social evils brought about by field-enclosure, urban expansion, famine or inflation, were not seen to be root causes of 'becoming' possessed. Not that these arguments are without weight. But, in the minds of contemporary society, the children were in fact, believed to be directly and intimately receptive to the spiritual. In the minds of many, the young and possessed were not misbehaving or chiding their superiors, they were victims of the Devil; they were not making-up far-fetched tales, they were experiencing and articulating a dialogue inspired by other-worldly prophecy. Furthermore, as Harsnett and his historians have argued, if the possession cases were in fact like stage-plays or the 'Pope's playhouse' in which religion became a 'pageant of puppittes' – then the children were the key cast. The young and possessed were not then breaking religious or spiritual authority structures, but were becoming and redefining them.

Young, Godly and Possessed: Demonic Possession and Religious Identity

We will now consider the explicit link between Puritanism, childhood and possession in the early modern period, returning to the stories of those who were young, godly and possessed. Here we will consider what possession stories can tell us about perceptions towards children at this time, and the way in which cases of the young and possessed became entangled in the controversial dialogue of Reformed belief. We will look at the cases relating to self-professed exorcist John Darrell, alongside two other most striking cases of Puritan dispossession, those of Mary Glover and Margaret Muschamp.[10]

Thomas Darling, whom we met briefly in the previous chapter, was 13 years old when he first met Darrell, whose identity within published accounts

---

[10]   Darrell worked on a range of cases. Here we will consider those involving children, including the cases of Thomas Darling and the Lancashire Seven. The case of Katherine Wright, a young girl, has been lost, and is only mentioned in Harsnett's *Discouery* (1599). The case of William Sommers (see John Darrell, *An apologie, or defence of the possession of William Somers, a yong man of Nottingham* (Amsterdam? 1599?) *STC* (2nd ed.) 6280.5) has been excluded, due to the fact that Sommers was a young man, aged 21 when he first came into contact with Darrell.

of the boy's dispossession case remained most discreet, almost to the point of anonymity. Thomas's demonic fits were, according to the tract describing the case, brought on when he was 'religiously occupied', and performed in front of a local audience. He, like the other victims here explored, oscillated between demonically afflicted and divinely inspired fits and visions. In between his torments, he begged 'his friends that were present to pray for him' and 'requested them to reade the scriptures, which they could not doe for weeping to behold his miserie'. In the guise of someone much older and wiser than his tender years, the child spoke calmly about his closeness to death, in a manner most similar to Protestant deathbed confrontations:

> With those that were good Christians, he took great pleasure to conferre; to whom he would signifie his daily expectation of Death, and his resolute readinesse to leaue the world, and to be with Christ: and all his loue to the world, he said extended thus farre, that (if God had so been pleased) he might haue loued to be a preacher to thunder out the threatenings of Gods word, against sinne and all abhominations.

Indeed, the boy put on something of a pious performance, side by side with his spiritual-accomplice, Jesse Bee, one of Darrell's associates and the possible author of the *Most wonderfull and true storie*. The man and young child worked together, Jesse Bee drawing the boy into a spiritually inspired battle; Bee coaxed, 'Thomas shall we take the sword with two edges and bid Sathan the Battayle'. The boy, being familiar with the Scriptural phrase, answered; 'if you will read, I will gladly heare'.[11]

Towards the end of his affliction, Thomas became so confident about his authority as a chosen, spiritual messenger and, somewhat surprisingly, about his elect status, he asserted: 'Auoyde sathan, I have vpon my head the helmet of saluation, and I am girded about with trueth. Iesus Christ hath shead water and bloud for my sins, & I sweat but water. O Lord thy apostles were whipt & scourged for thy trueth, & they departed, rejoycing that they were accounted woorthy to suffer for thy names sake. And now (O Lorde) I rejoyce that thou accountest me woorthie to suffer these cruell torments'. Then, lying on his back, this young and potential martyr for his faith, 'asked the standers by to sing the sixt psalm, and so they did, he singing with them verie cheerfully'.[12]

---

[11]   I.D., *The most wonderfull and true storie*, pp. 3, 3, 18.
[12]   I.D., *The most wonderfull and true storie*, pp. 28–9.

Whether or not he believed himself to be possessed, or whether he was acting out a scenario he *knew* would be typical, according to culturally accepted wisdom of someone who was possessed, is impossible to tell. Whatever the scenario, according to the text, Thomas gained an extraordinary amount of spiritual power, through which the author gives room to the notion that the child was able to construct his own identity, through which he presented himself as a godly agent and a willing martyr for the Puritan cause. Through piety and Scriptural eloquence, the child is depicted to have helped to orchestrate his own delivery. His gestures were acutely observed for signs of the child's godliness; whether such gestures were the product of forgery and cynical manipulation, or a more sincere effort to dispel perceived evil through pious action, they tell us much about the practice of early modern prayer. The boy would fall 'vpon his knees sodainely to prayer', and when deprived of speech 'hee would make signes of praying, with folded hands, sometime lifting then vp, and sometime striking then vpon his breast'.[13] Hence, the child was not depicted as a crazed instrument of demonic intrusion, but was, rather, an agent of godly authority, who was able to assure bystanders of his elect and divine status. It is quite probable that Thomas had never believed himself to be demonically possessed, or indeed had even intended to give that impression; but had rather wanted to construct himself as a 'godly' prophet.

One child whose identity became torn between demonic victim and godly seer was Mary Glover. Fourteen-year-old Mary captured the attention of religious, secular and medical authorities in the year 1603, when a tract detailing her possession and subsequent recovery, *A true and briefe report*, was published in London. Like many others of its ilk, the text reported a tale of malicious spiritual intrusion to a public greedy for such tales of sensational woe and wonder. Aside from the explicitly Puritan details, the story exposing Mary's possession was, as far as early modern cases of demonic intrusion went, fairly formulaic.[14] Mary was, supposedly, bewitched by an old woman, who had accused her of malicious gossip. The child fell so ill that the church bell was tolled for her, and the accused witch supposedly publicly rejoiced at the news of the girl's impending death. Mary suffered demonic affliction for over eight months, which, according to the tract, exceeded 'both arte and nature' in its extremity.[15]

Written by self-professed 'godly' author John Swan, the text told that, on the 16th of December 1602, Satan had departed from Mary Glover. Mary

---

[13]   I.D., *The most wonderfull and true storie*, pp. 3 and 5.

[14]   See the previous chapter.

[15]   John Swan, *A true and briefe report of Mary Glouers vexation and of her deliuerance by the means of fasting and prayer* (London, 1603) STC (2nd ed.) 23517, p. 1.

had thrown her hands high and 'wide a sunder', crying out, 'He is come, he is come ... The Comforter is come. O Lord, you have delivered me'.[16] According to the tract, which reveals an unusually detailed account of the process of dispossession, these were the dying words of her grandfather, Robert Glover, who was 'martyred' during the reign of Mary Tudor, as recorded in significant detail throughout various editions of Foxe's Book of Martyrs. Indeed, Robert Glover was a significant member of the early Protestant movement in England. He had married one of Hugh Latimer's nieces, and was burnt for his convictions on 19 September, 1555.[17] Hence, Swan presents Mary, like her grandfather, as the victim of persecution, both demonic and official, and simultaneously as a prophetic messenger, sent by God. The text's extreme detail and sense of purpose was derived from the fact that it was written as a reaction to contemporary anti-dispossession propaganda, evident when Swan complains; 'I am not ignorant, that one, very lately at Paul's crosse, spake much to the taxing of the Iudge, Iurie, and witnesses, and clearinge or acquittinge the witch'.[18] Indeed, Harsnett had, in his 1599 tract, ridiculed Darrell and his 'colleagues' Swan and George More, calling them, amongst other derogatory terms, 'devil-finders & devil-puffers, or devil-prayers'.[19]

The notion of Mary's providential martyrdom, inherited from her grandfather, and the dualistic perception of reception to both godly and demonic forces, is inherent throughout Swan's text. Throughout her dispossession her demonic fits and illnesses frequently gave way to more divinely inspired symptoms, such as prayer and prophetic insight. Mary was thus a site of demonic conflict and godly intervention, and above all a personification of Divine presence, or providence, on earth. When the child's body had become demonically infected, she displayed all the usual and distressing physical symptoms of one utterly possessed, as the text reads; ' ... with a pale dead colour of face and eyes closed (yet so, as you might perceiue the white of them to be turned vp) ... followed [by] dumbnes ... succeeded [by] an heaving or swallinge in the bellie, breast, and

---

[16]   Swan, *A true and briefe report of Mary Glouers vexation*, p. 47.

[17]   For details on Robert Glover, see his entry in the *DNB*; Susan Wabuda, 'Glover, Robert (*d.* 1555)', *Oxford Dictionary of National Biography*, Oxford University Press, 2004 [http://www.oxforddnb.com/view/article/10832, accessed 29 July 2014] See also his entry in 'John Foxe's Book of Martyrs', online version http://www.hrionline.ac.uk/johnfoxe. Various editions of Foxe's work reference Robert Glover, yet a lengthy account of his life and martyrdom exists in the *Book of Martyrs*, Book 11, pp. 1885–91.

[18]   Swan, *A true and briefe report of Mary Glouers vexation*, p. 5.

[19]   Samuel Harsnett, 'A Declaration of Popish Imposture', printed in F.W. Brownlow, *Shakespeare, Harsnett, and the Devils of Denham* (Newark: University of Delaware Press, 1993) p. 330.

throat'.[20] Furthermore, the young girl became 'wax pale coloured, weepinge, and answeringe faintly', whilst 'weepinge bitterly, wringing her handes extreamly, complaining of vnacustomed payne, yea casting out wordes of feare that God would not heare vs in calling on him for her so wretched a creature ...'.[21] In response, ritualistic methods were deployed in order to rid the young child of her possessing demon. 'She was advised to ... sitt about the midst of the Chamber, in a lowe wicker chaire, with her face towardes the fire, and her left side towardes the preacher'. Such spiritual performances were acted out in front of an audience of local witnesses, including notable magistrates, who read the Book of Daniel to the child, led by six ministers 'imployed ... [for] preachinge and prayer'.[22] Indeed, throughout this immense pain and suffering the young Mary became the site of earnest attempts of Puritan healing. Swan and his accompanying ministers recommended a course of conscientious fasting, prayer and Bible readings, which included, most appropriately, readings from the Book of Daniel, the young biblical prophet.

The depiction of the Puritan coterie that attended Mary's dispossession is what distinguishes this text from many others of its kind. Swan provides an immensely detailed description of the circle of godly spectators that surround the child, a group that included Mary's 'sober' parents, ministers and Swan himself. The awe-struck audience performed 'typically' Puritan acts of ritual and worship, they took detailed notes, they prayed, read from the Bible, sighed many 'hearty sighes' and they wept tears for the evil sins and cruel acts they beheld, as the tract reads; 'droppes of teares steale downe the cheekes of many'.[23] Most significantly, the group was most secretive about its doings. The meetings were very cloak-and-dagger, and at the closing of each day the group departed 'with mutuall consentes to meete the next morning at the time & place appointed ... in another place farr distant, for the more quyet and security to perform that good worke of prayer, fasting, and supplication'.[24]

Nonetheless, it is the depiction of the devout and pious Mary, and her intimate relationship with her anticipatory audience, that remains most significant to our

---

[20] Swan, *A true and briefe report of Mary Glouers vexation*, p. 16.

[21] Swan, *A true and briefe report of Mary Glouers vexation*, pp. 14–15.

[22] Swan, *A true and briefe report of Mary Glouers vexation*, p. 16.

[23] Swan, *A true and briefe report of Mary Glouers vexation*, p. 22; for an exploration into the nature of Puritan or 'godly' religiosity, and the sounds, actions and performances associated with spiritual worship, see John Craig's 'Psalms, groans and dogwhippers: the soundscape of worship in the English parish church, 1547–1642', in Will Coster and Andrew Spicer (ed.) *Sacred Space in Early Modern Europe* (Cambridge: Cambridge University Press, 2005) pp. 104–23.

[24] Swan, *A true and briefe report of Mary Glouers vexation*, p. 8.

purpose. During religious meetings held for the dispossession of Mary, the child was said to perform 'very seemely and comely reverence to such as were present', whilst she sat on a low chair, reading the Bible, 'whereof she made vse so long as she should, by turning to such chapters as were read, and to such textes as were handled such quotations as were cited: wherin if she at any time failed, either by greife of body, or infirmity of mynde, or meditation, or by fayling of sight ... then a woman sittinge by was ready alwayes in that behalfe to helpe her'.[25] Indeed, Mary was not only depicted as an intelligent, obedient and godly child, she was also presented as something of a child prodigy.

With the help of Divine insight and intervention, she recited a number of her own prayers, which were lengthy and spiritually elaborate affairs. The child, in a mood befitting of such Puritan perceptions of their own godliness, seemed whole-heartedly aware of her depraved and human nature, calling God to 'be mercifull vnto me and pardon all my sinnes, let them not stand vp as a wall to stoppe and hinder thy favours from me ... I haue been a vile wretch, and sinnfull creature, but deale not with me as I haue deserued ... though thou shouldest lett Satan kill my body, let him haue no power on my soule ... '.[26] Such exclamations were, perhaps, symptomatic of a child who was entering the first stages of youth, and therefore a wider spiritual awareness in relation to her own capability for sinfulness. Not only this, but Mary provided awe inspired onlookers with a knowledgeable interpretation of demonological thought, urging spectators to be forgiving towards the witch who afflicted her, blaming instead the Devil for her afflictions. The Devil, she professed, would in time suffer his retribution: 'Satan was herein thy rodde (o Lord) vppon me, and shee but the instrument, and as for the rodde when thou hast done with it, it shall be cast into the fire'. The child, furthermore, was seen in the text to be orchestrating her own recovery and redemption. After her long and agonising affliction, she spoke of feelings of spiritual renewal and rebirth: 'And now Lords graunt that begininge as it were a new, it would please thee to take me, even like a new borne babe, vnto thy good grace that so I may become a new creature: make me to hate sinne with a perfect hatred, and detest Sathan and his workes, and treade him vnder my feet as dyrte'.[27] Hence, the weak and sickly child presented to readers at the opening of the narrative, becomes in time a strong spiritual icon, a Puritan daughter and eloquent opponent of Satan. Perhaps her desire to be accepted by God 'like a new borne babe' demonstrated that she saw herself to be at the end of her

---

[25]   Swan, *A true and briefe report of Mary Glouers vexation*, pp. 9–10.

[26]   Swan, *A true and briefe report of Mary Glouers vexation*, p. 25.

[27]   Swan, *A true and briefe report of Mary Glouers vexation*, p. 49.

childhood, and on the fringes of a potentially more sinful youth. Yet, she was still presented by the author, significantly, as a child figure; as Swan concluded, it was a true case of God electing 'weake instruments to bringe downe the proud'.[28] Furthermore, prayers to Daniel, the child prophet, were also significant references to the importance of childhood in this case.

Mary, like the young Thomas Darling, became something of a mini-Puritan-martyr, a daughter sent from God to weave the old Jerusalem with the new, as Swan comments: 'I did in my prayer liken her, to an old grandmother of hers, Mary Magadalene, who though she was once a gazing stocke to many, yet afterwards, did leaue an honourable name behinde her to many generations: so now, I commend vnto this our Mary (to be had always in her minde and mouth) the songe of a more blessed Mary, the mother of our blessed Saviour'.[29] The possessed Mary was, then, in a rather obvious and clumsy attempt at a symbolic allegory, tied to the Marys of the Bible. Like Mary Magdalene, a once sinful character who had been cleansed of her 'seven demons', 'our' Mary was, too, redeemed of her sins, and in a sense reborn into the Christian covenant. Mary Glover was to remain then, an example to the pious; like Mary the mother of Christ, remembered through evensong, her memory and story would be an inspiration to the godly, and a warning to the sinful. Indeed, most significant to Mary's pious status was her family history. Mary was a descendent of the Latimer family, and grand-daughter of Protestant martyr Robert Glover. This was proof enough, according to the tract, of Mary's Divine and elect status.[30] She was not a sinful victim of Satan, or a misbehaving child, but rather a young and spiritual icon, a weeping and delicate victim of society's evil. This ideal 'Puritan' daughter was perhaps meant to be both a symbolic inspiration to the godly and a warning to the sceptical.

Words of Wisdom and Warning

Many reported cases of possession uttered words of warning, which incorporated an anxious awareness of the looming presence of Satan, as well as a conscious

---

[28]   Swan, *A true and briefe report of Mary Glouers vexation*, p. 56.

[29]   Swan, *A true and briefe report of Mary Glouers vexation*, p. 66.

[30]   See Chap. 2 for the notion that salvation and damnation were presented, by some Protestant writers, as states that could be inherited. Also, see Anna French, 'Disputed Words and Disputed Meanings: The Reformation of Baptism and Child Salvation in Early Modern England', in Jonathan Willis (ed.), *Sin and Salvation in Early Modern England* (Farnham: Ashgate, 2015).

knowledge of the imminent end of the world and Day of Judgement. Thomas Darling saw visions of fire, and had conversations with the Devil, who spoke to him in a voice 'small and shrill', while John Swan noted 'I imagine that ... [Satan's] mallice was rather growne greater towardes the end of his kingdome'.[31] Furthermore, Mary Glover's illness was related directly to worldly disasters, most particularly the plague of 1603, and was seen to be a warning of the retribution man was to suffer at the hands of God's agent, Satan. As Swan's text reads: 'Thus, while these, and other more weightie controversies continewe vndecided amongst vs, God hath ben provoaked at last to begin a controversie with vs, by sending a contagious sicknes, that hath turned our triumphs into dayes of heaviness: the which when and wher it will cease, he onely knoweth'.[32] Thus, Mary and Thomas's fits had an apocalyptic resonance. Satan was expected to increase in wrath before the end of the world, as tells the Book of Revelation. Children's bodies were therefore the site of an apocalyptic struggle between God and Satan, and throughout the texts the rhetoric of warfare predominates.

The words and violent gestures of these small children bore witness to foreboding pain and judgment, and echoed a contemporary condemnation of the sin-soaked nature of early modern society. Both Mary and Thomas came from highly religious families. Thomas's parents hoped that he would become a preacher; Mary's family attended sermons and meetings in outside parishes. The children's words, whether uttered by their own mouths, or given to them by author and text, gave voice to the struggles and tensions that were seen to exist within the spiritually fragmented and plague ridden world of early modern England. It was perhaps hoped that society would take heed of the warnings uttered by the spiritually small and vulnerable, as Swan urged, ' ... that so God may be pleased to call backe his Angell, whom he sent out to smite vs'.[33] Indeed, whether or not the words uttered by the young and possessed were truly their own, they tell us much about beliefs surrounding children, their spiritual status and authority, and their perceived receptiveness to both demonic and Divine forces. The young and possessed were not only 'acting out', or telling and re-patterning, a demonically motivated battle, they were also portrayed as mouthpieces of the 'godly'.

The belief that children were especially receptive to Divine messages was not an unusual one, as the following chapters on children and cases of godly prophecy will further explore. Similarly, in 1650, 11-year-old Margaret Muschamp

---

[31]   Swan, *A true and briefe report of Mary Glouers vexation*, p. 21.
[32]   Swan, *A true and briefe report of Mary Glouers vexation*, p. 5.
[33]   Swan, *A true and briefe report of Mary Glouers vexation*, p. 5.

fell into fits, during which 'God fed her with Angels food' and she saw many 'good things' in the 'likenesse of a Dove, and a Partridge'.[34] Both good and bad angels would attempt to speak to her, sitting upon each shoulder. Interestingly, such an image was derived from folkloric descriptions of good and bad angels. Furthermore, in order to meet her Divine companions, her mother dressed the child in white, before sending her to wait under a tree, in the family garden. The Angels, the child said, were 'bodyed like Birds, as big as Turkies ... [with] faces like Christians, but the sweetest creatures that ever eyes beheld ....'.[35] Upon the final day of her angelic visions, Margaret made a confident speech, telling spectators, ' ... I care not what the Divell can doe; I defie all the Divels in Hell'.[36] Strong words it seems, for a small child.

Indeed, the physical smallness and spiritual naivety of children meant that, within early modern social boundaries, the young were meant to be silent figures, neither seen nor heard. However, despite their physical smallness and young years, children did, at times, play a significant role within early modern religious life. Throughout many religious and spiritual histories, physical smallness or perceived weakness lend a form of strength to the perceived messenger. The weak and under-nourished children explored here were bestowed with the spiritual vigour traditionally reserved for stories of saints and miracles. God looked favourably upon the young – as the Bible tells, 'Out of the mouth of babes and sucklings' comes great strength and wisdom.[37] And as a result, the early modern mindset was attuned to listen to the wisdom that came from the small and pious mouths of these unconventional messengers. Young biblical prophets set the precedent for this form of religious discourse, in which the young and innocent were specially chosen by Divine will, in the words of unwilling biblical prophet Jeremiah, who said to God ' ... beholde, I can not speake, for I am a childe'; to which God replied, 'saie not, I am a childe: for thou shalt go to all that I shal send thee, and whatsoeuer I commande thee, shalt thou speake'.[38] From this belief in the moralistic wisdom and righteousness of the 'children of God', children like Mary Glover and Thomas Darling could derive much authority, through which they were able to not only challenge accepted social orders and flaunt their unusual social status in the face of their social superiors, but also to speak words of divinely inspired wisdom, as we will consider in the following chapters.

---

[34] Mary Moore, *Wonderfull newes from the north* (London, 1650) *Wing* (2nd ed.) M2581, pp. 3 and 6.

[35] Moore, *Wonderfull newes from the north*, p. 12.

[36] Moore, *Wonderfull newes from the north*, p. 19.

[37] Psalms 8: 2 and Matthew 21: 16.

[38] Jeremiah 1: 6–7.

Harsnett and the Popish Saga

However, the sixteenth-century possession sagas were not just a Puritan, or Protestant, phenomenon. Indeed, the 'young and possessed' were important tools of political propaganda and potential power for a variety of religious persuasions, however unorthodox in England at the time. It was not uncommon for parents of the demonically afflicted to dabble with a whole spectrum of religious persuasions, from Puritan and Catholic, to the 'superstitious' quack, in order to seek a cure for their child. The case of the Starkie family, or the 'Lancashire seven', explored above, highlights the spiritual struggles that could centre on cases of demonic intrusion. Indeed, the Starkie household, so we are told, witnessed the demonic affliction and spiritual dispossession of seven of its family members. The young son of the Starkie family was taken ill on his way to school, becoming 'compelled to shoute vehemently, not being able to stay him selfe'. His father, a Lancashire gentleman, sought highly unorthodox means of cure, looking for 'remedie without due regard ... [and] went to a Seminarie Priest'. However, according to the tract, the Catholic exorcist was of little help, as he 'had not then his bookes'. Hence Master Nicholas Starkie strayed further down the tangled path of spiritual unorthodoxy, this time seeking the assistance of Edmond Hartley, a local witch or cunning-man. Hartley agreed to help the family, and with the use of 'certayne popish charmes and hearbes' the children seemed cured.[39] Yet, the influence of the witch Hartley had negative affects upon the Starkie family. Indeed, Hartley's activities were somewhat worrying; he blackmailed the family for money, he attempted to 'kiss' a number of maid servants, and most disturbingly, he would venture out into the woods adjacent to the family home, 'where he made a circle a yard and a half around, with many crosses and partitions'. Concerned by such superstitious behaviour, Master Starkie sought the help of medical physicians, before finally visiting 'Doctor Dee at Manchester', who advised the father to gain the 'help and assistance of some godly preachers, with whom he should join in prayer and fasting for the help of his children'.[40]

---

[39]   George More, *A true discourse concerning the certaine possession and dispossession of 7 persons in one familie in Lancashire*, pp. 12–13.

[40]   More, *A true discourse*, p. 15. For information on the varied life and career of John Dee, see his *DNB* entry; R. Julian Roberts, 'Dee, John (1527–1609)', *Oxford Dictionary of National Biography*, Oxford University Press, Sept 2004; online edn, May 2006 [http://www.oxforddnb.com/view/article/7418, accessed 29 July 2014] Also John Dee, *John Dee's Library Catalogue*, (ed.) Julian Roberts and Andrew G. Watson (London Bibliographical Society, 1990).

Hence, the tract detailing the possession narrative forms part of a pro-Puritan and pro-Darrell propaganda. Written by Darrell's ally George More, the text complains of the 'maligne' work of the 'papists', further arguing that ' ... no marvel, for if the Church of Englande haue this power to cast out devills, then the Church of Rome is a false Church, for there can be but one true Church, the principall marke whereof ... is to worke miracles, and of them this is the greatest, namely to cast out Devills'.[41] With the assured assistance of the Puritan exorcists the Starkie children began to behave in a manner similar to the children explored above, and (as notable within the set of Darrell cases) very similar to the young Thomas Darling. Twelve-year-old John Starkie suffered fits, in which he 'shewed verie extraordinary knowledge'. During his trances he declared 'the straunge sinnes of this land ... denounced the fearfull judgments of God ... then exorted his parents, and the people there present to repent, that they might avoide all those grievous plagues'. After this profound announcement he 'made a most excellent prayer' for the Church, the Queen and for the 'subduing of her enemies, for the continuance of her life, and peaceable gouernment', for the upholding of true Gospel and all the people of God. The child's prayer continued for over two hours, and was, it was said, more excellent than that of a 'good preacher'. The boy then 'sunge a good peece of the 4 Psalme in a most sweete and heauenly tune, as ever might be heard'. The singing of a psalm seems to have been a trademark of the Darrell cases.[42] Furthermore, John Starkie performed this action 'in a traunce, his eyes being closed vp, and neither knew what he said nor did', much like Mary Glover.[43] Whether this trance-like state was seen to be induced by illness and demonic intrusion or by godly intervention is not clear. More probable is the notion that such symptoms were, in fact, taken to be signs of extreme godliness and purity. As argued before, Thomas Darling had 'fashioned' himself as a prophet; these children were sites of spiritual battle, in which God was seen to be defeating the Devil. They were also sites of religious performance; sighing, weeping, the closing of eyes, trance-like states induced by singing, religious recitation and prayer were all signs of godliness, and were

---

[41] More, *A true discourse concerning the certaine possession and dispossession of 7 persons in one familie in Lancashire*, pp. 4–5.

[42] Indeed, recent historiography has considered the importance of psalms to Protestant worship, and this importance is reflected in Darling's case. For work on music and worship see especially Jonathan Willis, *Church Music and Protestantism in Post-Reformation England: Discourses, Sites and Identities* (Farnham: Ashgate, 2010). Also, Alec Ryrie's *Being Protestant in Reformation Britain* (Oxford: Oxford University Press, 2013) considers the uses of psalms throughout.

[43] More, *A true discourse*, pp. 24–5.

parts of a 'Puritan' spiritual performance.[44] Indeed, the notion of performance within these cases, both Catholic and Protestant, is something to which we shall return below.

Nevertheless, despite the Puritans' 'successes' with this notorious case, they were still highly discredited by Harsnett and his more moderate party. As George More, rather despondently, wrote, ' ... there is a booke of a large volume latelie come out vnder the name of S.H. crossing and contradicting the whole course of proceeding for ... Darrels clearing, yoaking me also with him in this devilish legerdemaine (as they terme it) calling vs a couple of hypocrites, vsing also manie other badde termes'.[45] Indeed, when compiling his tract, George More had recently completed a two year prison sentence for such 'devilish' doings, a sure indication of the religio-political tensions surrounding these cases, and also of the seriousness with which they were dealt. Furthermore, when dealing with such instances of 'religious fervour', the potential penalties were not to be taken lightly. The Witchcraft Act of 1563 stated accused witches, in cases that did not involve death or murder, were to be rebuked by a year's imprisonment and the pillory. Yet, more starkly, those found guilty of 'conjuring' or exorcising spirits could be punished by death on the first offence.[46] This reveals that those who were perceived to be 'creating' religious hysteria were deemed more dangerous than those actually accused of practising witchcraft. For Catholics, an Act of Parliament passed in 1585 made Jesuits and seminary priests guilty of high treason, simply for standing on English soil, whilst those who sheltered them were guilty of felony, both crimes punishable by death.

Yet, despite such tensions, and the potential risks involved when evading the Church authorities, many parties, including those of Catholic persuasion, were prepared to 'throw in' their pennies' worth, and to offer healing to the victims of possession. Furthermore, there are significant cases in which other families sought various cures for the demonically inspired illnesses suffered by their little ones, within the competing market of the exorcising trade. Within such scenarios, the Catholic dispossession narratives were similarly formulaic, and the children, as centre-stage actors within such spiritual performances, were not much different.

Indeed, the case of William Perry, a 12-year-old boy from the county of Stafford, received much attention from contemporary audiences. The boy's case, a Catholic saga, reveals to us much about the competing agencies that were at

---

[44]   For singing and religious performance, see Craig's 'Psalms, groans and dogwhippers: the soundscape of worship in the English parish church, 1547–1642', pp. 104–23.

[45]   More, *A true discourse*, pp. 6–7.

[46]   Walker, *Unclean Spirits*, p. 44.

hand to alleviate parents of that distressing problem, the loud, misbehaving, disruptive young and possessed child. Accounts of the case were published by both Catholics and Protestants, although the Catholic cases only come to our attention through the Protestant version, and therefore it must be remembered that they come to us shaped and distorted by the prism of the Protestant press. This version took the form of an anti-Catholic attack, published in 1622, bearing the title *The boy of Bilson: or, A true discouery of the late notorious impostures of certaine Romish priests in their pretended exorcism*. The text provides details concerning the 'admirable guile and cunning' of young William, 'that boy', who pretended 'himselfe possessed of the diuell'. Furthermore, the text warns readers to 'Bee wise, and bee not hasty to beleeue'.[47] Indeed, when speaking of Catholic cases of dispossession, much emphasis was placed upon the notion of acting, drama and feigning, although this was possibly as much to do with the sheer spectacular and ritualistic nature of Catholic exorcism, as it was to do with the notion of the children themselves as actors. Indeed, for Bancroft, Harsnett and their followers, all such 'devil-puffers' were guilty of the same crime, that of pretence and religious perversion.

The case of William Perry and the events that unfolded around him was typically stereotypical and formulaic, if not a little story-like. Indeed, it bears striking similarities to Darling's case; it is very likely that William and his friends had read the case of the 'Boy of Burton'. Like Darling, when walking home from school William had stumbled into the path of a little old woman. When he did not acknowledge her the woman cursed him saying that he was a 'foule thing', at which words the child 'felt a thing to pricke him to the very heart'. He then grew ill and started falling into extreme fits. Subsequently, his parents sought the help of both local Puritans and Catholic priests.[48] The text details how 'diuers Puritans' came to him during the day, meaning the Catholic priests could not visit him until darkness had fallen. This again reveals something about the battle that took place, between Catholics and Protestants, over the bodies of these small children, in something of a spiritual underworld, submerged from the authorities. The Catholic observers commented upon the fact the while the 'Puritans were in place' the child was assaulted by visions of the Devil, in the form of a 'Black bird', while the Protestant commentators complained about the farcical and spectacular nature of the Catholic exorcists' performances.[49] Indeed, the Catholic methods of dispossession were somewhat more extreme

---

[47] R.B., *The boy of Bilson: or, A true discouery of the late notorious impostures of certaine Romish priests in their pretended exorcism* (London, 1622) STC (2nd ed.) 1185, sigs A3v–A4r.

[48] R.B., *The boy of Bilson*, pp. 45–6.

[49] R.B., *The boy of Bilson*, p. 51.

and performative than their Puritan counterparts. They would burn holy oil and candles, then read litanies, the Holy Gospel and the 'Exorcism of Saint Ambrose'; they gave the child holy water and oil to protect him from demons and witches.[50] In response, William vomited up pins, knitting needles, rosemary and walnut leaves. When frankincense was burned in the child's face, he would 'vehemently cry out that he was killed, burned and chocked ... ' and then, at length, he would drink 'vp the smoke, saying that [through it] he saw his Enemies tormented'.[51]

Mastery of the spirits, it seems, was mastery of the true faith. The exorcist took centre stage, while the child acted appropriately. In this instance the Catholics won the approval of William, who cried out that he would 'liue and dye a Catholicke, wishing father, mother, and all his friends to serue God'. When the priest asked the child to show 'how he would vse one dying out of the Romane Catholicke Church', the child fell into a fit, crying most bitterly, whilst biting the sheet. Similarly, at the mentioning of the words Luther, John Calvin and John Foxe he did 'performe after the same menner, but in a fiercer sort'. During one significant fit he decided that he had become 'perfectly himselfe' and he desired that all his belongings, his 'bookes, pennes, inke, clothes ... euery thing he had might be blessed' and wished his 'Parents, sisters, and brothers to ... become Catholicks; out of which faith, by God's grace, he said hee would neuer liue or dye'.[52] The child thus became the mouth-piece of such pro-Catholic propaganda, and with which the Catholics published their account of the case, entitled *A Faithful Relation*.

This significantly documented Catholic case does not exist in isolation; a similar scenario, which attracted the attention of Samuel Harsnett, was the Denham saga. Indeed, the information documenting the case comes from Harsnett's 1603 work, *A Declaration of Egregious Popish Impostures*, a tract written using the notes from the original events, and containing the accounts of four 'demoniacs' confessing to feigning their possession.[53] The case occurred between the spring of 1585 and the summer of 1586, when six demoniacs were 'dispossessed' by 12 Catholic priests in the houses of various Catholic recusants, mostly in the family home of Sir George Peckham of Denham, Buckinghamshire. The chief exorcist was the Jesuit William Weston, also known as Edmunds. Amongst the four confessions Harsnett details, two of the possessed were

---

[50]   R.B., *The boy of Bilson*, p. 47.

[51]   R.B., *The boy of Bilson*, p. 49.

[52]   R.B., *The boy of Bilson*, pp. 51–2.

[53]   For a discussion of Harsnett's intentions when writing this tract, and for suggested reasons behind the delay between these cases being reported and the publication of Harsnett's criticism, see Clive Holmes, 'Witchcraft and Possession at the Accession of James I'.

already Catholic, and were in fact young adults of 18. Yet, two victims, who were in the event converted to Catholicism, were servant girls Sara Williams, aged about 15, and her sister Frideswid, aged about 17. The young girls claimed that they had been both tricked and poisoned into believing themselves possessed of the Devil. Their exorcisms involved being seated and bound in a chair; being made to drink a 'holy' concoction containing oil, sack and rue, whilst being forced to breath in fumes from a dish of 'hallowed' burning brimstone. The girls, the Catholics professed, experienced visions of the 'Real Presence' and engaged in conversations with demonic familiars. They spoke of the power of Catholic relics and declared that Queen Elizabeth and her courtiers were the Devil's most obedient disciples.[54]

How, then, did the authorities, those such as Bancroft and Harsnett, react to such cases? The answer has, in fact, been considered in a small section of early modern historiography, much of it from a 'New Historicist' perspective, which seeks to relate cases of demonic possession to contemporary theatre. Indeed, it has been suggested that Harsnett deliberately tarnished cases of demonic possession with a theatrical stigma, in order both to discredit the supernatural work of the so-called healers, and to demystify the 'spectacular' symptoms and occurrences which were so intrinsic to such cases. Through such comparisons the demoniac and exorcist become merely actors on a stage, and the awe-struck witnesses simply an audience. Stephen Greenblatt has argued, in his article on 'Shakespeare and the Exorcists', that Samuel Harsnett sought to demonstrate that exorcism was an empty, dramatic gesture; a gesture intended to trick audiences into believing that they were indeed witnessing the 'ultimate confrontation between good and evil'.[55] According to Greenblatt, Harsnett achieved this aim by driving the exorcists, or at least the Catholic exorcists, into the realms of theatre. Hence Harsnett was 'determined to make the spectators see the theatre around them, to make them understand that what seems spontaneous is rehearsed, what seems involuntary carefully crafted, unpredictable scripted'. Furthermore, Harsnett sought to show that the exorcists were 'in the fashion of vagabond players, that coast from Towne to Towne' with their 'pageant of Puppits', in order to thoroughly empty the ceremony of its spiritual worth or political potential.[56]

---

[54] Harsnett, *A Declaration of egregious popish impostures*, pp. 35–42, 183, 211–12. D.P. Walker, *Unclean Spirits*, pp. 46–7.

[55] Greenblatt, 'Shakespeare and the Exorcists', p. 106.

[56] Harsnett, *A Declaration of egregious popish impostures*, pp. 20 and 149. See also Greenblatt, 'Shakespeare and the Exorcists', p. 106; for reactions to Harsnett's text see also Brownlow, *Shakespeare, Harsnett, and the Devils of Denham*, a text which originated as a

Such works have to be used with caution. Indeed, by its very nature, those seeking for the literary, and in this case the theatrical, within any form of source material are likely, through their very focus, to see the theatrical within the material. As a result, the religious or political significance, or even personal significance, of these cases can be somewhat ignored. Furthermore, it must not be forgotten that this notion of drama, or as contemporaries would have termed it 'counterfeiting', was nothing new, or indeed nothing particularly shocking to early modern audiences. Harsnett and his authorities dragged many confessions of falsity and lies from a variety of 'demoniacs', both Catholic and Protestant. These included Thomas Darling, William Sommers, Anne Gunter, as well as William Perry and the young people involved in the Denham saga.

We should also consider the role of children within this envisaged 'drama', for the children and young people themselves had a role to play, a role largely ignored by Greenblatt and his followers. Some of these children and youths openly acknowledged that they had, in fact, feigned their illnesses. They thus acknowledged that they were nothing more than actors or storytellers, actors who took centre stage within these unfolding dramas. What can the words and actions of these children reveal about their motivations? Greenblatt suggests that the children were depicted as weak victims, helpless at the hands of the exorcists and their propaganda campaigns, and he quotes Harsnett's descriptions of the young 'schollers'; who would 'frame themselues iump and fit vnto the Priests humors, to mop, mow, iest, raile, raue, roare, commend, & discommend, and as the priests would haue them, vpon fitting occasions ... in all things to play the deuils accordinglie'.[57] Such a situation was certainly possible, and indeed, within the Denham example, was most likely. However, this may not have always been the case. If, for example, we return to the case of William Perry, the child's own desire for authority and attention can clearly be seen.

Twelve-year-old Perry confessed to having feigned his possession on 8 October, 1620. The case of the 'Boy of Bilson' was compiled by Richard Baddeley, secretary to an official inquiry which aimed to expose Catholic priests involved in cases of spiritual intrusion. Baddeley's text, however, inferred that it was the Catholic priests who were the victims in this case, not the child. Indeed,

---

PhD Thesis at the Shakespeare Institute in Stratford, in 1963. Brownlow argues that the *Declaration* is flamboyantly anti-Catholic, but that it has a hidden agenda, aimed primarily at the Puritans, who were as inclined as Catholics to use demonic possession to propaganda the faith. For more recent research, see Clive Holmes, 'Witchcraft and Possession at the Accession of James I'.

[57]   Harsnett, *A Declaration of egregious popish impostures*, pp. 35 and 28. See Greenblatt, 'Shakespeare and the Exorcists', p. 107.

the theatrical and somewhat precocious Perry had, it was noted, concocted his illness with a mysterious elderly accomplice, known simply as Thomas. It was Thomas and William then, who willingly narrated, scripted and performed this drama, in front of large audiences of seemingly gullible witnesses. After Perry's confession, the accused witch, one Joan Clark, was proclaimed innocent in August 1620, and the authorities instead turned their attention to the boy. William was thus handed over to the Bishop of Lichfield and Coventry, and placed under close inspection in the Castle of Eccleshall. It seemed that William and the elusive Thomas had perhaps underestimated the swift change in public opinion, as King James's newfound scepticism took hold within learned and official circles. In order to find out whether or not the boy was authentically possessed, the Bishop read aloud the biblical verses that would, it was told, propel the child into extreme and violent fits. The child, upon hearing the offending verse (the opening verse from the Gospel of John) duly fell ill. When the boy recovered, the Bishop told him that he would read the same verse in Greek, causing the boy again to fall into fits. But in fact the Bishop had not read the correct verse, and the boy had been tricked into performance. Since the Devil was 'so ancient a scholer as of almost 6000 yeeres standing' he would have understood 'all languages in the world', including Greek. The Bishop then branded young William an 'execrable wretch, who playest the diuels part'.[58]

The child, however, did not relent easily; he feigned illness and coloured his urine with black ink in an attempt to resist discovery.[59] Yet, when such deceitful means failed, the boy then confessed, claiming that his accomplice, Thomas, had promised him he would no longer have to go to school by feigning such illnesses, and had taught him demonical skills and Catholic sentiments. The child had clearly enjoyed the fame and notoriety he had achieved, claiming that ' ... much people did resort vnto him, and brought him many good things'.[60] The Protestants now produced their own account of the case, *A True Discovery of the Late Notorious Impostures of Certain Romish Priests in Their Pretended Exorcism*.[61] The tract presents Perry's case as an unfolding farce, which contains all the ingredients of a good drama, one which should be 'hissed of the stage, for stale and grosse forgeries'. Indeed, the observer or reader of the Catholic account was to keep in mind that

[58]   R.B., *The boy of Bilson*, pp. 58–9.
[59]   R.B., *The boy of Bilson*, p. 60.
[60]   R.B., *The boy of Bilson*, pp. 69–70.
[61]   For a detailed background account and transcript of this source, see Almond, *Demonic Possession and Exorcism*, pp. 331–57; See Greenblatt, 'Shakespeare and the Exorcists', esp. pp. 108–9.

hee hath seen a Comedie, wherein the Actors, which present themselves, are these; A crafty old man, teaching the feats and pranks of counterfeiting a person Demoniacal and possessed of the Deuill the next, a most docible, subtle, and expert young Boy, farre more dextrous in the Practique part, than his Master was in the Theory; after him appear three Romish Priests, the Authors of seducement, conjuring their onely imaginarie Deuils ... and lastly, a Chorus of credulous people easily seduced, not so much by the subtletie of those Priests, as by their own sottishnesse.[62]

Hence, this notion of performance and drama reveals the extent to which children could, in fact, shape or fashion their own roles within such narratives. The rehearsed and scripted nature of such cases, and the potential authority a child could derive from them, reveals not only their cultural, religious and political significance; but also their overall significance in early modern society – children were, in a sense, deriving authority from a familiar and culturally accepted genre. They were utilising a form of authority available to them, in the form of culturally understood religious performances and stories, in order to express otherwise forbidden or discouraged ideas and levels of authority. As a result, these children were playing a significant part in unfolding religious and political dramas of the age, whether as innocent victims or as deceitful actors.

We have seen, then, the ways in which children could derive spiritual and religious authority, through the cultural space provided to them in publications about demonic possession. As Chapter 3 considered, this cultural space had a significant impact on the functioning of families and domestic space, and saw children behaving in a set of formulaic and familiar ways. As this chapter has considered, these texts also had a religio-political and public significance, through which the child 'actors', the demoniacs, provided a voice (a further voice) to the religious tensions that operated within the spectrum of faith that existed in early modern England. Protestants and Catholics of various shades of opinion dabbled within such cases, or propounded against them. Through this process we see the children involved in these cases thrust onto a very public stage, becoming temporarily notorious for their role in defeating Satan, or infamous for their forgeries. We see them playing dice with the Devil, in league with both Protestants and Catholics – and this role, this cultural space provided to children, is significant to perceptions of the young, as well as to the experiences of some children during this period. Indeed, one of the key reasons why children were seen to be likely actors in the possession cases, and why it was

---

[62]   R.B., *The boy of Bilson*, p. 9.

plausible that they could potentially have played such parts, was because it was widely believed within early modern society that children, due to their littleness of body and spirit, were receptive spiritual vessels vulnerable to the assaults of demons and even Satan himself. This perception would have applied itself, and been most relevant, to children living in early modern England – regardless of whether or not they had any direct dealings with the devil. This same tenderness, this spiritual vulnerability, also meant that the reverse situation was possible, as we have seen to some extent throughout the past two chapters. Children could be receptive to God, and could become mouthpieces of godly prophecy – and it is to these cases that we will now turn.

Chapter 5
Children of God: Cases of Child Prophecy

And it shalbe in *ye* last dayes, saith God, I wil powre out of my Spirit vpon all flesh, and your sonnes, and your daughters shal prophecie, and your yong me*n* shall se visions, and your olde men shal dreame dreames.[1]

Between 1580 and 1641 a story was circulated in Germany and England entitled (with some variations) *A prophecie vttered by the daughter of an honest countrey man*. It told of a young girl who returned from the dead to pronounce a prophecy to her contemporaries, in which she warned against the related sins of pride and vanity. Throughout the three traceable English versions of the tract, the names, dates and locations are changed. The same case was reported in tracts dating from 1580, 1614 and 1641, in locations as far ranging as 'Melwing' in Germany and Worksop in Nottinghamshire. Hence, an especially high level of doubt is cast upon the credibility of the story, both in terms of its participants and location. These issues will be explored below in some greater depth. However, the narrative and composition of the story itself, which remain highly consistent throughout each example and which present the child at the centre of this prophecy case as a vessel able to deliver divine messages, are of the highest significance to our purpose within this chapter. As before, whether or not these stories were true is not really important to our purpose, rather, what is most interesting is that fact that the stories provide us with information on the cultural spaces child figures, whether fictional or otherwise, could occupy in the early modern imagination. This chapter will explore the concepts of age and authority, and will argue that children in this period could be considered simultaneously to be sin-worn from birth and potential vessels for demonic spirits, as previously considered, and to be innocent or virtuous. It will explore how early modern children, depicted in these texts, were shown to be deriving spiritual authority through perceptions of their innocence and their perceived closeness to God. Indeed, cases of prophetic children were numerous and diverse; as well as the tale of the *daughter of an honest countrey man* printed in 1580, 1614 and 1641, there were also the 1581 published case of William Withers, who prophesied that the vain and 'fashion

---

[1]   Acts 2: 17, quoting Joel 2: 28.

conscious' members of sixteenth-century society would be punished by God for their excesses and the 1605 tract detailing the story of a young girl who was left deformed by attackers who also killed her brother, where through the assistance of God she found the individuals who wronged her, thus bringing about their trial and punishment. Similarly, many tracts on 'monstrous infants' who prophesied and warned spectators of their impending doom if they did not mend their ways were published during the sixteenth and seventeenth centuries.[2] Indeed, these cases will be explored throughout the next two chapters. The volume, notoriety and range of prophecy cases can help emphasise to us both the appetite for and awareness of ideas around child prophecy, and the potentially resulting perceptions of agency and authority.

The Worksop case, and others like it, is in this way emblematic of a wider trend. It reveals much about early modern beliefs concerning the life-course alongside age and authority structures, as well as providing us with a glimpse into a range of entwined ideas surrounding popular celestial fantasy and earthly desire. The tale tells of how a 'poore countrey maide', aged about 14 years, died suddenly. One day later the child miraculously returned from the dead for the space of five days, and during this time warned spectators of the perils they faced, comforted her grieving family, and provided awe-inspired onlookers with details of what they might hope to expect in the life hereafter. According to the girl, after her death:

> I was euertaken neere the bridge of the Brooke by a comely olde man, with a long gray Beard, who saluted mee ... said he to mee, come my louing Daughter, I must needes talke with thee, and tell thee that which as yet is hidden from thee ... So wee came to a faire costley forte, (no Princes Court like it, nor any earthly building to bee compared vnto it,) where we were let in. In which place, wee saw many bright Angels, shining like the beames of the sun all singing melodiously with cleare voyce ... But the olde man forbade me to speak vnto any. Forth with I was brought againe to the Brooke, where ... the old man willed me to rest contented,

---

2   See, for example, Eyriak Schlichtenberger, *A prophecie vttered by the daughter of an honest countrey man* (London, 1580) *STC* (2nd ed.) 21818; John Phillips, *The wonderfull worke of God shewed vpon a chylde whose name is William Withers, being in the towne of Walsham, within the countie of Suffolke* (London, 1581) STC (2nd ed.) 19877 and Anon, *The Horrible Murther of a young boy of three yeres of age, whose sister had her tongue cut out: and how it pleased God to reveale the offenders, by giving speech to the tongueles Childe* (London, 1606) *STC* (2nd ed.) 6552.

for this short time shall quickly haue an end, and within fiue daies thou shalt be brought againe unto this place.[3]

We see here that the girl has come back temporarily from the dead, presumably to tell onlookers of what Heaven may be like, and also to warn them of impending danger. We can also see that this child, whether or not she was a fictional character, was bestowed with great authority. As considered in the Introduction, and throughout the past two chapters, children in these cases demonstrated an authority which asked people to listen to their small voices, in person, potentially, if the stories are to be believed, but also to read their words (or the words given to them by author and printer). Children in possession cases were seen fighting and battling with the possession demons, becoming exemplars of divine worship and prayer when they eventually assail their possessor. The prophetic children receive a different form of attention and notoriety.

Indeed, where possession cases emphasised spiritual vulnerability, prophecy cases focused on pious authority, and they did so in a remarkably heterogeneous manner, with printed cases of prophecy exploring a very wide range of situations, environments and seers. Prophets, across post-Reformation Europe, and most especially 'popular' in the Lutheran context, could be men, women and children, usually drawn from the middling or lower ranks of society.[4] Yet, most pertinently for our own purposes, what is interesting is the fact that children were so well represented amongst the lists of prophets reported in cheap print – and that their young age did not seem to detract from the authority they were granted by speaking the word of God. Indeed, in some cases their youth appears to have been the chief cause of their notoriety and influence.

What is most significant about the account of the child of Melwing or Worsksop's vision, then, is what it can reveal to us about perceptions towards age relations. The opposite and corresponding spiritual roles of the old man and the young girl are particularly noteworthy. The notion that the very old and the very young were especially likely to hold spiritual or prophetic powers had a

---

[3]   T.I., *A miracle, of miracles* (London, 1614) *STC* (2nd ed.) 14068, sig. C2r; further accounts of this case were published in Eyriak Schlichtenberger, *A prophecie vttered by the daughter of an honest countrey man* and Anon, *The wonderfull works of God* (London, 1641) *Wing* (2nd ed.) W3377.

[4]   For details on the gender and age of prophets, as well as their popularity in Lutheran culture, see Jürgen Beyer, 'A Lübeck Prophet in Local and Lutheran Context', in Bob Scribner and Trevor Roper (eds), *Popular Religion in Germany and Central Europe, 1400–1800* (Macmillan, London, 1996) and his 'Lutheran Popular Prophets in the Sixteenth and Seventeenth Centuries: the performance of untrained speakers', ARV Nordic Yearbook of Folklore, 51 (1995), pp. 63–86.

heritage, much of which was biblically rooted. According to the Psalms, 'Out of the mouth of babes and sucklings hast thou ordained strength'. Furthermore, the Book of Joel and the Acts told that, in the last days, 'it shall come to pass ... your sons and your daughters shall prophesy, your young men shall see visions, your old men shall dream dreams'.[5] The Bible told that those at each extreme of the age spectrum were more likely to be close to God. This is perhaps understandable, if the life-course is envisaged as a circular process, through which humankind are believed to come from and return to God. The young and the old were, therefore, perceived to be more receptive to spiritual messages from beyond.

Perhaps the authority of the elderly is not so surprising to us. Old age was, in this period, a rarity; one to be respected and revered, or feared and despised. Indeed, witches and wizards were usually old women and men who perhaps stood out in a society made of, in terms of demographics, predominantly young members. It is this, as Keith Thomas has termed it, 'gerontocratic view' of society that would have, according to some historical interpretations, placed the young at the very bottom of the social pecking order. Thomas argued that whilst age was not necessarily as socially pivotal as status, wealth or gender, it has been seen as crucial in determining where one was to be positioned within the social spectrum – I would argue that age was as pivotal as gender and wealth, and would agree that it was crucial in determining your position in the social spectrum.[6] The old man described in the child's vision, for example, is granted unquestioned authority, celestial provenance no less. It could even have been that this elderly, bearded man, with his ministering manner, may have been received as a portrayal of God (such an image would have aroused significant disapproval amongst the reformed and the godly, but was more common in a Lutheran context).[7] Traditional stereotypes of God were of an old, wise man. If God was believed to be the most ancient of days, age certainly had an authoritative quality. That embodiment – that encoding – of the wisdom of age in the Lord himself reminds us that seniority was crucial in this period; but it should also emphasise the extent to which associations with spiritual or moral being – with learning or generosity, severity or justness – were externalised and embodied in representative individuals. That is, what was important was not necessarily the trappings of age (the beard, the bent frame, the wrinkled skin) but the characteristics associated with them, the spiritual *stage* – the

---

[5]   Psalms 8:2; Joel 2:28; Acts 2: 17. Walsham, *Providence in Early Modern England*, p. 209.

[6]   Keith Thomas, 'Age and Authority in Early Modern England', *Proceedings of the British Academy*, Vol. LXII (1976) pp. 205–48.

[7]   See, for example, Beyer, 'A Lübeck Prophet in Local and Lutheran Context'.

spiritual authority that came with age and experience, that was acquired through time and knowledge of God through a life well lived. Children were in a very different place on this age and authority spectrum. They did not have the experience, the knowledge or capacity, it was believed, to truly understand religion or to have faith in, to know, God. This then placed the young in a most precarious position, especially when so many died in infancy and childhood. Yet, as this work argues throughout, according to early modern beliefs, popular beliefs if you can forgive that term, children could acquire another form of spiritual status or agency – through their innocence. Children were untainted, innocent virgins, not yet stained by the sins of want or lust. This meant that if he so chose, God could reach out to the young, touch them with his divine finger, use children as vessels or as communicators. No set of early modern texts reveals such beliefs as much as those that detail childhood prophecy, which we will consider here.

Indeed, in examining these cases of prophecy and how they revolve around questions of age or authority, then, what strikes the historian is the extent to which this key faultline between physical and spiritual maturity has been missing from early modern historiography. Perhaps the quintessential statement of the traditional gerontocratic view of early modern society is Keith Thomas's article 'Age and Authority in Early Modern England', in which the early modern infant was seen to be like a small animal, with no capacity for imagination, emotion or reason. As children advanced in years and understanding their characters would mature. Age was progressive: wisdom, knowledge and social decorum came with its advancement. Hence, it only seems natural that authority should lie with those who have the most experience. This age-orientated social structure was reflected not just in the typologies of the 'wise old man' we have already explored, but in early modern cultural practices, evident, for example, in the fact that during church services the young were confined to the rear of the church, or to the aisles. Thus, dignity was fast tightened to perceptions of age, and the 'lower' social classes were regarded as childish and ignorant by their 'betters'. The 'childish', whether in terms of age or status, were to serve those who had acquired greater wisdom and thus authority. Such social belief systems were underpinned, Thomas argues, by theology, proverbial wisdom and science. The fifth commandment taught that one should 'Honour thy father and thy mother'; furthermore, theology taught that man was born evil, only able to be redeemed through a lifetime battle against sin and temptation, although admittedly other authorities agreed: Aristotle told that rationality developed over time, from the animal-like years of childhood through to adulthood; and contemporary humoral psychology suggested that the human body stabilised with age, humours would dry, and with this came the advancement of the soul.[8] It is this negative, age-related view of the social order that has, throughout social historiography on the family, tied children fast to such negative perceptions. Children and their subsequent childhoods are a modern phenomenon according to such historiographies, and they were scantly regarded throughout pre-modern periods.

We might begin to wonder, however, how this framework relates to cases of prophecy, which, as we have seen, set considerable and unusual store by the words of children. Indeed, Thomas himself allowed for the idea that children presented in the stories could, in some circumstances, gain authority. Whilst the concepts of maturity and the acquisition of authority cannot be torn apart nor unravelled, there is another side to this situation, one which has been barely developed in the last 30 years. The work of Thomas and others remains important and central to our understanding of early modern culture in general, but in exceptional and yet relatively common cases such as those of the child prophets it begins to break down, revealing a more nuanced and gradated picture. If we return to the story of the child prophet, or indeed to many of the stories considered in the previous or the following chapters, it can be seen that the child too had authority, albeit one derived from her close encounter with the godly figure. In the German story which began this chapter, the child's authority was displayed in a variety of ways. Firstly, the young girl had, according to the tracts, visited Heaven: she had witnessed the life hereafter. This very notion gave the child an extraordinary amount of spiritual authority. Not only this, her body was the site of a miracle. She had returned from the dead to forewarn those she knew in life of their impending judgement. Finally, and perhaps most significantly, once the child had declared her message, she was able to return to Heaven, and to reassure her family of her fate. She was therefore viewed as a symbol of the potential to be saved, and of the potential pathway to heaven provided by godly behaviour or by ceding to her message. This gave the child, whether she was fictional or otherwise, symbolic authority.

Alongside the notion that children were born both in and through sin and were therefore sinful, ungodly creatures, was an alternative vision: one which saw children as innocent and untainted – or at least, innocent once they had undergone baptism. We have seen the flipside of this belief already at work in the vulnerability of the demoniacs; in the cases of the child prophets, they seem conversely more open to the divine rather than diabolic intervention. Children,

---

[8]   Exodus 20: 12; Deuteronomy 5: 16; Thomas, 'Age and Authority in Early Modern England', pp. 205–48.

whilst they had not had chance to acquire knowledge or spiritual wisdom, had instead their innocence. Such a perception was tightly bound with perceptions of mental naivety and physical virginity; children had not been educated about the world around them, and they had not been tainted by it either. Such innocence enabled children, according to such perceptions, to be especially receptive to the spiritual world. Stories about the mystical or magical nature of children derived much from traditional folklore and fairytales, beliefs which became entwined with Protestant beliefs about godly providence. Whilst children could not know of God through experience or through learning, they could know Him, and be assured of his protection, simply due to their spiritual innocence – an innocence and assurance 'sealed' or symbolised by godly baptism.[9]

Beliefs surrounding prophecy and visions, in which children and young people featured strongly, provide an important window through which to glimpse early modern perceptions concerning the relationship between childhood and spiritual authority, and thus to reshape our wider comprehension of early modern culture's 'gerontocracy'. During the early modern period it had long been believed that virginity and innocence were the keys to clairvoyance. Village sorcerers, for example often used the young to gaze into crystal balls and to make contact with the spirits of the dead. Indeed, a Hertfordshire clothier, who had suffered many thefts from his shop, attempted to discover the identity of the thief using the spiritual powers of the young. He went out after midnight with his crystal, accompanied by a young boy or girl to act as a spiritual intermediary, or scryer; 'for they say it must be a pure virgin' to gaze into the crystal.[10] Alexandra Walsham has noted, in her work on beliefs surrounding providence, that children and adolescents were seen to be 'inherently sacred and psychic'; a child was able to act as an 'aerial and antenna for receiving special transmissions from heaven'.[11] Furthermore, reports of 'prophetic' orphans found in fields or woodland, or mysteriously hidden under walls were not uncommon. Such stories are closely related to fairytales involving starveling elves and changelings, who were believed to replace the bodies of abducted children.[12]

The trope of the authorised child was thus not so unfamiliar a one to the early modern imagination. Indeed, this spiritual power and immediacy did

---

[9]   See Introduction.

[10]   This case is mentioned by Thomas, no date is given, see *Religion and the Decline of Magic*, pp. 255–6; see also Walsham, *Providence in Early Modern England*, pp. 209–10.

[11]   Walsham, *Providence in Early Modern England*, pp. 209–10.

[12]   See Chapter 6 below, under 'Crime, Retribution and Children'; Thomas, *Religion and the Decline of Magic*, pp. 728, 731–2; Walsham, *Providence in Early Modern England*, pp. 209–10.

not necessarily stop during early childhood, and could continue through to adolescence. According to the words of a Southampton Wizard in 1631, 'when a spiritt is raised none hath the power to see yt but children of Eleaven or Twelve yeares of age or such as are true maides'.[13] Indeed, perceptions of innocence, most typically virginity, could apply to adolescents as well as young children.

Indeed, Thomas's article argued that it was in imitating adults – that is, foreshortening their own childhood – that children could gain rare occasions of authority. Whilst children did not generally gain authority, being as they were trapped and restricted by age-old social conventions which dictated that childhood and youth were like 'apprenticeships' for life, they could, through imitation of adult behaviour, gain respect. According to Thomas, although children were not especially valued within early modern communities, such a 'relative devaluation of childhood' lent itself to a 'preference for precocious infants who rapidly assumed the externals of adult behaviour, revealing themselves to be pious or learned before their time'.[14]

We have already seen that prophetic children were often depicted as just that – their 'adultness' was remarked upon but not to the extent of pretending away their childishness. Nevertheless, whilst many children and youths at this time were behaving in 'childish' or 'juvenile' ways – throwing stones, breaking things, cursing, shouting and disrupting church services – in the midst of such behaviour were those who *did* behave in a more ordered manner.[15] This inevitably raises the question, if the best-behaved children were those who imitated adults, what kind or adult behaviour were they imitating? The source material, as will be explored below and as we have already seen to some extent in the confessional jousting of the possession debates, suggests that the behaviour being adopted by some children and youths was in fact that of godly culture. If this was indeed the case, this raises a further predicament. Were early modern perceptions of childhood virtue connected with Puritan or Reformed culture? If this were true, then the argument would lend itself to the now much-revised historiographical notion that the modern, 'civilised' concept of childhood grew out of 'middle class' culture and pedagogical developments starting in the sixteenth century.[16] Was, then, Puritanism linked with new ideals about childhood (and was it,

---

[13]   R.C. Anderson (ed.) *The Book of Examinations and Depositions, 1627–1634*, Publications of the Southampton Record Society, 31 (Southampton, 1931) pp. 104–5.

[14]   Thomas, 'Age and Authority in Early Modern England', p. 210.

[15]   Ibid., pp. 210–18.

[16]   Ariès, *Centuries of Childhood*; for the relationship between Puritanism and childhood, see C. John Sommerville, *The Discovery of Childhood in Puritan England* (Athens and London: The University of Georgia Press, 1992).

therefore, linked to proto-bourgeois notions of child-rearing)? This chapter will now move on to explore and challenge some of these theories.

Children of God: A Historical Background to Childhood Spirituality

It would, of course, be inaccurate to assume that the Reformation brought about complete changes to the way children were perceived from the sixteenth century onwards. The belief that children could act as spiritual envoys or intermediaries was far from novel at this time. The view that children had the ability to acquire special spiritual status was a long founded one, not least because it had biblical precedents. We have already noted that the Psalmist wrote quite clearly on this matter: 'Out of the mouth of babes and sucklings hast thou ordained strength'; likewise, the Gospel of Matthew reassured that, 'Iesus said vnto the*m*, Yea ... By the mouth of babes and sucklings thou hast made perfite the praise'.[17]

Late medieval Catholicism had embraced the belief that children were more often chosen as divine intercessors than adults. Children and adolescents were commonly featured in festive rites, dressed as angels and seen to be leading processions. Children could be venerated as prophets, or more simply as miracle children. The Feast of the Holy Innocents was, in particular, a time when the role of children was festively marked. Regions as diverse as fifteenth-century Tuscany, Castile, Catalonia, Florence and Henrician England reported instances in which popular and much-celebrated prophets and seers had been children, or those on the verge or in the middle of puberty. Before considering English examples of post-Reformation 'holy children', then, it is useful to look at the historical context to these belief-systems within early modern Europe.

Catholic Saints and prophets were much more visceral than any objects of Protestant attention; they cried tears and shed blood and sweat, while Catholic worshippers flocked to renowned shrines in order to experience this form of direct and palpable devotion. They were, quite simply, expressions of the direct workings of God in the earthly world. Within such patterns of high-drama-devotion, everyday people were temporarily elevated from their usual social positions, to occupy, for a short period of time, a position of temporary authority. Such occurrences were associated with festive rites, such as sacred plays, saints' days and festivals. Children, the most innocent members of society, were often seen to be mirrors of God's word, and their special spiritual insight could provide instructions for dealing with imminent disaster. Indeed, children

---

17   Psalms 8:2; Matthew 21:16.

were the most vulnerable victims within disasters such as plague and famine, and child prophecies occurred more frequently during such times.[18] In this way, what people supposedly heard from the mouths of Saints and prophets can act as a reflection of their deepest fears and desires.

In late Medieval and Renaissance Florence and Spain, for example, 'child-holiness' was drawn into the very ritualistic, highly emotional public displays of devotion that were typical of Catholic festive rites. The young formed an integral part of such celebrations. Children were especially privileged, and would walk in prominent place at the front of religious processions.[19] In fifteenth-century Florence social confraternities were created for boys. On festival days they formed processions in which some of the children were dressed as angels. Clothed distinctively in white these children presented the image of innocence to the Florentine public. They were depicted as asexual beings, a dramatic representation of innocence.[20] Indeed, late medieval and early modern Catholic culture was one in which innocence could be effectively institutionalised, and the outward patterns of the pious, the orders of monks and nuns, was reflected in the behaviour of post-Reformation popular prophets.[21] Childhood innocence and piety were similarly reflected by choosing boys to act out sacred plays; the innocence of youthful actors aptly fitted the narratives of biblical or hagiographical stories.[22]

In Spain the differences between ages were marked by a subtle use of terminology. Young girls between the ages of nine and ten were known as *niños*; by the age of twelve they were *moza*, *mozuela* or, if past puberty, *moza niña*. *Mozas* could, potentially, be tempted by sin, hence their purity had to be carefully preserved, by ensuring that such girls avoided occasions for sin, such as dances. Children, most especially girls, who had preserved their physical innocence, through appearance or experience, beyond the number of years generally expected were especially favoured, and were reassured that they would receive reward in Heaven for their pure and pious modesty and virtue.[23] Of course, Spanish culture and Catholicism was much removed from traditional English culture:

---

18   William A. Christian Jr, *Apparitions in Late Medieval and Renaissance Spain* (Princeton University Press, Princeton, New Jersey, 1981) p. 220.

19   Christian, *Apparitions in Late Medieval and Renaissance Spain*, p. 215.

20   Christian, *Apparitions in Late Medieval and Renaissance Spain*, p. 223.

21   See also 'holy anorexia' exploration below.

22   Richard C. Trexter, 'Ritual in Florence: Adolescence and Salvation in the Renaissance', in Charles Trinkhaus and Heiko A. Oberman (eds), *The Pursuit of Holiness in Late Medieval and Renaissance Religion* (Leiden: Brill, 1974) pp. 222–9.

23   Christian Jr, *Apparitions in Late Medieval and Renaissance Spain*, p. 218.

Spanish Catholicism in particular was marked by a more rigorous 'policing' of female sexual honour. Yet, early modern ideas of innocence can still be applied to post Reformation culture in England. Indeed, the notion of *appearing* to be young, whether through sheer chance or even through ritualistic self-starvation, alongside the idea of being *presented* as young by tract and pamphlet writers, in order to mark out and suggest innocence, was a significant idea within English texts. The importance of appearing to be child-like, bodily and spiritually, and thus to possess innocence, runs throughout this work.

English receptiveness to 'Continental' or traditional Catholic ideas did not stop at hungry young women, however. The Festival of Saint Nicholas and the Feast of the Holy Innocents were key features of the Catholic ritual-year, celebrated each year on December 6 and December 28, and both centred on the role of children.[24] The custom was observed in England as late as the reign of Mary Tudor. Saint Nicholas was considered to be the patron saint of scholars and of youth. One of the most important aspects of the festival was the election of the Boy Bishop, or 'Episcopus Choristarum', a young chorister chosen by fellow choristers who would also dress-up as officers to the chosen Bishop. The role of the Boy Bishop centred upon the notion, both comic and socially distinctive, of the inversion of social norms. The children would be 'ledde with songes and daunces from house to house, blessing the people and gatheryng of money; and boyes do singe masse and preache in the pulpitt'.[25] While the sight of a young child, dressed as a junior Bishop complete with miniature surplice, pastoral staff in hand and a mitre on his head, was most probably vastly amusing to early modern sensibilities, the child was also endowed with more serious and meaningful duties. Indeed, Boy Bishops and Priests were allowed to preach full sermons, which were given meaningful messages, in which childhood concerns were often paramount, and through which child piety and innocence were strongly and clearly emphasised. A sermon preached by a Boy Bishop in Gloucester Cathedral told: 'prayse ye childerne almighty God ... The children ... whiche lacke dyscrecyon, use of reason, and parfyght cognycyon, and yet attayne to the ende that is prepared for mannes blysse'.[26]

---

[24] For details on popular culture and rituals, see Peter Burke, *Popular Culture in Early Modern Europe* (London: Temple Smith, 1978), esp. chapter 2, part 7, 'The World of Carnival'.

[25] John Gough Nichols (ed.), *King Henry VIII's Proclamation against Holy Innocent's festivities, The Camden Miscellany, 7th volume*. M.DCCC.LXXV.1, includes 'Two Sermons Preached by the Boy-Bishop', pp. xx–xxi.

[26] Nichols, ed., *King Henry VIII's Proclamation*, pp. 3–5.

Furthermore, the special spiritual status of children, and the intricate relationship between childhood, innocence and spiritual cleanliness or purity was emphasised, with the support of biblical passages:

> ... in as moche as Cryste sayth in the Gospell 'suffre ye childerne to come to me, for of suche the kingdom of heven is fulfylled', ... it is not oonly understonde those that bene chylderne of age, but those that bene chylderne pure in clennesse from synne and malice. (Cor xiiij) ... And in this fourme alle maner of people and al maner of ages in clennesse of lyf ought to be Pure as childerne.[27]

During the Reformation, apart from a brief lapse under Mary I, the childhood piety, or perhaps more fittingly, frivolity, surrounding the Boy Bishop was actively forbidden, as were any forms of celebration coinciding with the day of the Holy Innocents. Henry VIII's proclamation against the festive rite found the fact that 'children be strangelie decked and apparayled to counterfeit priestes [and] bishoppes' especially distasteful, and at the expense of 'the pure and sincere religion of Christe'.[28] Furthermore, the supposed piety underpinning such festive occasions did not go unsuspected by members of local religious communities. Especially critical were the supporters of the Protestant Reformation. Indeed, in 1556 Gertrude Crokhay of London was accused of not opening her door to the Boy Bishop and his youthful fraternity. She claimed, in her defence, that this was because, as an abstainer from the Catholic Church, she knew 'no saynt Nicholas ... For S. Nicholas is in heaven', and saw only her neighbour's son at the door. However, she also added that she was 'afrayd of them that came with him to haue had my purse cutte by them. For I haue heard of men robbed by Saint Nicholas'.[29]

Such doctrinal and liturgical changes, however, could not so easily deal with the social or cultural functions of parts of this Catholic inheritance. It is clear that within Catholic culture there was a direct and immediate relationship between these festivities and social order. Such inversions of the natural age and authority orders could, in turn, strengthen and clarify accepted religious and social modes of behaviour. The world was, effectively, 'turned up-side-down' during festival periods.[30] These short but intense moments of chaos strengthened the correct

---

[27]   Nichols, ed., *King Henry VIII's Proclamation*, pp. 3–5.

[28]   Nichols, ed., *King Henry VIII's Proclamation*, p. xxi.

[29]   John Foxe, *Book of Martyrs*, online version: http://www.hrionline.ac.uk/johnfoxe, Book 12, 1583 edition, pp. 2144.

[30]   For more information on this idea see Burke, *Popular Culture in Early Modern Europe*.

social order – God spoke through the weak, he used them to convey messages and to convey innocence – once these messages had been heard it was time to return to acceptable modes of behaviour, and for children and the rest of the temporarily socially venerated to return to their normal roles and lives. How far, then, were such patterns able to continue within post-Reformation England? Were, as Alexandra Walsham argues, traditional modes of belief allowed to continue in a distinctly Protestant dress? Most significantly to our purpose, what happened to the child prophet and to notions of the holy child? As we have seen, the figure of the pious and holy infant did not go away. But, to return to the suggestion in the prophecy cases of a godly influence, to what extent did child prophets play a separate sort of role in the Protestant context?

Precocious Godliness: King Edward VI as the New Josiah

One of the most significant and highly influential Protestant examples of a holy child was the young King Edward VI (1537–1553), known affectionately by some of his subjects as 'England's treasure'.[31] Whilst he was not in any particular sense a 'popular prophet', and was not endowed with any such powers of intercession (as was typical for the holy infants in polemical works), royal officials nevertheless played upon and reshaped the role of child prophet as a form of political propaganda.[32] Edward was an example of a prophetic, inspirational child; his holy identity had been entirely constructed for him, thus depicting how the royal court envisaged a child prophet of the royal variety *should* be. The fact that this identity was not necessarily a realistic one for a nine-year-old boy was not admitted, revealing something about the power of iconic stereotyping, and the construction of identity that was made possible through polemic literature at this time. Furthermore, this was an image created by the arch-Reformers that surrounded Edward – suggesting at the very least a radical watering-down, in this new paragon of childish spiritual authority, of the 'Catholic inheritance' and of traditional belief in general.

Edward, the 'Boy King' was said to be re-treading the footsteps of biblical precedents: he had God on his side. In the traditional historiographies of the period, England had already been punished for their misdemeanours

---

[31]   See Dale Hoak, 'Edward VI (1537–1553)', *Oxford Dictionary of National Biography*, Oxford University Press, 2004 [http://www.oxforddnb.com/view/article/8522, accessed 15 May 2007].

[32]   For example, see Kevin Sharpe, *Selling the Tudor Monarchy: Authority and Image in Sixteenth-Century England* (London: Yale University Press, 2008), Ch. 7.

by the negative and sometimes catastrophic reigns of adult kings, such as Harold Godwinson, Edward II, Richard II and Henry VI. However, a freshly reformed, Protestant England had the opportunity to redeem itself, under the rule of the innocent and holy child King.[33] Edward's holy or prophetic nature was staged on a range of levels. Firstly, the central feature of the political and polemical propaganda that surrounded Edward was the notion that his kingship represented the prophetic return to the style of leadership held by the Old Testament Kings. Comparisons between Edward and the boy kings of the Old Testament were frequent throughout his six-year reign and beyond.[34] Edward was compared to positive regal models, including Moses, David, Jehoshaphat and Josiah, the noble princes of God's people. Most especially, however, Edward was compared to Josiah (2 Kings: 22–23).[35] Josiah was the king of Judah and a zealous reformer and iconoclast – they were thus presented as the boy kings who 'purged their land of idols'.[36] He was just eight years old when he began to reign and he stayed in power for 31 years in Jerusalem. In this way, Edward became the godly channel for a new chosen people, a boy whose voice carried the word of God and therefore unique and transformative authority.

Edward and his England were seen to be continuing an age-old legend, through recreating the religious struggles of the Old Testament in sixteenth-century England. The princely role-models usually cited came from the historical books of the Old Testament that dealt with the establishment and degeneration of the kingdoms of Israel and Judah, mainly 2 Kings and 2 Chronicles. As part of this religio-political paradigm, the English King was to model his character and policy upon that of a Jewish King of the Ancient world. Edward was also sometimes presented as another Old Testament figure, that of Solomon, both because of the associations with profound wisdom, but also due to the notion that Solomon was able to build the Temple of Jerusalem, unlike his father David (or, as some Tudor writers put it, Solomon and Edward were able to build the Church, unlike their fathers, David and Henry VIII). For some contemporaries, those disapproving of Edward's Reformation, other Old Testament cast, such as Ahab, may have been seen as more appropriate. [37] Within such a bibliocentric world view, such a prospect was not as unusual as it may sound; the Scriptures

---

[33]   Stephen Alford, *Kingship and Politics in the Reign of Edward VI* (Cambridge University Press, 2002) pp. 50–51.

[34]   Diarmaid MacCulloch, *Tudor Church Militant* (London: Allen Lane, 1999) pp. 62–3.

[35]   Alford, *Kingship and Politics in the Reign of Edward VI*, p. 34.

[36]   Diarmaid MacCulloch, *The Boy King: Edward VI and the Protestant Reformation* (London: Palgrave, 2001) p. 14.

[37]   MacCulloch, *The Boy King*, p. 14.

were believed to be a source of never fading truth, and Edward, in the guise of a new, prophetically constructed Josiah, was to continue the Christian war against the powers of Antichrist.[38] This was the Protestant view of history, and was one in which there existed two worlds, those of God and the Devil (again, we might perceive the Janus face of prophecy and possession). Such was this shared system of meaning, which was to shape the perceptions of Edward's short reign for many years to come. The use of biblical names and features appealed to an audience which was fully versed in biblical concepts. Indeed, much of the audience would have been living directly through such conceptions. The power of the word and the biblical precedent were vital ingredients to all reports of holy prophecy at this time.

However, the association between Edward and Josiah was not to be taken to the end of its hoped conclusion, as Edward was to suffer an inconveniently untimely death. Nevertheless, even through his early death Edward continued to be sanctified: through death came idealisation and martyrdom. Edward was perceived as young, innocent and too good for this world. He thus was released through a good, Protestant death, however much chaos and destruction his premature demise caused for a spiritually fragmented England. Yet, his politically engineered identity was one which brought biblical ideas and precedents into the forefront of sixteenth-century political propaganda and religious opinion, and his example as a child prophet cannot be justly forgotten in this exploration of early modern England's 'holy children'. Indeed, it might seem crucial in the shaping of, and the stoking of interest in, the new form of authorised child we have been exploring here.

The notion that children had a special spiritual status, then, continued after the Reformation. This was often due to their perceived purity, their innocence and virginity: they were free from the taints of the world. Beliefs concerning the spiritual status, or special powers, of children after the Reformation formed part of a set of beliefs in divine providence. Stories were circulated in which children had witnessed visions, experienced visitations or had returned from the dead. Like Edward himself, in such cases children were granted a form of divine agency; they were pronouncing the words of God and becoming miniature messengers for God's voice on earth. Other cases, often involving infants (or 'monstrous births', as they were known), saw the bodies of children themselves becoming the message to be observed – children were being used and shaped by

---

[38]   Christopher Bradshaw, 'David or Josiah? Old Testament Kings as Exemplars in Edwardian Religious Polemic', in Bruce Gordon (ed.), *Protestant History and Identity in Sixteenth-Century Europe, Vol. II, The Later Reformation* (Hants: Aldershot, 1996) p. 77.

God as ominous messages of warning. This afforded the Protestant version of the sacred child a rather more active and participatory role in their drama: rather than symbol, they were representatives, preaching and even sermonising in the style of their ministers. Indeed, vocalisation was a recurring motif in the stories which depicted child prophets.

Tales rooted in folklore and later in notions of divine providence saw children as the innocent voices who would bring resolution to a corrupt world. Children who had suffered cruelty or murder would return to haunt those who wronged them; those who had been left unbaptised would refuse to rest; and those who were poor and poverty stricken would witness privileged visions of Heaven – indeed, we will consider these examples in the following chapter. Within such cases these children, the most vulnerable members of society, would be seen to bring about some form of just resolution. Those who had been injured or killed would name their attackers; those who had remained unbaptised would demand a name; and the poor would be assured of their salvation and of riches in Heaven. Much like the festivities surrounding the Boy Bishops, the stories and morality tales concerning prophetic children brought resolution and confirmed existing patterns of social order, and also served to comfort those who had lost children to early death – again, we will move on to develop these ideas further in Chapter 6.

Within such perceptions, images of childhood innocence and sweetness were combined with the blighting of early promise embodied in Edward's own story, to create the hope that children who were snatched so young from the world would be assured of heavenly peace. However, within popular culture there was also much doubt and suspicion surrounding child salvation, as was especially true for infants.[39] This uncertainty was evident, for instance, in the tortured debates around the baptism ceremony, considered in Chapter 2, in which perceptions of children and hopes for their salvation were cast in considerable doubt. Children were no longer offered a definite hope of salvation at the font, as they were in Catholic culture, so efforts to educate them from the earliest possible age, as well as a desire to find stories or beliefs which cast children in roles which promised potential salvation or which provided the cultural space to imagine children with spiritual agency, became evermore important – as this work considers throughout.[40] A key contention of this monograph is that

---

[39]   Jacqueline Simpson, 'The Folklore of Infant Deaths: Burials, Ghosts and Changelings', in Gillian Avery and Kimberly Reynolds (eds), *Representations of Childhood Death* (London: Macmillan Press, 2000) p. 11.

[40]   See Introduction and Chapter 2, also see Anna French, 'Disputed Words and Disputed Meanings: The Reformation of Baptism, Infant Limbo and Child Salvation in

this ambivalence surrounding the spiritual status of children was reflected, and acted out, in the cases of prophecy and possession: that ways and means were found to circumvent gerontocratic norms, doctrinal orthodoxy, and the physical vulnerability of children themselves, in order to dramatise – either on page or for real – the liminality of child spirituality. Child prophets, following the example of Edward VI and in contrast to the anxiety of demonic influence in the possessed, offered evidence that God could reach and save even the youngest, most vulnerable members of society. For the remainder of this chapter, therefore, we will consider how such providential tales continued to be circulated within Protestant England, exploring cases of providence in which children become mouthpieces for God within the world.

Children and Cases of Providential Prophecy

> ... neyther signes nor tokens in the firmament, as comets, blasing starres ... scarce and terrible lightnings, this blate ... starre which appeareth at this present, God's heauie iudgements against us for the use of sinne, can cause vs to crye out with David and to confesse we haue sinned, straunge tokens are nothing regarded, Earth-quakes are made none account off, great floods and inundations of waters are accounted trifles, alas what shall I say, if euer people deserued the fulnes of Gods indignation.[41]

In early modern England cases of child-related 'miracles' were recast into ideas and beliefs about godly prophecy and providence. Through these narratives they became more than figures saved by the grace of God, but also the providential mouthpieces of God. Godly providence was an aspect of early modern Calvinist belief, explored most notably by Alexandra Walsham. Protestant providentialism was, Walsham argues, a 'tissue of beliefs about the intrusion of supernatural forces in the earthly sphere.'[42] Furthermore, such beliefs were not confined to the lofty views of the ecclesiastical elites, but were incorporated into the nexus of popular socio-religious views and outlooks. As Walsham concludes:

Early Modern England', in Jonathan Willis (ed.) *Sin and Salvation in Early Modern England* (Farnham: Ashgate, 2015).

[41] John Phillips, *The wonderfull worke of God shewed vpon a chylde whose name is William Withers, being in the towne of Walsham, within the countie of Suffolke* (London, 1581) STC (2nd ed.) 19877, sig. A6v.

[42] Walsham, *Providence in Early Modern England*, p. 328.

... there was a constant two-way flow between published texts and oral tradition, so were sermons and inexpensive ephemera symbolically linked, caught in a complex and mutually enriching equilibrium. Seepage and haemorrhage occurred in both directions. The world of the pulpit and edifying tract was by no means inherently at odds with the world of commercial publishing and the titillating broadside.[43]

Indeed, these spiritual views were flexible and adaptable, and can be seen within a range of early modern texts, including those relating to the role of childhood – the perceived relationship between children and God as well as a wide range of other natural occurrences; as one text phrased it:

> Many are the wonders which haue lately happened, as of sodaine and strange death vpon ... persons, strange sights in the Ayre, strange births on the Earth, Earthquakes, Commets, and fierie Impressions, with the execution of GOD himselfe from his holy fire in heauen ... [44]

All this offers one more key with which to unlock the prophecy cases. In January 1581, for example, the case of William Withers was published in London. God had struck again and his Divine finger was clearly discernible within the earthly world, and this time it pointed to the sin and abominable evil apparently evident within Elizabethan England – or more precisely, within Suffolk. The text, like many other works on sin and prophecy, told that, 'God ... [has] bent his bow of displeasure against vs, fethered the consuming arrowes of our destruction, whet his sword, and set in the fullness of his furie'. Hence, God would make trees fruitless and cause crops to fail, and:

> by this present example, not far from hence, but within the bondes of Suffolke, giuen by a child of xj. yeres of age, who with great vehemencie cryeth, that the end of al things is at hand, threatning our destruction, except wee speedely repent, the which God graunt for his sonnes sake.[45]

The pamphlet told that, during the Christmas of 1580, an 11-year-old boy from the county of Suffolk had fallen into a trance. For 10 days the young William Withers had remained silent, existing without communication, or any form of nourishment. Very similar to the swoons reported in some of the cases

---

43   Ibid., p. 327.
44   T.I., *A miracle, of miracles*, sig. A3v.
45   Phillips, *The wonderfull worke of God*, sig. A4r–v.

of demonic possession explored in the previous chapters, he lay in a trance, not eating and temporarily mute. The boy would speak only once every 24 hours, to declare the 'most straunge and rare thinges, which are to come', to the 'great admiration of the beholders' and to the 'greefe of his parentes'.[46] He warned an audience of locals and notaries of the perils they faced; 'the rypenesse of our sinnes' he spoke, was so great 'that without spedie repentance the day of our destruction' was surely at hand. Most fearfully, 'brotherly loue', he pronounced, was 'strangled, the bowels of compassion and pitie were shut vp ... [and] neighborly affection was changed to flattery'.[47] Humans, thundered the child, were making themselves 'bondmen to the deuill'; 'Pittie is made an outcast, conscience is drowned, compassion is buried'.[48] Strong words, it seems, for such a small person.

This 'Prodigall childe' was thus perceived to be a vessel, used to express and enact God's wrath to the sinful people of England.[49] In a similar fashion to the cases of demonic possession, when he did speak his words reflected thorough Scriptural knowledge and were delivered with an immense physical strength, signalling spiritual interference; 'the threateninges of God he publisheth by the authoritie of the Scriptures in such sorte as though he were a learned Divine, & when he speaketh his voyce seemed to bee of such power that all the bedde shaketh, to the astonishment of the hearers'.[50]

The notion that William Withers was an agent of godly providence on earth was clearly put forward within the 1581 tract. It was seen that God had sent this child directly to warn society of its sins and to remedy the social evils of the age; 'he hath raised vp a second Daniel, a yong child of xi. yeres'. The child was thus an 'instrument giuen to vs by the prouidence of God, if it may be to waken vs out of the perilous slumber of our sinne'.[51] The sheer concept of God raising a second Daniel of Israel – known for his dramatic encounter with the Lions Den – in a child, of fairly humble origin, dwelling in Suffolk, is striking. Yet, this is by now a familiar pattern, of course: young biblical prophets set the precedent for this form of religious discourse, in which young and innocent 'lambs of God' were

---

46 Phillips, *The wonderfull worke of God*, cover and sig. A7v. For a detailed analysis of this case, see Walsham's article '"Out of the Mouths of Babes and Sucklings": Prophecy, Puritanism, and Childhood in Elizabethan Suffolk', in Diana Wood, *The Church and Childhood*, the Ecclesiastical History Society, Vol. 31 (Oxford: Blackwell, 1994), pp. 285–99.

47 Phillips, *The wonderfull worke of God shewed vpon a chylde*, sig. A7v.

48 Phillips, *The wonderfull worke of God*, sig. A5r–A6r.

49 Phillips, *The wonderfull worke of God*, sig. A7r.

50 Phillips, *The wonderfull worke of God*, sig. A8v.

51 Phillips, *The wonderfull worke of God*, sig. A8r.

specially chosen by Divine will; in the words of the unwilling biblical prophet Jeremiah, who said to God: ' ... behold, I cannot speak, for I am a child'; to which God replied; 'Say not, I am a child: for thou shalt go to all that I shall send thee, and whatsoever I command thee thou shalt speak'.[52]

From this belief in the moralistic wisdom and righteousness of the 'Children of God' (so distinct, as we can now see, from the wisdom of the old man considered at the start of this chapter), children like William Withers and the young girl in the German pamphlet with which we began this inquiry could derive much authority, through which they were able to challenge accepted social orders, and flaunt their unusual status in the face of their social superiors. One vice about which the young William Withers had seemingly become particularly agitated was that of pride, evoked most clearly through contemporary styles of dress. Also like the German cases explored at the opening of this chapter, the case of William Withers criticises vanity, as reflected in frivolous clothing: 'gaye garmentes of purple collour, are euery where', yet 'needie brethren, which want of foode are oft times readie to perish in the streets'.[53] Men, Withers raged, had become like 'monsters' and women 'shamelesse wantons'. The seemingly eloquent young boy even went so far as to taunt one bystander, despite his being superior in age and social standing, for his 'great monstrous ruffes', (or extravagant collar) for it would be better for him to 'put on a sackcloth & mourn for his sinnes, then in such abhominable pride to pranke vp himselfe like the diuels darling'. In response, the young man, supposedly, 'sorrowed & wept for his offence, rent the bande from his neck, tooke a knife and cut it in peeces and vowed never to weare the like againe'.[54] Whether or not these words were truly those of an 11-year-old boy and his remorseful bystanders, we will never know. Nevertheless, as we have explored these cases we have also reconstructed early modern belief systems, and the status that could be acquired by a child within them – or even by a fictional child-character that existed only in the spiritual imaginarium of the people bound by those systems. Whether or not that child was truly a well-known member of the religious community, or rather an invention or embellishment of the press, the image remains a powerful one: that of a young child, fasting and abstaining from nourishment; weeping tears and shouting in the face of social hierarchies for the sins of his generation.

To bring this tour through the vexed landscape of the early modern child prophet full circle, we can now properly return to the case of the German girl,

---

52 Jeremiah 1: 6–7.
53 Phillips, *The wonderfull worke of God shewed vpon a chylde*, sig. A5r.
54 Phillips, *The wonderfull worke of God*, sig. B2r.

first introduced at the opening of this chapter. The case, *a prophesie reuealed by a poore countrey maide*, contains a miracle story in which the hand and words of God are seen to be clearly presented through the actions of a young girl. The case appeared in two other English publications; the 1641 anonymous publication *The wonderfull works of God* and also in an earlier and less expanded story, Eyriak Schlichtenberger's *A prophecie vttered by the daughter of an honest country man* in 1580.[55] Here, we will refer to the more detailed 1614 edition. The story is a fairly complicated one, which ends in a providential warning against vanity; one which is pronounced by the child, who returns from the dead in order to evoke the most extreme reaction from communities of readers.

It is also significant to note that such cases of popular prophecy were most common in and typical of German, or Lutheran, culture. As we have seen, popular Lutheran belief systems reinterpreted traditional, Catholic beliefs in saints and miracle stories – opting instead for tales of popular prophets. Here we see stories in which ordinary, humble folk, stumbled upon old men with beards or witnessed visions of angels dressed in white. These prophets were not just children, but adult men and women as well. Interestingly, typical symptoms would include falling into ecstasy, fits, becoming ill, becoming temporarily mute, and then later theologically eloquent. Such symptoms were similarly reported in English culture – although in such instances also just as easily interpreted as instances of demonic intrusion or interference, as has been considered.

These German 'popular prophets' warned against crimes such as pride (often involving overly indulgent dress), usury, avarice or fornication. Such stories became a part of the Lutheran system of repentance and forgiveness, much like their Catholic predecessors. Visions and visitations tended to occur most readily at times of calamity or social uncertainty, such as war, plague or famine – reflecting attempts to gain control – and as a result they can be used as a 'barometer' of social opinion. Such stories were circulated in pamphlets and sermons, thus becoming fairly standardised and formulaic. Furthermore, such belief systems were often reintegrated back into 'official' Church culture: witnesses would report their visions to ministers, who would use their stories within their own preaching.[56] In the ways we have explored, such ideas were also able to penetrate and be adapted by English culture, partly through the spread of popular ideas and stories by the printing press – hence all those multiple additions, and the transmutation of Melwing into Worskop.

---

[55]   See T.I., *A miracle, of miracles*, sig. C2r; further accounts of this case were published in Schlichtenberger, *A prophecie vttered by the daughter of an honest country man* and Anon, *The wonderfull works of God*.

[56]   See Beyer, 'A Lübeck Prophet in Local and Lutheran Context', pp. 166–81.

The tale of the 'Poor Country Maid' begins by recounting a most everyday and hopeful event, that of a wedding celebration. The bride and groom were of humble origin, yet the groom's master organised and funded the wedding in a style and manner only accustomed to those of higher social standing. The bridegroom's humble and spiritually eloquent sister is the character at the centre of the story, and she provides God with an amiable and angelic vessel through which to relay his message.

The day after the celebrations, the 14-year-old sister visited the wedding house with a friend. They wanted to see the daughter of the man who had funded the wedding, the 'worshipfull Maister George von Ramyttes', mistress Annys. The 'two maides sate downe by her, where together they conferred of many matters, especially as concerning their attire and apparell'. Indeed, the bridegroom had ensured that his younger sister was well-dressed for the occasion – perhaps more luxuriously clothed than was fit for her social position. The child had been able to wear 'a silk upper-body with which shee had dressed her selfe as handsomely as shee might, and withall she wore the best ... apparel ...' In response, the more wealthy Annys 'beganne to floute at her, saying: can thy father cloath thee thus, and seeme so poore'. To this the innocent child humbly answered, 'my poore father hath alwaies to his power apparelled me: but this which you see, my Brother hath bestowed on mee, to doe him honestly at his marriage ... And though wee bee poore in goods, I trust God will make vs rich in Spirit ...'[57] At this, the humble child left the room, leaving the other 'somewhat vaine-glorious' girls to continue discussing their apparel. It was further said that:

> The poore Countrey maide that knew no Prince, nor had any such attire to boast of, [and so] held her peace, accounted her selfe with her povertie, as acceptable before God, as the richest or fayrest of those fine Dames present: saying inwardly to her selfe, God is a iealous God, he hateth Pride, he punisheth the vnrighteous, he comforteth the poore, which haue no delight therein: and maintaineth them that are continually bent to the seruice of him.[58]

However, during the third day after the marriage, 'all the ioy was turned into heauinesse', when each of the three girls died in the same afternoon. Before the children were due to be buried, the mother of the poor maid, while her neighbours prepared her daughter for burial, asked if she could see her child one more time;

---

[57]   T.I., *A miracle, of miracles*, sig. B4r.
[58]   T.I., *A miracle, of miracles*, sig. C1r.

... so they went al together, to see the dead Corpses (which had been laid foorth, the full space of two and twenty houres) and the mother lifted vp the sheets, sighing, purposing then to take her last farewell, and sight of her deare Daughter, whom she so tenderly loued.[59]

However, there came a shock to the child's mother and the spectators, as the child 'as one awaked from a slumber, raised vp herselfe, and with a milde and cheerefull countenance, spake vnto her mother'. She said, in response to the mother's grief;

My most deare mother, why haue you sinned so sore against GOD: you haue made me sorrowfull many times, but bee you content, GOD hath forgiuen all, for I am sent as a messenger to you, and within fiue daies I shall returne againe to the place I come from, where I shall liue in all peace.[60]

Such words echo the popular belief that, if a mother grieved too much for a lost child, they would never be able to find peace in Heaven. Many folktales exist in which mothers are said to have visions of angelic-like children playing in Heaven. Among these children they recognise their own child weeping. When asked why they do not play with the others, the sorrowful child answers that the mother's pain keeps them from being happy, and from finally being able to be released from the skeins of earthly life.[61] Such stories were part of a folk-lore or popular culture which helped grieving parents to come to terms with the loss of a child.

Unsurprisingly, the sudden sight of the German maiden shocked and 'amazed' those who witnessed her. They noted that whilst the 'Maide was seldome before seene to be merry, They now perceiued her more cheerefull, and with a pleasant ... countenance'.[62] She was also much more confident in her speech, asserting:

Beloued Christians, wonder not that I haue been a short time from you: but be thankfull to God, that he hath certified you by sundry signes, how the ende of the world is at hand, and the day of rest comming to reioyce vs ... [63]

---

[59] T.I., *A miracle, of miracles*, sig. Cv.

[60] T.I., *A miracle, of miracles*, sig. Cv.

[61] See Simpson, 'The Folklore of Infant Deaths: Burials, Ghosts and Changelings'.

[62] T.I., *A miracle, of miracles*, sig. Cv.

[63] T.I., *A miracle, of miracles*, sig. Cv–C2r.

Most interesting, though, is her description of where she had been after death: was it that she had seen Heaven, where she saw a 'costley forte' and 'bright Angels shining like the beames of the sun'? Similarly, had she been guided by a God-like figure, the 'comely olde man, with a long gray Beard'? The old man willed the child to 'manifest (vnto the Penitent) the mercy of GOD, and to say vnto the world, that he is bent to wrath: cheefly to those that despise, and giue no credite to his examples'. The girl was thus a warning, sent, the pamphlet argued, to 'admonish vs from the detestable Pride, which is heere maintained, because before GOD you shall finde it Damnable'.[64] Furthermore, the child was at hand to warn spectators what exactly the punishment would be, a message so strong in its conviction, that it deserves a full consideration:

> If you amend not, and turne to GOD, hee will forthwith send on you a generall alteration, and such an one, as not onely men, but Birds of the ayre and all liuing things, shall tremble at his wrath. Warres shall greatly greeue the earth, and they shall destroy Countreyes and people: men shall bee most greeuously chased from their houses, and most miserable murthered. And before this happen, there shall come a great Dearth: and then GOD will take his owne that haue turned vnto him, not suffering them to see this miserie: but those that liue after, shall truely feele the wrath of God, so that those which remaine in the third yeere, shall well say, where haue you beene, that you are not yet destroyed. Many for feare shall Decay: there shall bee great Earthquakes, through which Townes and steeples, Castles, fortes and houses shall be throwen down on heapes. Then shall follow such mishap, as is not necessary to be spoken of, for the sin of the people is abhominable & curses before God.[65]

As a result of this strong apocalyptic message, put forth profoundly not by the old man of the story but instead by such a small child, local people supposedly began to change the way they dressed. According to the text, clothes in the style the 'vaine-glorious' girls had been seen wearing became 'loathsome to all persons, whereby none shall be able to weare them'. Further, people were said to have travelled to see the clothes, and the bedroom of the girl, so much so that it was walled in, in an attempt to prevent the attention. While the child was still alive, learned men (perhaps even ones with beards) were said to have visited her to discuss spiritual matters. Finally, before she returned to Heaven, she asked to receive the sacrament. On 6 October, 1613, 'betweene one and two

---

64   T.I., *A miracle, of miracles*, sig. Cv–C2r.
65   T.I., *A miracle, of miracles*, sig. C2r.

of the clocke, pattently sitting in a Chayre, she committed her soule to God, and yeelded vp the Ghost'.[66] A hefty message, for such a small child.

The use of child prophets as a form of salve – like King Edward, a channel of godly wisdom inspiring hope in a people – is evident, too, in this story's treatment of child death. That anxiety around child salvation revolved around questions of child mortality and predestination: was a parent's child bound for Heaven or Hell? Whether or not this child's death was as 'triumphant' and peaceful as expressed here would not have been the significant point. Rather, what is most important is the way the death was represented. This was, by Protestant standards, a good death.[67] It was peaceful, pious and observed by attentive witnesses. It also made an impact – spectators were inspired into religious fervour. In this way, the potential for children to die well and at least demonstrate outward signs of election, or for less Reformed parents to suggest strongly in their visions of Heaven their own salvation, are encoded in the person of the child prophet. The unusual spiritual agency granted to children expressed and answered a key spiritual anxiety of the period. Child death was not an unusual occurrence. This does not mean, as this work has sought to show, that parents became immune to the deaths of their children, or that they did not bond with them. Rather, it meant that parents had to find alternative ways of coping with such occurrences. Early modern society, deeply religious in essence, philosophised about the early deaths of their children; they used the resources they had at hand – religion, faith, folklore and stories – in order to make sense of the often cruel world around them. Hence, depictions of childhood death, such as those explored in the case of the German maiden, were presented as triumphant. Philippe Ariès wrote about such depictions of death, which have been described by others as the 'conceptual equation of death with the beautiful'.[68] There was an appreciation of the beauty of death, for it preserved the child at the height of his or her innocence. Children would be delivered straight to heaven, before the world around them could taint them.[69] This does not signify a lack of care towards the young, but

---

[66] T.I., *A miracle, of miracles*, sig. C2v–C3r.

[67] For detailed consideration of a 'good Protestant death' see Ralph Houlbrooke, *Death, Religion and the Family in England, 1480–1750* (Oxford: Oxford Studies in Social History, 1998).

[68] Elisabeth Bronfen, *Over Her Dead Body: Death, Femininity and the Aesthetic* (Manchester: Manchester University Press, 1992) p. 87.

[69] Gillian Avery and Kimberly Reynolds (eds), *Representations of Childhood Death* (London: Macmillan Press, 2000), pp. 7–8; Ariès, *Centuries of Childhood*, p. 87. Idealised depictions of childhood death were not the only interpretation of such occurrences. Some interesting work has been undertaken on the high incidence of child and adolescent suicide in the early modern period. In such cases children were given no funeral or marked burial,

serves to reminds us that attitudes towards children, birth and death are, in part, culturally constructed – resting on a plethora of cultural understandings – such as religion and story-telling. The child prophet had spiritual authority not just within the story – admonishing and inspiring better behaviour – but amongst those who read it, since they could perceive in the tale answers to the questions posed by the doctrines of Reformed Protestantism, which had for instance minimised the consolatory aspects of the baptism rite.

To conclude this chapter, then: stories of prophetic children reveal important aspects of religious perceptions towards the young during the early modern period. Firstly, according to ideas put forward in the texts, children could gain much notoriety, attention and authority by becoming religiously inspired. Such stories saw children trespassing against normal boundaries of childhood behaviour, and perverting accepted social hierarchies. They were, in a sense, turning the world upside-down. The spiritual advice decreed by the young and pious was not far removed from the religious teachings issued each week in Sunday sermons. Indeed, as considered in Chapter 1, and throughout this work, there was a clear theme of 'sermonising' in the words given to these young children, through which we see these cases reflecting and adopting motifs, messages and lessons which were similar to those congregations received from the minister at the altar, emphasising the strong ties between the so-called spheres of 'popular' and 'learned' culture. Yet, they were coming straight from the mouths of physical and social inferiors – the supposedly socially silent. This made what the children in the stories said all the more stark. The authority of these children was fleeting and temporary, in a sense borrowed. They were, however, being used as vessels by the highest authority possible – to spread messages from God.

Secondly, this tells us something about the nature of early modern perceptions of childhood. The cases of the prophets sit side by side with those of the demoniacs, and pose serious questions about how children could be seen to be receptive both to the purest messages and the most depraved. Children, it seems, were thought to be capable of tuning into both godly and demonic forces, and could act as receptive vessels for both extremes of spiritual force. The examples explored here reveal something about the dualistic nature of childhood, so perceived. Children were capable of both great good and potential evil. Childhood was, then, seen to be a period of limbo, uncertainty and spiritual instability – reflecting the anxieties and fears of parents and authorities in a post-

---

and were believed to go straight to hell, see Terence R. Murphy, 'Woful Childe of Parents Rage': Suicide of Children and Adolescents in Early Modern England, 1505–1710', *The Sixteenth Century Journal*, Vol. XVII (Issue 3) Fall 1986, pp. 259–70.

Reformation landscape where many of the old consolations, and even old forms of control, had been swept away. This explains, perhaps, why such a significant amount of printed material at the time focused its energies on educating and taming the young – a disordered youth would threaten the future of both society and Christendom at large.

Finally, on a wider level, such cases reveal something about the nature of religion post-Reformation. Whilst the child prophet formed part of an all-pervasive Protestant belief in godly providence, not necessarily a recycling of old beliefs nor older patterns of piety resurfacing in a distinctively Protestant dress, as Alex Walsham has argued for beliefs in providence and prophecy more widely – in these cases we can also see evidence of old cultural tropes and symbols (boy bishops and such visions of child authority) being adapted to suit new ideas and purposes within popular culture. Most especially, such ideas and concepts related to the child messenger or authority figure helped Protestant families to negotiate the potential anxieties of reform, most especially those surrounding the tense and contested spiritual status of children, cast into doubt by Protestant predestinarianism and new teachings about baptism, as outlined in the second chapter. Despite rival Protestant ideologies, which scorned any form of belief touching upon magic, fortune or 'popish superstition', such cases of providence, omen and demonic intrusion, speak of a world in which perceptions of the 'supernatural' remained highly prevalent, if somewhat transformed. This reveals a world in which proverbs, traditional wisdom and folklore continued and blended with new forms of faith. Beliefs in the 'magical' and 'mystical' abilities of children formed part of *both* traditional and reformed faiths. The stories explored in the past three chapters challenge the notion of polarity within Reformed culture – polarity both in terms of the differences between old and new faith, and polarities between good and evil within the early modern world. The early modern child had, through encapsulating both good and evil, and by perverting accepted social boundaries, the ability to temporarily turn the world upside-down and inside-out, but also to console, knit together and inspire. Their outlandish behaviour and perceived 'otherness' reasserted the value of good social order, and yet could also rally the faithful to new – and better – ways of living and practising faith. Having so performed, however, children returned to their rightful place, a silent world, in which we neither see nor hear any more of them. As a result, what became of these young prophets, once they resumed their normal lives, we can never know. What we can, see, however, is the extent to which they mattered to their parents, societies and cultures, their significance and not entirely subordinate role in the spiritual life of Reformation England. In the next chapter, we will turn to one of the most troubling aspects of childhood for contemporaries: the monstrous births, infant deaths and other vexed complexities that surrounded the tiniest, most innocent, and yet most spiritually vulnerable, children of all.

Chapter 6
Sin, Providence, and the Judgement of Children

We have seen that the prophetic child offered a trope or a type through which the anxieties of the age – both around children and infants specifically and salvation and damnation more broadly – could be personified and refigured. Cases of prophecy suggested God's purpose in the world, but also offered agency to those usually without it, soothing perhaps a sense of predestinarian hopelessness. As we will see in this chapter, the prophetic capacity of children could also offer evidence that justice could be similarly attained in *this* world: that infants and children could communicate God's judgements in the earthly as well as the heavenly realm, and to similarly consolatory effects.

In this chapter, then, we will consider the role of children in literature surrounding the solving of crime and the bringing about of retribution; and then we will move on to look at 'monstrous births', cases in which the children themselves bore the punishment for society's evil. As in the previous chapter, we see again evidence of beliefs that children could be used as messengers from God, or as vessels through which both godly and demonic forces could communicate with the earthly world. Hence, the cases in this chapter, as in the other chapters in this book, continue to reveal to us the cultural space that could be occupied by children in early modern culture, and in many senses, in early modern 'popular' soteriologies. For, as has been established, stories surrounding children in this period reflect early modern anxieties surrounding the changing beliefs about salvation – child salvation in particular. These tales emphasise potentially comforting beliefs, which see children occupy positions of spiritual authority, fight demons, reflect the blessings of God and right the wrongs to which they have been subjected. As will be argued here, the stories to be considered in this chapter emphasise something else perhaps more acutely than the previous possession and prophecy cases – they reveal the continuation of some beliefs and cultural tropes, such as, for example, the notion that punishments should fit the crime, in a moral sense, thus reflecting previous beliefs in Purgatory. But they also reveal to us that these familiar ideas within popular culture were being used and shaped within popular Protestantism to represent new, Protestant beliefs – they were in many senses providing a comforting salve for the potential harshness of predestinarianism. Indeed, as considered earlier, Protestant beliefs in predestination could be especially harsh on the young.

The sources in which this material is contained are popular tracts, exaggerated texts which feed on forms as diverse as fairy tales and medical treatises; they are vivid and vernacular, and offer a window into the mindsets of the period, even as they prove at times distractingly unusual. Nevertheless, it is possible to perceive in the disparate truth-telling of these children many of the qualities and causes we have already identified: openness both to virtue and to sin, and an over-riding interest in salvation, particularly since Reformed faith had brought the vulnerability of the infant soul into even greater relief. As we have seen throughout this book, age was a crucial tool and signifier that contemporaries used to understand their world; these distinct and specific instances of providential children, then, allow us relatively clear windows into that mode of perception, and offer us the opportunity to illustrate the ways in which youth was not always the least authoritative of the various social positions of the period. Indeed, it could occasionally be the most spiritually potent of all.

Crime, Retribution and Children

Narratives of child prophecy often formed part of wider literature on crime and murder, which of course covered stories of the misdemeanours and the unfortunate fates of individuals on all points of the social, age and gender spectrums.[1] The roles of children in such cases were tightly bound with ideas surrounding divine agency and retribution, with God using children to solve crimes or to bring justice upon those who had done wrong – again we see ideas about childhood innocence as a means through which to be close to divine messages or to predict and detect signs other individuals could not. Such ideas were certainly not new, and although the sources explored here contain clear elements of Protestant culture, they have traditional influences too, reflected in medieval and early modern literature, traditional beliefs about purgatory and even popular folktale, as will be explored in this chapter. As considered in the

---

[1]   A comprehensive overview of crime literature and the forms and patterns crime narratives tended to take can be found in Peter Lake, 'Deeds against Nature: Cheap Print, Protestantism and Murder in Early Seventeenth Century England', in Kevin Sharpe and Peter Lake (eds), *Culture and Politics in Early Stuart England* (Basingstoke: Macmillan, 1994) pp. 257–83.

previous chapter, although all social groups were equally represented in cases of prophecy, what is interesting in such cases is that children, the usually socially silent, were given a certain level of equality. Through these narratives we see children equally represented as potential vessels of godly messages – we see them prophesying and thus, in many senses, sermonising – or, as relevant in the narratives to be explored here, we see children solving crimes, prophesying and bringing about just resolution, retribution and punishment. Although, again, the credibility of these stories can be cast into doubt, what is most interesting is that the social space existed for children to be imagined in this way – if the cases do represent some grains of truth, they provide a wonderful opportunity to 'hear' the voices of early modern children.

Fitting punishments to sins was a favourite pastime of some Renaissance writers – most famously, the various circles of Dante's Hell shaped themselves around the infractions of those who inhabited them. The concept of the child being a vessel for God's judgement, particularly against those whose crimes involved harming children, was a long-standing one by the time of the Reformation. Indeed, Chaucer's *The Prioress's Tale*, part of *The Canterbury Tales*, reflects such beliefs. The story tells of the plight of a young child, murdered on his way to school by a Jew, and of his mother's grief upon finding her son dead. When the child was about to be buried, he miraculously and briefly returned to life, in order to bring justice upon the one who had wronged him:

> Upon this beere ay lith this innocent
> Biforn the chief auter, whil the masse laste;
> And after that, the abbot with his covent
> Han sped hem for to burien hym ful faste;
> And whan they hooly water on hym cast,
> Yet spak this child, whan spreynd was hooly water,
> And song *O Alma redemptoris mater!*[2]

The text tells of how the child could only gain peace if the murderer could be brought to justice, without it, the boy's soul would wander restlessly and would not be able to enter heaven. Such examples reveal to us the familiar nature of these ideas, and the fact that these tropes had a long history. As we will see in the cases to be explored below, this belief that children had a role in bringing wrong-doers to justice continued in both Protestant crime and prophecy literature – the notion of the innocent child as 'crime solver' was a cultural trope that stubbornly

---

[2]   Chaucer, *The Prioress's Tale*, p. 380, Fragment VII, lines 635–41.

continued in post-Reformation culture – familiar ideas then, in which the message was slightly different. In the Protestant cases to be explored the children generally are not dead, but they nevertheless seek the punishment of those that have wronged them, or who have committed crimes, in order to bring about a just resolution. We see children using their innocence, and their receptiveness to godly messages, to accuse murderers, to witness bodily or physical 'miracles' (sudden speech when it was not previously physically possible for example) or even cases in which the very birth of a baby was in itself a message to onlookers to repent, and to amend their ways.

Within Catholic, pre-Reformation cases, such solutions often involved the spirit of the dead child returning to right the wrong to which they had been subjected, or even attempting to get revenge. Folklore told stories about the souls of unbaptised infants returning as butterflies or moths, birds at dusk, or restlessly wandering the skies as will-o-the-wisps, fairies or pixies. These malicious spirits were believed to be ill-omened and dangerous to travellers.[3] Unbaptised babies, it was believed, would return to punish their mothers, and they were believed to be heard screaming near the place where they died. Some of the Breton Ballads tell of a mother who bore seven babies to her own father; she killed each of them in secret, without baptising them, before hiding their bodies in various confined places – usually under the floor or in a wall. One day she found a priest in order to confess her crimes. In form of penance, he told her to spend seven years, one for each child, locked in a chest. During this time the ghosts of her dead children returned to her as piglets, tearing her to pieces, drawing as much blood as the water that would have been needed to baptise them. According to the tale the mother dies, but through her penance gains salvation for each child and for herself.[4]

Here we see again, of course, the concept that the punishment should fit the crime – but also that the souls of the aggrieved were not without avenues of retribution. Such stories, or morality tales, helped societies to explain, justify and understand the plights of young souls snatched before their time. They served as warnings to parents who might consider doing wrong by their children. They also provided comfort in the other direction, by assuring listeners that child spirits could gain salvation and recognition despite their fleeting time on earth. Protestant culture, however, taught that ghosts or miracles such as returning from the dead (as in the case of *The Prioress's Tale*) were impossible. Nevertheless, despite and because of this shift in what was seen to

---

3   Simpson, 'The Folklore of Infant Deaths: Burials, Ghosts and Changelings', p. 15.
4   Simpson, 'The Folklore of Infant Deaths: Burials, Ghosts and Changelings', p. 16.

be acceptable, Protestant popular culture found alternative ways to deal with crimes and wrongs committed against children – crime literature and stories in which justice was sought for child victims was one of these ways. By doing so, these narratives again placed children in a protected space – reflecting, and yet ordering, contemporary anxieties surrounding the spiritual status of the young.

All of these urges – to explain, to console, to punish – are visible in the curious sub-genre of the early modern child detective. The murder pamphlet was a common genre between 1580 and 1640. They were usually hastily written, short and gruesome in detail – the unpleasant and disgusting designed to shock, both to entertain and often to reassert correct order by providing a glimpse of the alternative chaos. Crime literature is a difficult genre to consider, as it served a multitude of purposes. Like previous texts considered in this work, it may or may not have been related in some way to true events. It was designed to be dramatic, to simplify the division between good and evil. It had simplistic stock characters representing good and evil, in order to entertain. As Peter Lake has written, such pamphlets served four main purposes: to titillate and entertain; to correct and strengthen ideas about social order by *inverting* them with captivating stories; to explore ideas about the Devil, and to consider and reflect notions of providence and divine justice. That is, quite aside from the reality of their cases, the drivers of these stories – their assumptions and underlying structures – reflect, relate and amplify the mindsets of their writers and readers.

Whether or not such literature was written with religious intention, however, seems to have confused early modern historians. Tessa Watt, for example, chose not to include murder pamphlets in her work on cheap print and religion in the sixteenth and seventeenth centuries.[5] Yet, Keith Thomas has identified a level of Protestant, or even Puritan, beliefs within such literature.[6] Here, it will likewise be argued that such crime literature could contain a strong religious message, mostly involving ideas of divine providence – of the action and agency of God's will in the world. Indeed, as Lake argues, such literature was often dualistic, representing a battle between God and the Devil. As he writes:

> For over against the forces of sin and the devil was ranged the awesome power
> of divine providence. As it was described in the pamphlets, the resulting struggle

---

[5]   Tessa Watt, *Cheap Print and Popular Piety, 1500–1640* (Cambridge: Cambridge University Press, 1991).

[6]   For works on crime, see Peter Lake, 'Deeds against Nature: Cheap Print, Protestantism and Murder in Early Seventeenth Century England', pp. 257–83; James Sharpe, *Crime in Early Modern England, 1550–1750* (London: Longman, 1984); Thomas, *Religion and the Decline of Magic*, chapters 3 and 4.

amounted to a species of pseudo-Manichaeanism – a view of the world stretched tight between God and the devil, with the room for human agency left between them constricted and confined at times almost to nothing.[7]

That is, the conventions of the murder pamphlet created an exaggerated space in which God's judgement – and the role of selected children in enacting it – can be seen in particularly sharp relief. One early seventeenth-century pamphlet records the plight of a young girl and her brother in Hertford during the year 1605. The text, entitled *The Horrible Murther of a young boy of three yeres of age*, tells of how an elderly woman called Mother Dell and her adult son kidnapped two smartly dressed children. The girl was aged about four, the boy 'not three yeares of age'. The children were noticed by a local tailor, due to their unusual clothing. Mother Dell and her son murdered the young boy in front of his sister; they then brutally cut out the girl's tongue, before supposedly leaving her in a hollowed tree trunk. The girl was left for dead, yet she survived due to godly providence. God, who had:

> ... preserued Daniel in the Lions den, and made the blinde to see, the lame to goe, and the dumbe to speake, did not onely preserue the life of this childe, but also did giue vnto her an extraordinarie strength and vigor, whereby she was able, and did make such a noyse ... that a man heard her ... he pulled her out of the tree.[8]

However, the passer-by took fright at her bloody appearance, and ran away. The text then tells of how the child wandered for four years, begging for food, unable to speak or to explain how she had been injured. Yet:

> ... the Lord who had reserued her, both to bring so monstrous a murder, and cruell a massacre to light, and also to make manifest his almightie power to many misbeleeuing and vnbeleeuing miscreants ... he, I say; as may most euidently appeare, did both preserue her, and prouide for her.[9]

As the text tells, God had greater purposes for the young girl, and the case was not to remain unsolved. Indeed, he made it so the girl returned to Hertford.

---

[7]   Lake, 'Deeds against Nature: Cheap Print, Protestantism and Murder in Early Seventeenth Century England', p. 270.

[8]   Anon, *The Horrible Murther of a young boy of three yeres of age, whose sister had her tongue cut out: and how it pleased God to reveale the offenders, by giving speech to the tongueles Childe* (London, 1606) *STC* (2nd edn) 6552, pp. 1–5.

[9]   Anon, *The Horrible Murther of a young boy of three yeres of age*, pp. 1–5.

At first, she wandered the streets, unaware of the town's significance. Then, she discovered the house of Mother Dell, at which moment she supposedly began screaming, attracting the attention of local onlookers, including the tailor who had spotted the two children four years earlier. Mother Dell and her son were put into jail, suspected of their involvement in the disappearance of the children. Meanwhile, the young girl grew physically stronger in the care of the local community, eating good food and enjoying the company of other children. It was then that her 'mightie miracle' occurred. As the text reads, 'But now (Gentle Reader) let mee intreate thee as thou readst, not onelye to admyre and wonder, but to prayse & magniffie the mightie maker and preseruer of vs all, for his great mercy and might shewed to this poore childe, in this next succeeding action ... .'

The child had been playing in a yard with other children, when a cock began to crow, 'like as a bird of the same name and nature, vsing the selfe same note, [that] put Peter in minde that hee had denied his maister, from which his remembrance sprung his true and heartie repentance'. The playing children began to imitate the bird, when the speechless girl joined them, singing 'coke-adoodle doo'. From this point on the girl was able to speak 'so plainly that they all vnderstoode her'. The child was then asked who had cut out her tongue and killed her brother, to which the girl could answer. The child was brought to court in the August of 1606, at which case the jury sentenced Mother Dell and her son to death.[10] Through this story the young girl was able, through godly providence, to gain some justice for both herself and her brother – although there was a more pragmatic course to justice that other cases of prophecy we have seen (involving returning from the dead, for example), as in this case, the perpetrators of individual crimes are brought to trial. Hence, in the prophecy cases we have been considering, we see children defending their innocence and purity, and gaining justice against those who had wronged them – thus restoring social order and bringing about a just resolution. It was perhaps a case, then, of justice restored in *this* life, rather than, as in traditional tales, of influencing the soteriological destination of the soul, which would have flown in the face of Protestant predestinarianism a little too awkwardly, thus reflecting Protestant beliefs, and the notion that traditional cultural tropes could be pulled apart, altered and re-shaped to communicate new ideas.

There was clearly an appetite for this particular kind of working-out of the dilemmas of Protestant soteriology: traditional forms were being used to push forward and to make more palatable new ideas. This was especially true during

---

[10] Anon, *The Horrible Murther of a young boy of three yeres of age*, pp. 5–9.

especially sensitive aspects of the life-course, such as childhood. Interestingly, the same case was published in a further tract in 1606, this time entitled *The most cruell and bloody murther committed by an Inkeepers wife*. As the title suggests, in this version 'Mother' or Annis Dell, was not a widow. In this more gruesome case, female thief Annis Dell and her son kidnapped an entire family. Despite the pleas of the father, Dell murdered the pregnant mother and the brother, before cutting out the tongue of the girl. The tract places the story of the murdered boy and his abused sister firmly in the context of godly providence – a doctrine that helped to make sense of a world in which chance and disaster could wreak havoc:

> This Historie then so liuely expressing the mortalitie of mans life, that to the highest belongs a graue, assoone as the lowest, and that man himselfe is a witnesse to himselfe, how vncertaine are his daies ... that a Spider is able to choake vs, a haire to stifle vs, and a tile falling on our heads to extinguish vs, and in that moment when we least expect so sudden Calamities.[11]

In the face of such uncontrollable calamity, however, God's hand could often be seen, etching celestial purpose onto what would otherwise be the inexplicable twists of fate: 'but in ye meane time such as is the iust iudgment of God, to the plague of murtherers, and terror of them that delight in bad, the dumbe shall speake ere they escape vndiscouered'.[12]

As in the previous version, the girl, here named Elizabeth, miraculously overcame her physical impairments to regain the power of speech, here striving vigorously and courageously against those who had wronged her and her innocent sibling. She gave evidence 'as boldly in accusing, as wonderfull in speaking' saying that 'since God had lent her a speech by miracle, shee would with that inspired breath follow the law of them, & haue their bloods lawfully, who stole away her brother'.[13] Of further interest is the dualistic language used to describe the child victims and their attackers. The children are 'faire', 'little ones', 'poore', 'innocent'; whereas, by contrast, the murders are 'villaines', 'wretches' and 'monstrous'. Furthermore, it is Mother Dell, not her son, who was seen as the worst offender in this crime; Mother Dell the 'whore', 'beast', 'monstrous female' and 'strumpet'. This reveals something about gender roles. It was far more of an inversion against the laws of nature and of morality for a woman to wrong a

---

[11]   Anon, *The most Cruell and Bloody Murther committed by an Inkeepers wife, called Annis Dell, and her sonne George Dell* (1606), sig. A2r.

[12]   Anon, *The most Cruell and Bloody Murther committed by an Inkeepers wife*, sig. B3v.

[13]   Anon, *The most Cruell and Bloody Murther committed by an Inkeepers wife*, sig. C1v– C2r.

child. Women, by nature, should, it was believed, be nurturing and protective towards the young and innocent. Such texts speak of fears surrounding women who had broken away from the binds of patriarchy – the stories, through the use of drama and inversion, speak of the dangers surrounding women who did not stick to such systems of obedience and motherhood. The case also, as do the other examples considered, emphasises the ongoing anxiety about child salvation, and this intermeshing of new Protestant and traditional beliefs.

This case was not unusual, either in its gritty violence or consolatory aspect. A further case in which a child stands for truth and justice, although less miraculous and more pragmatic in emphasis, is told in the 1595 publication *A most horrible & detestable murther committed by a bloudie minded man vpon his ovvne vvife and most strangely reuealed by his childe that was vnder fiue yeeres of age*. This short pamphlet tells of how a man from the county of Sussex murdered his wife one evening, while his young son was in bed. The man attempted to hide his crime by burning down the family's house, while the boy Ralph was still inside. Neighbours, hearing the child's cries, rescued the boy and discovered his mother's body. The child then 'called after the name of his father brought before them, and required to tell when his father came home'. The boy, 'without any blushing feare (as commonly is seene in children) tolde them that his father came home when his mother was a bed, and first vsed some churlish speech vnto hir, then he drew out his knife, cut hir throate and so left hir: describing in good order the bignes of the knife ...'.[14] This is a different kind of agency or authority to the child prophets of the previous chapter: the boy in this tale is not imparting secret knowledge obtained directly from God; rather, he is speaking a virtuous truth derived from events he had witnessed, and about which it had been assumed he would remain silent. If the boy is not quite a classical prophet, then, we might still perceive in him the virtue of honesty, and the purity of intention, that can characterise the divinely inspired words of that figure.

Certainly, the text perceives him as a virtuous actor. Here again, we see a young child bringing about order and resolution, and solving a 'bloody' crime within early modern murder and prophecy tales. These tales reveal the fear of inversion: inversions which included adults harming the innocent, when it was seen to be the duty of elders to care for those younger and more vulnerable.

---

[14] Anon, *A most horrible & detestable murther committed by a bloudie minded man vpon his ovvne vvife and most strangely reuealed by his childe that was vnder fiue yeeres of age* (London, 1595) *STC* (2nd edition) 17748, sig. A3v.

Such stories clearly had an audience and a relevant place within early modern popular culture, and more significant to our purpose, they tell us much about early modern childhood. Again, as has been mentioned, they reveal a keen and at times desperate desire to make sense of the world, and also to resolve uncertainties and heal disorder. As a result, the tales gave children a voice and a place within a society in which they were vulnerable for a whole host of reasons, be they biological, spiritual or social. As in the narratives themselves, in these tracts and pamphlets children are marshalled to respond to that which immediately concerns them: a survivor of an attempt at murder can claim her revenge, so a child prophet can resolve the thorny questions of child salvation that so vexed contemporaries. Perhaps the murder ballads, with their easy, dualistic form and almost fairytale logic, offer the starkest – if most simplistic – example of how early modern culture attempted to square these soteriological circles.

As Marina Warner has considered in her work on fairytales, the hunger for fairytales, particularly within pre-modern societies, can seem to 'offer the possibility of change, for beyond the boundaries of their improbable plots ... these sudden swerves of destiny, created the first sustaining excitement of such stories'. Hence, fairytales could 'remake the world in the image of desire'; they helped people to view the world how they would like it to be, and to write out evil and misfortune. The wonders of such tales are that, although bad things occur – such as violence, and death – they are later healed and restored to life or good health. Hence, within such marvels and prodigies there is a basic disregard for logic, tales come to an orderly conclusion and the characters seem to return to their normal lives.[15] Such characteristics can be seen in the texts discussed here, from *The Prioress's Tale* through to the later, early modern popular texts. The tales are pious and they aim to inspire devotional feelings within readers. Indeed, the texts verge on hagiography in terms of style. They have innocents who are impossibly good, 'young', 'tender', little', and villains who are impossibly bad, uncomplicated and evil. This might not hold much of the reality of contemporaries' lives – but it speaks at volume about the intense concerns contemporaries had about children, and their need to find ways to empower them against the sin and damnation to which they were uniquely vulnerable. More complex, but no less rooted in this vulnerability to bodily and spiritual assault, were the cases of the youngest possible of children who physically, rather than verbally, attested to God's judgement on earth: the 'monstrous births'.

---

[15]   See Marina Warner, *From the Beast to the Blonde* (London: Chatto and Windus, 1994).

A 'Looking Glasse' for Sin: Monstrous Births and Providential Omens

... every man may let this fearefull monster or token of God, be unto him a looking glasse, whereby to amend his life, and repent.[16]

Cases of childhood prophecy and notions of justice secured by the young were not restricted to older children, who with their power of speech were able to shape or take active part within such narratives. A further genre of popular prophecy was centred upon the role of newly born infants, or to use early modern terminology, 'monstrous births'. Alexandra Walsham's work on providence in early modern England has considered the idea that 'morality and embryology' could be readily interlocked within the early modern mindset. A mindset in which 'God sometimes encoded a particular message in the contorted limbs and tumorous growths of these unfortunate infants, projecting onto their diminutive bodies a silhouette of the sins which had infested the body politic'; furthermore, Walsham argues, commentaries on such spectacles drove early modern moralists to externalise 'their own prejudices and obsessions'.[17]

The mysteries surrounding childbirth, with its understandable precariousness, as well as the emphasis on the importance of childbirth for the continuity of Christendom, understandably led contemporaries to believe that children were gifts from God. The birth of a healthy baby within a family was seen to be a blessing, whereas the reverse situation – struggles with conception, with bringing a pregnancy full-term or failing to give birth to a healthy child – were often viewed by many as potential punishments, especially by those of a 'godly' disposition.[18] Within such a scheme of beliefs, children who were born not sickly, but instead as, according to texts reporting the cases, unseeingly monstrous and not even human, were viewed as a terrible sign that something was seriously wrong. Children born ugly and deformed were interpreted not just as a correcting punishment from God, but as a direct indication or warning of God's anger, or even, more threateningly, as a sign from Satan. Such providential signs fitted two main groups. Firstly, these children, it was believed, could be sent, in a macroscopic sense, as a warning of social evils – as a punishment for society at large. Secondly, monstrous births could be viewed in a microscopic sense: as a direct and personal punishment for the sins of particular parents.

---

[16]   Anon, *Gods handy-vvorke in vvonders miraculously shewen vpon two women, lately deliuered of two monsters* (London, 1615) *STC* 11926, sig. A5v.

[17]   Walsham, *Providence in Early Modern England*, pp. 194–5.

[18]   For a comprehensive overview of early modern perceptions of childbirth, see especially David Cressy, *Birth, Marriage and Death*, especially pp. 16–21.

Within this chapter such signs of divine wrath will be dealt with separately, due to their significant and differing implications.

Indeed, when 'monsters' were born as a symbol of God's anger towards the social evils of mankind, they were regarded, however unsightly the spectacle, as a direct message from the hands of God. Such signs of godly providence were indications of God's 'fatherly affection, shewed unto us Christians, in that he forewarneth us to flie from the wrath to come'.[19] Whilst God's anger was directly impressed on to these sorry infants, they were providing Christian society with the warnings needed to 'speedily repent', or 'tokens of his wrath to forewarne thee'.[20] Thus, they were to be read as warnings, rather than punishments necessarily – they were seen as a window through which early modern society might be able to catch a glimpse of the sins they had committed, and more pertinently, to perceive what God thought of such sinful behaviour. So again, we see various strands of beliefs expressed through such cases. We have in these cases, as seen in the previous stories we have considered, an illustration of early modern beliefs in providence and prophecy, and we also have evidence of further cases in which children echo God's purpose, or in which their tender bodies and small voices (for, as we will see, these monstrous babies were sometimes prone to giving lengthy speeches) are used by God, or by spiritual forces, to speak to society on earth. Indeed, like the young and possessed and the young prophets, these babies were again physical manifestations of messages from the spiritual world – and of the perceived 'openness' and receptiveness of the young. Simultaneously, these cases also provide further examples of stories which reflect the tensions which existed around infants and young children – infancy was a very vulnerable stage, as has been established – and one cannot help to perceive in the tales of the monstrous babies traces of anxiety surrounding childbirth and infancy, especially when the tender aspects of these lifecycle events went wrong.

However, the birth of a monstrous infant could also be taken as a direct punishment when parents had sinned against God. The notion that God would directly indicate his wrath upon particular individuals, striking the womb of the mother in order to snatch any worldly joy or pleasure, was a particularly harsh one, with little room for images of future forgiveness. Such a fact seems to have

---

[19]   Anon, *Gods handy-vvorke in vvonders*, sig. A2r.

[20]   Anon, *Gods handy-vvorke in vvonders*, sig. A2r; and, Anon, *A true relation of the birth of three monsters in the city of Namen n. Flanders, as also Gods judgement vpon an vnnaturall sister of the poore womans, mother of these abortiue children* (London, 1609) *STC* 18347.5, sigs. A3r–v. For similar cases of monstrous birth and godly providence see also John Barker, *The true description of a monsterous chylde, borne in the Ile of Wight* (London, 1564) *STC* (2nd ed.) 1422.

been reflected by both the treatment of the parents, and subsequently the child, after the occurrence of such a birth. Those who bore 'providential omens' became the focus of much social amazement, much like the possessed and prophetic children we have already encountered, and the stories of such infants were put to press with suitably moralistic prayers and 'messages to the reader'. The children themselves were regarded with much curiosity; commentators detailed the exact span of their lives, often noting that the infants had passed away peacefully, usually after they had been baptised (which is in itself most interesting).[21] The lives of these babies were pitiful; their fleeting time on earth and untimely deaths became undignified moments which attracted amazement, again evidencing the appetite for texts of this sort, and the clear cultural space that existed for the notion of the prophesying child. Yet, reports of such children were not as grim as those who were believed to born as a direct result of parental sin.

Turning to the cases themselves, we will first consider the popular literature that interpreted unusual births as signs or indications of God's displeasure towards mankind, the accumulative sin of society, turning next to the theme of individual punishment. In almost all of such reported cases, the child's peculiar disfigurement was directly related to the particular cause of God's displeasure, in a sense the punishment was designed to fit the crime – very much like the cases of children and crime considered above. One case of twins, born in Kent, was said to reveal God's anger concerning the 'great Decay of harty love and charytie'. It was said that the case of the infants, joined at the face, 'one as it were imbrasynge the other', reflected mankind's 'faulse Dyssemblynge'.[22] In another similar case, a child born with 'ruffes' about the neck, which was said to indicate God's anger at the vain and sumptuous fashions of the age – a message remarkably similar to the story of the '*daughter of an honest countrey man*' considered in the previous chapter. This particular pamphlet warned the women of England:

> in ruffes do walke to oft:
> Perswade them stil to bere in minde,
> this childe with ruffes so soft.[23]

---

[21] See especially Anon, *The true description of two monsterous chyldren borne at Herne in Kent*, which noted that 'They were booth women chyldren and chrystened, and lyued halfe a daye. The one departed afore the other almoste an houre' (London, 1565) *STC* (2nd ed.) 6774, one sheet.

[22] Anon, *The true description of two monstrous chyldren borne at Herne in Kent*, one sheet.

[23] H.B., *The true discripcion of a childe with ruffes borne in the parish of Micheham in the cou[n]tie of surrey* (London, 1566) *STC* 1033, one sheet.

The connection between unusual births and criticisms of fashion, most usually female fashion, was a common one.[24] One tract fittingly entitled *God's handy-work in wonders*, argued that monstrous births were 'mockeries of their pride that boast of their purple and rich cloathing, when an arme from heaven can strike them in a moment'.[25]

Such providential 'stories' reveal aspects of Protestant belief similar, in their soteriological function at least, to those belonging to traditional Catholicism. The notion that God's wrath was projected onto an infant's body, as a punishment directly mirroring a particular crime, reflects similar perceptions to Catholic beliefs in Purgatory. Indeed, the images of Purgatory portrayed in Eamon Duffy's *Stripping of the Altars*, in which the souls of sinners are graphically depicted to be undergoing tangible and physical punishments, punishments to befit the crimes committed, bear similarities to the images of these deformed babies. In Purgatory, in the words of Duffy, 'the proud are brought low by the burden of immense rocks on their shoulders, the gluttonous waste away from famine, the avaricious are pinioned to the earth by their longings for the things of earth'.[26] Similarly, the limbs of the infants were seen to be directly twisted, as both a punishment of and warning against worldly sin. Babies were born with ruffles and frills, in 'lustful' embraces. Most significantly, the importance of both Purgatory and these providential warnings was to provide spiritual hope and a means towards salvation.[27]

The belief that prophetic children were born to punish the sin of an immoral society, a microscopic representation of macroscopic issues, was far from the complete picture. Such providential omens were part of an entire genre concerning elements of nature, seemingly twisted and corrupted by God's angry fingers. Contemporary literature was saturated with tales of unusual animals, deformed birds, frightening fish left on beaches by low tides, trees creaking with sighs of woe.[28] Stories of infants, and their relation to the human condition as well as apocalyptic fervour were frequent; popular superstition combined with Protestant perceptions of godly omnipotence to help form such providential beliefs. Providential tales were a legitimate and orthodox part of Protestantism.

---

[24]   See also the anonymous ballad, *the true reporte of the forme and shape of a monstrous childe, borne at Muche Horkesleye a village about three myles from Colchester, in the countie of Essex* (London, 1562) *STC* 12207, one sheet.

[25]   Anon, *Gods handy-vvorke in vvonders*, sig. A3r.

[26]   Duffy, *The Stripping of the Altars*, p. 344.

[27]   For Duffy's descriptions of pre-Reformation beliefs in Purgatory, see Duffy, *The Stripping of the Altars*, pp. 338–78, especially pictorial images numbers 127, 128.

[28]   See in particular, Walsham, *Providence in Early Modern England*, pp. 167–224.

Indeed, the word 'providence' was clearly in common usage, as one contemporary commented: 'most manifest it is therefore ... that whatsoever hath bene, is, or shall be to proceede, either Celestial or Terrestriall, can not be without the fore-ordinance and providence of God'.[29] It was perhaps true that traditional Catholic beliefs persisted, reinterpreted into the particularities of the Protestant faith – traditional superstition remoulded. Indeed, in addition to the dressing-up of old belief in new dress that has been described by Walsham, there is also in all this the reverse: new beliefs in old dress, traditional narratives and their structures being employed to assess and interrogate the difficulties posed by Reformed belief. With Purgatory gone, but children still vulnerable both physically and spiritually, the stories of monstrous births – like the other examples of youthful spiritual agency this book considers – offered contemporaries a familiar toolkit with which to reorient their children's suddenly shifted soteriological states. Children and infants could be messengers from God, could be His agents and, conversely, carriers of sin – and therefore not so passive as Reformed liturgies might have at first suggested. We see in these stories not just a survival of cultural tropes or forms but a working-out of new ones.

Indeed, the visions of such infants were embraced into popular Protestant beliefs and culture. The short lifetimes of such children were not without purpose or a sense of awe and respect. The messages of godly providence they delivered, many pamphlets urged, should be heeded and acted upon: 'The monsterous and unnaturall wayes of these chyldren and Dyvers lyke brought foorth in our dayes ... [are] not onelye for us to gase and wonder at, as things happenyng either by chaunce, or els by naturall reason'; society should *not* 'judge god onely offended wyth the parentes of the same, for some notoryous vyce or offence reygning alone in them', but rather should heed the warning as 'lessons & scholynges for us all ... who dayly offende as grevously as they do; wherby god almyghtye of hys greate mercy and longe sufferaunce admonysheth us by them to amendmente of our lyves'.[30] Such children were sent as an 'ensample to us of the great wrath of GOD, because of our manifold and great sinnes, which now a dayes in every place doth beare sway, as cursing, swearing, Blaspheming of God, whoredome, Drunkenesse of the like'.[31] Hence, these children offered contemporary society the chance of redemption and forgiveness – in other

---

[29] Stephen Bateman, *The doome warning all men to the iudgemente wherein are contayned for the most parte all the straunge prodigies hapned in the worlde* (London, 1581) STC (2nd ed.) 1582, Dedication, sig. ¶ ii r–v.

[30] Anon, *The true description of two monstrous chyldren borne at Herne in Kent*, one sheet.

[31] Anon, *Gods handy-vvorke in vvonders*, sig. A5v.

words, of agency amidst what at face value could have otherwise seemed an unforgiving theology of salvation.

Monstrous births literally embodied this process of working-out. For instance the term 'out of the mouths of babes and sucklings', applies acutely to one, naturally impossible, case reported from Flanders. The tale provides something of an unrivalled example of the belief that infants and children, due to their innocent or spiritually uncomplicated state, could be more receptive to the will of God, and thus capable of foretelling mystical prophecies. According to the Flanders report, one devout and humble woman had given birth to three unusually proportioned infants, one son and two daughters. Not only were the bodies of these children literally 'read' for signs of prophecy, they also spoke words of godly warning. The first child to be born, a daughter, 'that had such dressings, and attyre on the head, by the nature of flesh, as women haue made by art of Bonelaces ... cryed with a shrill voyce' the words 'thou Creator, that gauest me this forme & life, let me not liue here in this world of Pride, of Lust, of Murther, and all wickednesse: returne me suddenly to what I was: for here (I know) is nothing but calamity'. After this fairly miraculous account, the child immediately died.[32] The second child, a son, was born with 'a strange misshapen head, hauing upon the backe of his right hand, the fashion of a deaths head: And this child sayd, that Dearth and Plague should couer the whole World, and that they were sent to giue notice of it to all men'. After his pronouncement, 'speach and life left him together'.[33] The last of the triplets to be born, a daughter, also spoke words of wisdom, in something of a grand finale to the entire providential message. She was born 'hauing about the necke, a Ruffe laced, and cuffes about the wrests, like the Ruffe, all of flesh, so artificiall in nature, as if nature in her first work had intreated Art to help her'. This child said 'that God would punish the world suddenly, for our manifold transgressions: and sayd moreover, that they three were sent to forewarne us of the Lords coming; and then straight dyed'.[34] Out of the mouths of babes indeed. The deformed bodies of such children were thus taken to be an indication of things to come; of plague, death and punishment – to affect a vain, fashion conscious society – and a forewarning of the impending Apocalypse and final day of judgement. Hence, a true indication as to the ominous and prophetic status a young child could receive in Protestant England. Furthermore, we can again see how Protestant providentialism and

---

[32]   Anon, *A true relation of the birth of three monsters in the city of Namen n. Flanders*, sigs A4v–Br.

[33]   Anon, *A true relation of the birth of three monsters in the city of Namen n. Flanders*, sig. Br.

[34]   Anon, *A true relation of the birth of three monsters in the city of Namen n. Flanders*, sig. Br.

English popular culture actively embraced and continued ideas which Reformed theologians rejected as relics of superstition and popery.

Such signs were to be revered as a true indication of God's displeasure and purpose. As in the contrast between demoniac and prophet, these unsightly spectacles revealed godly purpose in less than perfect children. The suggestion that such occurrences were due to natural factors, as some 'biological' tracts published throughout Europe were beginning to claim, was to undermine God and the purpose of his nature.[35] Indeed, some tracts attempted to suggest earthly causes for such births. Ambrose Paré's *The workes of that famous chirurgion Ambrose Parey*, for example, contained four pictures of devilish creatures women had supposedly given birth to. It argued that 'monstrous creatures ... of sundry forms are ... generated in the wombs of women ... [such] as frogs, toads, serpents, lizzards'. This was blamed on physical factors, such as a bad diet, or even the wrong amount of food: 'For it happened whilest they fed on fruits, weeds and trash, and such things as were of ill juice, they generated a putride matter ... and consequently opportune to generate such unperfect creatures'.[36] The tract details the contrasting examples of two Italian women, one rich and the other poor; 'that in one moneth brought forth each of them a monstrous birth'. The poor woman, the wife of a tailor, 'brought forth a thing so little, that it resembled a Rat without a taile; but the other a Gentlewoman, brought forth a larger, for it was of the bignesse of a cat; both of them were black', and as soon as they were born they 'ran up high on the wall, and held fast thereon with their nailes'. Other physical factors blamed for such monstrous births were centred upon the fact that women's bodies were naturally weak and 'certainely very subject to putrefaction and corruption, and consequently opportune to generate such unperfect creatures'.[37]

However, such physical or natural explanations were hotly disputed by authors of providential works. As one early seventeenth-century tract entitled *God's handy-work in wonders* argued, prodigious births were not:

> ... simple or meere mistakings in God as if like a bungler in some common trade ...
> no, hee receiueth no lesse honour from the shape of a Monster, than from the
> rarest piece of beautie, that euer was out of the earth; no, we are all but one piece

---

[35] The notion that monstrous births could be due to natural circumstances perhaps softened the belief that God would deliberately subject ignorant or sinful parents to the harsh punishment of an unwell child.

[36] Ambroise Paré, *The workes of that famous chirurgion Ambrose Parey translated out of Latine and compared with the French* (London, 1643) STC (2nd ed.) 19189, p. 763.

[37] Ambroise Paré, *The workes of that famous chirurgion Ambrose Parey*, p. 763.

of clay, and as the Potter pleases, so are the vessels made, some to the base vses, and others to noble.[38]

Each individual was made for a purpose. God was responsible for all of his creation, and even those elements which were hideous to the eye were sculpted by God for his ultimate purpose:

> If God had from the beginning of the world made all creatures beautifull, and in their perfect shape, his glory had not bin so great: but as white sets off blacke, so these contrary colours in the creation of man, sometimes fayre, sometimes deformed, express the skill, power, and omnipotency of the great Master, in whose hand it lyes to make a Begger, or a king, a beautifull body, or a monstrous, and to fashion thee or me as ugly, as that wretched shape.[39]

The second form of monstrous birth cases was, as mentioned above, those that blamed the children's deformities on the sins of the parents themselves. Indeed, in the words of one contemporary, 'to punish the sinnes of some particular parents, God from time to time striketh the womb of the mother, and doubleth his curse, not onely in making her to bring forth with pain ... but to bee delivered with fearefull and horrid shapes, to astonish the beholders, and affright the sinfull breeders'.[40] There existed a fairly developed strand of opinion that argued that ungodly parents could be directly punished by receiving the shameful spectacle of a deformed child. As one anonymous commentator harshly noted, 'wormes [are] bred out of our owne corruption; and to punish the sinnes of some particular parents'.[41] Furthermore, 'what man (unlesse the hammers of hell continually beat vpon his heart to harden it) being a father to a son or daughter so blasted in the natiuity, but would at sight of such a horror fall downe and die with sorrow'. Indeed, such a father would continually 'curse' himself, 'that euer his sinnes were so blacke and monstrous' to move God to such extreme wrath. The worst scenario was if such a child would grow into youth and adulthood, as the tract cruelly questioned, 'say such a childe should live to call him father, how vnpleasing were the sound? The very name of *this is my sonne*, should presently strike him cold to the heart, with, *this is my shame*; or rather, *this is my sinne*'.[42] The connection between God's vengeance upon cruel or sinful

---

38   Anon, *Gods handy-vvorke in vvonders*, sig. A3r.
39   Anon, *Gods handy-vvorke in vvonders*, sig. A3r.
40   Anon, *Gods handy-vvorke in vvonders*, sig. A3v.
41   Anon, *Gods handy-vvorke in vvonders*, sig. A3v.
42   Anon, *Gods handy-vvorke in vvonders*, sig. A3v.

parents, and the disfigurement of a child was seemingly well established: 'Gods owne fingers shall crush the loynes in the wombe, and set his markes of fearefull diuine vengeance, on the brest of an vnborne Babe, to turne it into a Monster ... a revenge and punishment for some extraordinary sinnes in the Parents'.[43]

In cases where the sin of individual parents was held responsible for the deformed state of the monstrous children, the style of writing was substantially different in tone. Rather than being a sign of providential wonder, for which contemporary commentators thanked God, both child and parents were instead regarded with suspicion and contempt. The vices of the parents were listed and pored over, in a warning to others. Furthermore, the child was granted little status, regarded more as an animal than a human. Indeed, in such cases, the humanity of the infant was often disguised; pictures of animalistic shapes or small demons visualised descriptions of hideous monsters that bore little resemblance to human infants. In one such case reported from America, John Winthrop, governor of the Massachusetts Bay Colony in the 1630s and '40s, told of the story of the alleged heretics, also suspected of witchcraft, Anne Hutchinson and Mary Dier. The unfortunate Anne Hutchinson was said to have laboured with 'thirty monstrous births or thereabouts, at once; some of them bigger, some lesser, few of any perfect shape, none at all of them ... of humane shape'.[44]

Perhaps here more than elsewhere we perceive the gerontocratic assumptions which were otherwise undermined by cases of spiritually potent youth: the babies were seen to be mere adjuncts to their parents' spiritual experience. Mary Dier's births were, similarly, of little resemblance to usual human form: 'mistris Dier brought forth her birth of a woman child, a fish, a beast, and a foule, all woven together in one, and without a head'.[45] It was argued that their sin was reflected in such judgements: 'how the wisdom of God fitted this judgement to her sin in every way, for look as she had vented misshapen opinions, so she must bring forth deformed monsters'.[46] Hence, this was seen to be a direct and immediate punishment from God: 'Then God was pleased to step in with his casting voice, and bring his owne vote and suffrage from heaven', as 'clearly as if he had pointed with his finger'.[47]

---

[43] Anon, *Gods handy-vvorke in vvonders*, sig. A3v–A4r.

[44] John Winthrop, *A short story of the rise, reign, and ruine of the 'Antinomians', Familists and Libertines, that infected the Churches of Nevv England* (Cambridge, 1644) *Wing* (2nd ed.) 3095, Preface.

[45] Winthrop, *A short story*, Preface.

[46] Winthrop, *A short story*, Preface.

[47] Winthrop, *A short story*, Preface.

Such representations of God's pure wrath were dehumanised. They were often denied a natural death or baptismal blessing, but were instead killed by shocked onlookers. Indeed, such an incident was reported, in various chronicles detailing 'straunge prodigies' for a doom-thirsty audience, to have occurred in Holland. One unfortunate woman had supposedly given birth to a devilish creature, reported to have had 'a roughe bodie hairie and blacke ... two feet like peacocks, [eyes which] shined like fire and were very great ... a tayle like an oxe, tow bending hornes of his heade, in stead of handes, clawes like a hawke'.[48] This monstrous birth, dehumanised by both onlookers and author through descriptions of its animalistic features, was deserving of none of the usual rituals associated with birth, and was thus subject to an untimely death. As the chronicle states, 'not long after it was delivered, but sodainely the monster ranne under the bed ... to the great feare of manye among them it was smothered to deathe betweene two beddes'. In another reported case, a woman from Flanders gave birth to a monster

> with a crooked nose, a long round necke, terrible eies, a sharpe taile, and wonderfull quick of the feet. As soone as it came into the light it filled the whole room with a noise and hissing, running to every side to finde out a lurking hole wherein to hide its head, but the women which were present, with a joynt consent fell upon it, and smothered it.[49]

Such deaths were presented as natural and justified – and amounted to little more than the literal quashing of sin. Potentially, we could attribute such behaviour to cases of infanticide, or to early modern attempts to understand abnormal births or miscarriage.[50] These monstrous births were viewed as, in the words of one commentator, 'moales in nature ... sticking on her cheeke to disgrace her'.[51]

Monstrous birth narratives also absorbed some fairly theologically problematic concepts, including that of the self-fulfilling oath. One tale, recounted on numerous occasions during the seventeenth century, was that of a Dutch woman whose drunken and adulterous husband, in a fit of rage, wished she might 'beare the Devill of Hell'. Subsequently, the woman gave birth to a demonic creature, animalistic in form, with cloven feet and a bird-like face.[52] Another work, *The secret miracles of nature in four books*, argued that the

---

48   Bateman, *The doome warning all men*, p. 401.
49   Paré, *The workes of that famous chirurgion Ambrose Parey*, pp. 763–4.
50   Bateman, *The doome warning all men*, p. 401.
51   Anon, *Gods handy-vvorke in vvonders*, sig. A3.r
52   For accounts of the tale see *Ibid.,* sig. B1r–v.

mother's imagination could help to determine the gender or appearance of an unborn infant:

> ... for if she conceive in her mind, or do by chance fasten her eyes upon any object, and imprint that in her mind, the child commonly doth represent that in the outward parts ... For such is the power of imagination, that when the woman doth intentively behold any thing, she will produce something like that she beheld ... So if some of our women, seeing a Hare, bring forth a child with a hare-lip; so some children are born with flat Noses ... and ill shaped of all the body, because the woman when she conceived the child, and in the time she was big of it, had her eyes and mind busied upon some monstrous creature.[53]

Alexandra Walsham has argued that such stories reveal much about early modern fears and beliefs in the power of maternal fantasy, and the unstable and uncontrollable nature of the female mind.

Indeed, the connection between human shame and the spiritual status of the newly born seems to have been an extremely important segment of early modern beliefs surrounding pregnancy, childbirth and infancy. Furthermore, this aspect of understanding has been barely acknowledged by historical research. Such shame seemingly took many forms. In particular there were deeply inherent fears surrounding human physicality; the inheritance of sin from Adam and Eve, as described in Genesis, combined with a fear and mistrust of the female body. Alongside such views there existed a strong strand of belief which judged the human imagination to be immensely influential upon the physical state and moral wellbeing of an unborn baby. Through such beliefs we can trace traditional ideological beliefs mingled with limited medical understanding, to create a situation in which thoughts or figments of human imagination were believed to shape the physical and spiritual character of a child.

This placed infants and youths yet again at the heart of a central theological faultline of the period, revolving around questions of sin and salvation which

---

[53] Levinus Lemnius, *The secret miracles of nature in four books* (London, 1658) *Wing* L1044, pp. 10–11. This text also contains some interesting details on ideas surrounding conception and gender, arguing that, 'sometime when the mans seed falls on the left side of the womb that is ordian'd for the procreation of females, there will be something in it that is but half man, and will be fairer, and whiter, or smoother and less hairy than is convenient for a man to be, or the voice will be small, and sharp, or the chin will be bare and bald, and the courage will be lesse. Again, if the seed be cast into the right side of the womb, it may be a girle begotten; but because she is conceived in the place ordained for the male, she will ... [have] strong limbs, very tall, a swart countenance, a hairy chin, a ruder face, a strong voice, and a bold and man-like courage'.

were not easy to answer. Popular forms of literature, however exaggerated or untrustworthy, speak to the widely shared anxieties of the time: that children were vulnerable to sin, but also potentially carriers of divine judgement; that God's will was in action in the world; and that despite and because of their spiritually liminal status children might be a particularly potent focus of this agency. In this way, even the dehumanised monstrous births were gifted with a form of authority, tacitly condemning the spiritual failings of their supposed betters – but also, in the way of the children seeking revenge against murderers, able to reprove and rebalance the sins of the earthly world according to the demands of the standards of the heavenly one. Whether demoniac, prophet or monstrous birth, our children had, it seems, been loaned authority by God – and each in their own way, in narrative form or vivid parable, offered either consolatory or condemnatory signposting for vexed parents through the thickets of Reformed soteriology.

Chapter 7

Conclusion

To conclude, this book has contributed to and informed some of the most recent historiographical directions taken by early modern history, most especially the history of demonic possession and divine prophecy, the 'lived experience' of early modern religion and the history of childhood. *Children of Wrath* has drawn these three areas of historical interest together, to offer a scholarly exploration of the dialogue between each area of discourse.

Throughout this book we have witnessed the duality of early modern childhood, or at least the dual perceptions early modern people held towards children. We have considered the ideals of childhood and of parenthood, set out for parents to read in familial advice literature, and also what happened when these ideals potentially broke down. Indeed, as part of this process we have found that children, although often invisible within the literature from the early modern world, were not always silent. We can read about children in various texts from the period, but through the cases of demonic possession and divine prophecy explored here, we can witness children in something of a new light: we can 'hear' what were presented as their voices, their utterances and their responses. We can witness children imagined as often violently unquiet, vocally present. Whether or not the words of these children, as recorded in the texts, were true accounts of children's experiences and voices, or whether they were rather shaped by writers and publishers in a manner to fit or shape their audiences' preconceptions, does not alter the fact that these recurrent ideas and tropes provide a window through which to glimpse, at the very least, early modern perceptions of the young.

Through these instances of possession and prophecy, children are depicted shouting and writhing, sick and starving, in prayer and contemplation. We see them within their communities – alongside their parents, peers and elders, as such onlookers attempted various ways to normalise the children's behaviour. Yet, if we look a little more deeply into these events, as this book has done, we can see more than sick children, the possessed or (according to early modern perceptions) the spiritually afflicted – we can see more than children lying on their beds, praying for mercy or redemption. We can instead perceive such children under a peculiarly bright spotlight, as children at the centre of unfolding dramas, as key actors in these significant early modern events.

As has been explored, considering demonic possession, and even divine prophecy, as cases of unfolding drama is not new. Stephen Greenblatt, Clive Holmes and more recently Brian Levack have all considered the symbolic similarities between the staging of early modern possession cases and the early modern playhouse: possession cases were like dark and unfolding dramas, which grew out of the same period as playwrights such as Shakespeare and Marlowe.[1] Slightly seedy, yet enigmatic and captivating, these devilish and divine dramas held the focus of audiences, within families, communities, and on printed pages.

However, unlike previous studies on possession and prophecy cases, this book has considered the key actors within these events: the children. As has been explored, children commonly featured as either victims of demonic displeasure or agents of divine fingers at work within the world. Their smallness combined with spiritual naivety and emotional softness made them, early modern society believed, particularly prone, susceptible or vulnerable to the various aspects of the spiritual world. Whether or not the printed words on pages truly reflected the words and actions of the children involved in these narratives is not really the point of consideration here, but rather, what is most interesting is the fact that these texts featured children in these ways – that they produced and created the cultural space for children to exhibit these characteristics. No other historiographical work has considered such an aspect of early modern childhood – or at least, early modern perceptions and constructions of childhood.

With that in mind, then, if we look again at these cases – as this book has done – we see these child actors in positions of spiritual authority or even notoriety. Thomas Darling and Alexander Nyndge are able to play key roles in delivering themselves from the grasp of the Devil; like child prophets such as William Withers, they are spiritually adept and knowledgeable, reassuringly confident in their spiritual accomplishments, and thus, the reader is inclined to assume, confident of their salvation.[2]

One cannot underestimate the importance of such 'characters' within early modern culture. As has been considered throughout this work, the soteriological status of children was brought into question during the Reformation and post-Reformation periods, due to the doubt Protestant reforms placed on the efficacy of the baptismal blessing. No longer did the spiritual washing of the baptismal

---

[1]   Greenblatt, 'Shakespeare and the Exorcists'; Holmes, 'Witchcraft and Possession at the Accession of James I'; Levack, *The Devil Within*.

[2]   I.D., *The most wonderfull and true storie;* Nyndge, *A true and fearefull vexation;* Phillips, *The wonderfull worke of God.*

ceremony assure Christians in England (those who were loyal to the state Church, at least) of the spiritual safety of the souls of children. Infants and children, like all human souls, were hostage to the indeterminable will of God, through the doctrine of predestination. For early modern society, to contemplate the notion that infants and young children could be damned, regardless of whether or not they had been baptised, would have been most difficult. The children in these cases, with their spiritual heroics, provided comfort and assurance to a society which feared the awkward spiritual status of its young.

Recent historiography has put forward the notion that far from being something to fear, or to cause pastoral difficulties, the doctrine of predestination could actually provide comfort and assurance to believers – it was designed to prevent anxiety over the need to do good works, and placed emphasis on true faith, which those who felt themselves to be godly could profess and exhibit.[3] Nevertheless, as this work has argued, this was not necessarily the case for the young. Whereas the doctrine of predestination may have provided comfort to active believers, for parents of young children, whose offspring had not yet had the chance to learn about God or true faith, the potential soteriological destination of a child who died young was painfully ambiguous. Hence, the spiritual status of the early modern child was often confused and uncertain, and in the wake of the English Reformation became an issue of urgent interest.

Part of the response to such anxieties, as this work has considered, was for advice manuals to put forward the notion that salvation could be 'inherited' – by children from their godly parents. Another culturally adopted solution was the concept of the strong child, spiritually confident and uniquely in touch with the divine – young, godly and possessed. Of course, at the other end of the spiritual spectrum which involved this attempt to intuit a spiritual agency for the young was that they were also necessarily open to the temptations of the Devil: it was possible to be possessed by demons as much as it was by the Holy Spirit. This is perhaps why the children in both types of case act so similarly: ultimately, they are afflicted by the same closeness to the spiritual, regardless of which spirits choose to access them.

The attempted negotiation of the difficulties of Reformed theology, then, opened out a series of roles for children which became popularly understood – one assumes not just by the adult audiences of cheap print, but perhaps also by the children who began to exhibit their characteristics. That is, possession, prophecy and the children featured in these stories offer us a fascinating insight into the domestic piety of the period. Hence, as well as contributing to historiography on

---

3   See especially Dixon, *Practical Predestinarians* and Hunt, *The Art of Hearing*.

early modern possession and prophecy, and the connections between these two sets of ideas, this book has also added to recently scholarly work on the theme of Protestant religion as a 'lived experience'.

Taking all these things into account, it is perhaps surprising that the study of early modern childhood, and most especially the religious experiences of children, has been generally under-represented in the work of early modern scholars. This work contributes to recent explorations which have sought to address this historiographical gap. Works such as Hannah Newton's *The Sick Child* and Lucy Underwood's *Childhood, Youth and Religious Dissent* (which was going to print as this work was being finalised) – and now this present volume – have attempted to begin explorations into what it might have been like to be an early modern child, and how children experienced some of the most significant shifts and social upheavals in the early modern world – those centred around religious change.[4] This work has shown how great emphasis was placed on the words of children, and upon the origin of those words, whether they were believed to be demonic or divine – which in turn placed significant import and authority on this supposedly silent part of the community.

Children featured more prominently than we may have assumed in the lived experience of early modern religion, and could even become objects of spiritual fame and notoriety. Most significantly, despite the fact that early modern theology taught society about the inherent sinfulness of children, and that Protestant authorities as well as Puritan ministers adopted strict forms of religious education for the young, in practice the religious experiences of children were negotiated, with the help and commitment of adults. Far from simply being seen and not heard, or routinely cast into the mould of sinful child in need of education, children were rather listened to, guided, instructed and encouraged in their religious life and experiences.

---

[4]   Newton, *The Sick Child*; Underwood, *Childhood, Youth and Religious Dissent*.

Bibliography

Early Modern Printed Texts

Ainsworth, Henry, *A Seasonable, or, A Censure upon a dialogue of the Anabaptists intituled, A description of what God hath predestined concerning man* (London: 1651) *Wing* (2nd ed.) A813.

Barker, John, *The true description of a monsterous chylde, borne in the Ile of Wight* (London, 1564) *STC* (2nd ed.) 1422.

Bateman, Stephen, *The doome warning all men to the iudgemente wherein are contayned for the most parte all the straunge prodigies hapned in the worlde* (London, 1581) *STC* (2nd ed.)1582.

Bentley, Thomas, *The sixt lampe of virginitie conteining a mirrour for maidens and matrons* (London, 1582) *STC* (2nd ed.) 1894.

Chrysostom, John, *The disclosing of a late counterfeyted possession by the deuyl in two maydens* (London, 1574) *STC* (2nd ed.) 3738.

Church of England, *The booke of the common prayer and administration of the sacramentes* (London, 1549) *STC* (2nd ed.) 16270.

———— *The boke of common praier, and administracion of the sacramentes* (London, 1552) *STC* (2nd ed.) 16286.2.

———— *The booke of common praier, and administration of the sacramentes* (London, 1559) *STC* (2nd ed.) 16292.

Cleaver, Robert, *A godly forme of household* (London, 1603) *STC* (2nd ed.) 5385.

Darrell, John, *An apologie, or defence of the possession of William Somers, a yong man of Nottingham* (Amsterdam? 1599?) *STC* (2nd ed.) 6280.5.

———— *The replie of Iohn Darrell* (England? 'Imprinted by the English secret press', 1602) *STC* (2nd ed.) 6284.

Dent, Arthur, *A Pastime for parents; or A recreation to passe away the time, containing the most principall grounds of Christian religion* (London, 1609: Cf. first edition 1603) *STC* (2nd ed.) 6624.

Downame, John, *The Christian Warfare* (London, 1604) *STC* (2nd ed.) 7133.

Fleming, Abraham, *A straunge and terrible wunder wrought very late in the parish church of Bongay* (London, 1577) *STC* 11050.

Gifford, George, *A dialogue concerning witches and witchcraftes* (London, 1593) STC (2nd ed.) 11850.

A glasse for householders (London, 1542) *STC* (2nd ed.) 11917.

Gods handy-vvorke in vvonders miraculously shewen vpon two women, lately deliuered of two monsters (London, 1615) *STC* (2nd ed.) 11926.

Gouge, William, *Of Domesticall Duties, Eight Treatises* (London, 1622: Cf. first edition 1612) *STC* (2nd ed.) 12119.

H.B., *The true discripcion of a childe with ruffes borne in the parish of Micheham in the cou[n]tie of surrey* (London, 1566) *STC* (2nd ed.)1033.

Halewill, George, *An apologie of the povver and prouidence of God in the gouernment of the world* (Oxford, 1627) *STC* (2nd ed.) 12611.

Harsnett, Samuel, *A Declaration of egregious popish impostures* (London, 1603) *STC* (2nd ed.) 12880.

———— *A discouery of the fraudulent practises of Iohn Darrel* (London, 1599) *STC* (2nd ed.) 12883.

Hildersham, Arthur, *CLII Lectures vpon Psalme LI, preached at Ashby-Delazouch* (London: 1635) *STC* (2nd ed.) 13463.

The Horrible Murther of a young boy of three yeres of age, whose sister had her tongue cut out: and how it pleased God to reveale the offenders, by giving speech to the tongueles Childe (London, 1606) *STC* (2nd ed.) 6552.

I.D., *The most wonderfull and true storie, of a certain witch named Alse Gooderige* (London, 1597) *STC* (2nd ed.) 6170.7.

James I, King of England, *Daemonologie* (Edinburgh, 1603: Cf. first edition 1597) *STC* (2nd ed.) 14365.

Jocelin, Elizabeth, *The mothers legacie to her unborne childe* (London, 1635: Cf. first impression 1624) *STC* (2nd ed.) 14625.7.

Jorden, Edward, *A briefe discovrse of disease called the suffocation of the mother* (London, 1603) *STC* (2nd ed.) 14790.

L.P., *strange and wonderfull news of a woman which lived neer unto the famous city of London who had her head torn off her body by the divell* (London, 1630) *STC* (2nd ed.) 20322.3.

Latimer, Hugh, *27 sermons preached by the ryght reuerende father in God ... maister Hugh Latimer* (London, 1562) *STC* (2nd ed.) 15276.

Leigh, Dorothy, *The mothers blessing, Or the godly counsaile of a gentle-woman not long since deceased, left behind for her children* (London, 1616) *STC* (2nd ed.) 15402.

———— *The mothers blessing, Or the godly counsaile of a gentle-woman not long since deceased, left behind for her children* (London, 1627: Cf. first edition 1616) *STC* (2nd ed.) 15405.

Lemnius, Levinus, *The secret miracles of nature in four books: learnedly and moderately treating of generation, and the parts thereof, the soul and its immortality, of plants and of living creatures, of diseases, their symptoms and cures, and many other rarities* (London, 1658) *Wing* (2nd ed.) L1044.

Loyer, Pierre, *A treatise of spectres or straunge sights, visions and apparitions* (London, 1605) *STC* (2nd ed.) 15448.

Magomastix, Hieronymus, *The strange vvitch at Greenvvich, (ghost, spirit or hobgoblin) haunting a wench* (London, 1650) *Wing* (2nd ed) S5920.

Merbecke, John, *A booke of notes and common places* (London, 1581) *STC* (2nd ed.) 17299.

Moore, Mary, *Wonderfull newes from the north* (London, 1650) *Wing* (2nd ed.) M2581.

More, George, *A true discourse concerning the certaine possession and dispossession of 7 persons in one familie in Lancashire* (Middelburg, 1600) *STC* (2nd ed.) 18070.

Morton, Richard, *Phthisiologia or, A Treatise of consumptions* (London, 1694) *Wing* (2nd ed.) M2830.

The most Cruell and Bloody Murther committed by an Inkeepers wife, called Annis Dell, and her sonne George Dell (1606) *STC* (2nd ed.) 6553.

A most horrible & detestable murther committed by a bloudie minded man vpon his ovvne vvife and most strangely reuealed by his childe that was vnder fiue yeares of age (London, 1595) *STC* (2nd ed.) 17748.

The most strange and admirable discouerie of the three witches of Warboys (London? 1593) *STC* (2nd ed.) 25019.

Nyndge, Edward, *A booke declaringe the fearfull vexasion, of one Alexander Nyndge. Beynge most horriblye tormented wyth an euyll spirit In the yere 1573* (London: 1573) *STC* (2nd ed.) 18752.

——— *A true and fearefvll vexation of one Alexander Nyndge being most horribly tormented with the deuill* (London, 1615: Cf. first edition 1573) *STC* (2nd ed.) 18753.

The office of Christian parents shewing how children are to be gouerned throughout all ages and times of their life (Cambridge, 1616) *STC* (2nd ed.) 3180.

Paré, Ambrose, *The workes of that famous chirurgion Ambrose Parey translated out of Latine and compared with the French* (London, 1643) *STC* (2nd ed.) 19189.

Perkins, William, *Christian oeconomie, or, A short survey of the right manner of erecting and ordering a familie according to the Scriptures* (London, 1609) *STC* (2nd ed.) 19677.3.

———— *A Discovrse of the damned art of witchcraft*, (Cambridge, 1608) *STC* (2nd edn.) 19697.

Phillips, John, *The examination and confession of certaine wytches at Chensforde* (London, 1566) *STC* (2nd ed.) 19869.5.

———— *The wonderfull worke of God shewed vpon a chylde whose name is William Withers, being in the towne of Walsham, within the countie of Suffolke* (London, 1581) STC (2nd ed.) 19877.

Price, Sampson, *The Two Twins of Birth and Death* (1624) *STC* (2nd ed.) 20334.

R.B., *The boy of Bilson: or, A true discouery of the late notorious impostures of certaine Romish priests in their pretended exorcism* (London, 1622) STC (2nd ed.) 1185.

Rhegius, Urbanus, *An homely or sermon of good and euill angels* (London, 1593: Cf. first edition 1583) *STC* (2nd ed.) 20846.

Schlichtenberger, Eyriak, *A prophecie vttered by the daughter of an honest countrey man* (London, 1580) *STC* (2nd ed.) 21818.

Scot, Reginald, *The discouerie of witchcraft* (London, 1584) *STC* (2nd ed.) 21864.

To Sions Virgins: or A Short Forme of Catechisme of the Doctrine of Baptisme (London, 1644) *Wing* (2nd ed.) T1385.

Swan, John, *A true and briefe report of Mary Glouers vexation and of her deliuerance by the means of fasting and prayer* (London, 1603) STC (2nd ed.) 23517.

T.I., *A miracle, of miracles ... Also a prophesie reuealed by a poore countrey maide* (London, 1614) *STC* (2nd ed.) 14068.

The true description of two monstrous chyldren borne at Herne in Kent (London, 1565) *STC* (2nd ed.) 6774.

A true relation of the birth of three monsters in the city of Namen n. Flanders, as also Gods judgement vpon an vnnaturall sister of the poore womans, mother of these abortiue children (London, 1609) *STC* (2nd ed) 18347.5.

The true reporte of the forme and shape of a monstrous childe, borne at Muche Horkesleye a village about three myles from Colchester, in the countie of Essex (London, 1562) *STC* (2nd ed.) 12207.

Wanley, Nathaniel, *The Wonders of the Little World* (London, 1673) *Wing* (2nd ed.) W709.

Whitford, Richard, *A werke for housholders* (London, 1530) *STC* (2nd ed.) 25425.

Wilburn, Percival, *A checke or reproofe of M. Howlets vntimely shreeching in her maiesties eares* (London, 1581) *STC* (2nd ed.) 25586.

Winthrop, John, *A short story of the rise, reign, and ruin of the 'Antinomians', Familists and Libertines, that infected the Churches of Nevv England* (London, 1644) *Wing* 3095B.

The wonderfull works of God (London, 1641) *Wing* (2nd ed.) W3377.

Transcriptions of Primary Sources

Adams, Thomas, 'The White Devil: or the Hypocrite Uncased' (1612), printed in Martin Seymour-Smith (ed.) *The English Sermon, 1550–1650: Volume I* (Cheshire: Carcanet Press, 1976).

Anderson, R.C. (ed.), *The Book of Examinations and Depositions, 1627–1634*, Publications of the Southampton Record Society 31 (Southampton, 1931).

Augustine, *Concerning the City of God against the Pagans*, trans. Henry Bettenson (London: Penguin, 1984).

Becon, Thomas, *The Catechism of Thomas Becon, Parker Society* (ed.) John Ayre (Cambridge: Cambridge University Press, 1844).

Bullinger, Heinrich, *The Decades of Henry Bullinger, The Fourth Decade, The Parker Society*, (ed.) Thomas Harding (Cambridge: Cambridge University Press, 1851).

Calvin, Jean, (ed.) John Baillie, John T. McNiell and Henry P. Van Dusen, *Library of Christian Classics; Calvin, Institutes of the Christian Religion*, vol. 2 (London: SMC Press, 1961).

Chaucer, Geoffrey, *The Prioress's Tale*, (ed.) A.C. Cawley, 'The Canterbury Tales' (London: J.M. Dent, 1996).

Dee, John, *John Dee's Library Catalogue*, (ed.) Julian Roberts and Andrew G. Watson (London Bibliographical Society, 1990).

Donne, John, 'A Sermon, Preached at a Christening, on Ephesians 5.25, 26, 27', (ed.) George R. Potter and Evelyn M. Simpson, *The Sermons of John Donne, Vol. 5* (Berkeley and Los Angeles: University of California Press, 1959).

Goodwin, Thomas, *The Works of Thomas Goodwin, Sometime President of Magdalene College, Oxford*, Vol. 2 (Edinburgh: James Nichol, 1861).

Gough Nichols, John (ed.), *King Henry VIII's Proclamation against Holy Innocent's festivities, The Camden Miscellany, 7th volume*. M.DCCC. LXXV.1, Introduction by Edward F. Rimbault.

——— (ed.), 'Two Sermons Preached by the Boy-Bishop', The Camden Miscellany, 7th volume. M.DCCC.LXXV.1, Introduction by Edward F. Rimbault.

Secondary Sources

Alford, Stephen, *Kingship and Politics in the Reign of Edward VI* (Cambridge: Cambridge University Press, 2002).

Almond, Philip C., *Demonic possession and exorcism in early modern England: contemporary texts and their cultural contexts* (Cambridge: Cambridge University Press, 2004).

Anglo, Sydney, *The Damned Art: Essays in the Literature of Witchcraft* (London: Routledge and Kegan Paul, 1977).

Ariès, Philippe, *Centuries of Childhood* (London: Penguin, 1960).

Avery, Gillian, and Kimberly Reynolds, *Representations of Childhood Death* (London: Macmillan Press, 2000).

Baker, Ian S., 'Do ghosts exist? A summary of parapsychological research into apparitional experiences', in John Newton (ed.), *Early Modern Ghosts, Proceedings of the Early Modern Ghosts conference* (Centre for Seventeenth-Century Studies, University of Durham, 2002).

Bardsley, Sandy, 'Sin, Speech, and Scolding in Late Medieval England' in Thelma Fenster and Daniel Lord Smail (eds), *FAMA: The Politics of Talk and Reputation in Medieval Europe* (Ithaca and London: Cornell University Press, 2003).

Baun, Jane, 'The Fate of Babies Dying Before Baptism in Byzantium', in Diana Wood (ed.), *Studies in Church History, 31, The Church and Childhood, Papers Read at the 1993 Summer Meeting and the 1994 Winter Meeting of the Ecclesiastical History Society* (Oxford: Blackwell, 1994).

Beyer, Jürgen, 'Lutheran Popular Prophets in the Sixteenth and Seventeenth Centuries: the performance of untrained speakers', ARV Nordic Yearbook of Folklore, 51 (1995).

——— 'A Lübeck Prophet in Local and Lutheran Context', in Bob Scribner and Trevor Roper (eds), *Popular Religion in Germany and Central Europe, 1400–1800* (Macmillan, London, 1996).

Bloch, Marc, and S. Guggenheim, 'Compadrazgo, Baptism and the Symbolism of a Second Birth', in *Man* 16 (1980).

Bradshaw, Christopher, 'David or Josiah? Old Testament Kings as Exemplars in Edwardian Religious Polemic', in Bruce Gordon (ed.), *Protestant History and Identity in Sixteenth-Century Europe, Vol. II, The Later Reformation* (Hants: Aldershot, 1996).

Brigden, Susan, 'Youth and the English Reformation', reprinted from *Past and Present* (95) 1982 in Peter Marshall (ed.), *The Impact of the English Reformation 1500–1640* (London, Arnold, 1997).

Briggs, K.M., *The Anatomy of Puck, An Examination of Fairy Beliefs among Shakespeare's Contemporaries and Successors* (London: Routledge and Kegan Paul, 1959).

Bronfen, Elisabeth, *Over Her Dead Body: Death, Femininity and the Aesthetic* (Manchester: Manchester University Press, 1992).

Brown, Sylvia (ed.) *Women's Writing in Stuart England, The Mothers' Legacies of Dorothy Leigh, Elizabeth Joscelin and Elizabeth Richardson* (Stroud: Sutton Publishing, 1999).

Brownlow, F.W., *Shakespeare, Harsnett, and the Devils of Denham* (Newark: University of Delaware Press, 1993).

Burke, Peter, *Popular Culture in Early Modern Europe* (London: Temple Smith, 1978).

Canepa, Nancy, *Out of the Woods: the origins of the literary fairy tale in Italy and France* (Wayne State University Press, 1997).

———— *From Court to Forest: Giambattista Basile's 'La Cunto De Li Cunti' and the Birth of the Literary Fairy Tale* (Wayne State University Press, 1999).

Christian, William A. Jr, *Apparitions in Late Medieval and Renaissance Spain* (Princeton University Press, Princeton, New Jersey, 1981).

Clark, Stuart, *Thinking with Demons* (Oxford and New York: Oxford University Press, 1997).

———— (ed.), *Languages of Witchcraft: Narrative, Ideology and Meaning in Early Modern Culture* (Hampshire and London: Macmillan, 2001).

Cohn, Norman, *Europe's Inner Demons: The demonization of Christians in medieval Christendom* (London: Pimlico, 1993).

Collinson, Patrick, *The Elizabethan Puritan Movement* (London: Cape, 1967).

———— *The Religion of Protestants: the Church in English Society, 1559–1625* (Oxford: Oxford University Press, 1982).

———— *The Birthpangs of Protestant England: Religious and Cultural Change in the Sixteenth and Seventeenth Centuries* (Basingstoke: Macmillan, 1988).

———— *Richard Bancroft and Elizabethan Anti-Puritanism* (Cambridge: Cambridge University Press, 2013).

Coster, Will, 'From Fire and Water, the Responsibilities of Godparents in Early Modern England', in Diana Wood (ed.), *Studies in Church History: Church and Childhood* 31 (1994) 301–12.

———— 'Purity, Profanity and Puritanism: the Churching of Women, 1500–1700', in W. Sheils and D. Wood (eds), *Studies in Church History: Women in The Church* 27 (1994) 377–87.

———— '"Tokens of Innocence:" Infant Baptism, Death and Burial in Early Modern England', in B. Gordon and P. Marshall (eds), *The Place of the*

Dead in Late Medieval and Early Modern Europe (Cambridge University Press, 2001).

———— *Baptism and Spiritual Kinship in Early Modern England* (Farnham: Ashgate, 2002).

Coster, Will, and Andrew Spicer (eds), *Sacred Space in Early Modern Europe* (Cambridge: Cambridge University Press, 2005).

Craig, John, 'Psalms, groans and dogwhippers: the soundscape of worship in the English parish church, 1547–1642', in Will Coster and Andrew Spicer (eds), *Sacred Space in Early Modern Europe* (Cambridge: Cambridge University Press, 2005).

Cressy, David, *Birth, Marriage and Death: Ritual, Religion, and the Life-Cycle in Tudor and Stuart England* (Oxford: Oxford University Press, 1997).

Cunningham, Hugh, *Children and Childhood in Western Society Since 1500* (London: Longman, 1995).

Darnton, Robert, *The Great Cat Massacre, and Other Episodes in French Cultural History* (London: Penguin, 1984).

Dixon, Leif, *Practical Predestinarians in England, c. 1590–1640* (Surrey: Ashgate, 2014).

Duffy, Eamon, *The Stripping of the Altars: Tradition Religion in England 1400–1580* (Yale University Press, 1992).

Durston, Christopher, and Jacqueline Eales, *The Culture of English Puritanism, 1560–1700* (Basingstoke, New York: Palgrave Macmillan, 1996).

Ellis, F.S. (ed.) *The Golden Legend, or lives of the Saints* (London: The Temple Classics, 1900).

Esdaile, Katharine A., *English Monumental Sculpture Since the Renaissance* (London: Society for Promoting Christian Knowledge; New York and Toronto: Macmillan, 1927).

Fenster, Thelma and Daniel Lord Smail, *FAMA: The Politics of Talk and Reputation in Medieval Europe* (Ithaca and London: Cornell University Press, 2003).

Fletcher, Anthony, 'Prescription and Practice: Protestantism and the Upbringing of Children, 1560–1700', in Diana Wood (ed.), *Studies in Church History, 31, The Church and Childhood, Papers Read at the 1993 Summer Meeting and the 1994 Winter Meeting of the Ecclesiastical History Society* (Oxford: Blackwell, 1994) 325–46,

Forster, Marc R. and Benjamin J. Kaplan (eds), *Piety and Family in Early Modern Europe: Essays in Honour of Steven Ozment* (Farnham: Ashgate, 2005).

Fox, Adam, and Daniel Woolf, *The Spoken Word, oral culture in Britain 1500–1850* (Manchester and New York: Manchester University Press, 2002).

Freeman, Thomas, 'Demons, Deviance and Defiance: John Darrell and the Politics of Exorcism in late Elizabethan England', in Peter Lake and Michael Questier (eds), *Conformity and Orthodoxy in the English Church, c. 1560–1660* (Woodbridge: Boydell Press, 2000).

French, Anna, 'Possession, Puritanism and Prophecy: Child Demoniacs and English Reformed Culture', *Reformation* 13, (2008).

——— 'Raising Christian Children in Early Modern England: Salvation, Education and the Family', *Theology* 116 (2) (2013).

——— 'Disputed Words and Disputed Meanings: The Reformation of Baptism, Infant Limbo and Child Salvation in Early Modern England', in Jonathan Willis (ed.), *Sin and Salvation in Early Modern England* (Forthcoming, Farnham: Ashgate, 2015).

Gammon, Vic, 'Child Death in British and North American Ballads from the Sixteenth to the Twentieth Centuries', in Gillian Avery and Kimberly Reynolds, *Representations of Childhood Death* (Macmillan Press, 2000, London).

Gennep, Arnold Van, *The Rites of Passage* (London: Routledge & Kegan Paul, 1960).

Gibson, Marion, *Possession, Puritanism and Print: Darrell, Harsnett, Shakespeare and the Elizabethan Exorcism Controversy* (London: Pickering and Chatto, 2006).

Gittings Clare, *Death, Burial and the Individual in Early Modern England* (London: Routledge, 1988).

Gordon, Bruce (ed.), *Protestant History and Identity in Sixteenth-Century Europe, Vol. II, The Later Reformation* (Hants: Aldershot, 1996).

——— 'Malevolent ghosts and ministering angels: apparitions and pastoral care in the Swiss Reformation', in Bruce Gordon and Peter Marshall (eds), *The Place of the Dead, Death and Remembrance in Late Medieval and Early Modern Europe* (Cambridge: Cambridge University Press, 2000).

Gordon, Bruce, and Peter Marshall (eds), *The Place of the Dead, Death and Remembrance in Late Medieval and Early Modern Europe* (Cambridge: Cambridge University Press, 2000).

Green, Ian, 'For Children in Yeeres and Children in Understanding, the Emergence of the English Catechism under Elizabeth and the Early Stuarts', *Journal of Ecclesiastical History* 37 (1986) 397–425.

——— *The Christian's ABC: Catechism and Catechizing in England c. 1530–1740* (Oxford: Clarendon, 1996).

Greenblatt, Stephen, 'Shakespeare and the Exorcists', in *Shakespearean Negotiations* (Berkeley and Los Angeles, University of California Press, 1988).

Griffiths, Paul, *Youth and Authority, Formative Experiences in England, 1560–1640* (Oxford: Clarendon Press, 1996).

Griffiths, Paul, Adam Fox and Steve Hindle, *The Experience of Authority in Early Modern England* (London: Macmillan, 1996).

Haigh, Christopher, 'The Recent Historiography of the English Reformation', *Historical Journal* 25 (1982) 19–33.

––––––– 'Success and Failure in the English Reformation', *Past and Present* 172 (2001) 28–49.

Hardman Moore, Susan, '"Such perfecting of praise out of the mouth of a babe": Sarah Wright as Child Prophet', in Diana Wood (ed.), *Studies in Church History, 31, The Church and Childhood, Papers Read at the 1993 Summer Meeting and the 1994 Winter Meeting of the Ecclesiastical History Society* (Oxford: Blackwell, 1994) 313–24.

Holmes, Clive, 'Witchcraft and Possession at the Accession of James I: the publication of Samuel Harsnett's "A Declaration of Egregious Popish Impostures"', in John Newton (ed.), *Witchcraft and the Act of 1604* (Leiden, Boston: Brill, 2008).

Houlbrooke, Ralph, *The English Family, 1450–1700* (London: Longman, 1984).

––––––– *Death, Religion and the Family in England, 1480–1750* (Oxford: Oxford Studies in Social History, 1998).

Hunt, Arnold, *The Art of Hearing; English Preachers and Their Audiences, 1590–1640* (Cambridge: Cambridge University Press, 2010).

Hutton, Ronald, *The Rise and Fall of Merry England: The Ritual Year, 1400–1700* (Oxford: Oxford University Press, 1994).

––––––– 'The English Reformation and the Evidence of Folklore', *Past and Present* 148 (1995) 89–116.

Jackson, Kenneth, *The Gregynog Lectures 1961; The International Popular Tale and Early Welsh Tradition* (Cardiff: University of Wales Press, 1961).

Johnstone, Nathan, *The Devil in English Culture c.1549–c.1660* (University of Kent at Canterbury, 2000, unpublished PhD thesis, held at the British Library).

––––––– 'The Protestant Devil: the Experience of Temptation in Early Modern England', *Journal of British Studies* 43 (April 2004) 173–205.

––––––– *The Devil and Demonism in Early Modern England* (Cambridge: Cambridge University Press, 2006).

Joyce, Patrick, *Democratic Subjects, The Self and the Social in Nineteenth-Century England* (Cambridge: Cambridge University Press, 1994).

Karant-Nunn, Susan, *The Reformation of Ritual: An Interpretation of Early Modern Germany* (Abingdon: Routledge 1997).

————— *The Reformation of Feeling: Shaping the Religious Emotions in Early Modern Germany* (Oxford: Oxford University Press, 2010).

Lake, Peter, *Moderate Puritans and the Elizabethan Church* (Cambridge University Press, 1982).

————— 'Deeds against Nature: Cheap Print, Protestantism and Murder in Early Seventeenth Century England', in Kevin Sharpe and Peter Lake (eds), *Culture and Politics in Early Stuart England* (Basingstoke: Macmillan, 1994).

————— *The Antichrist's Lewd Hat: Protestants, Papists and Players in Post-Reformation England* (New Haven and London: Yale University Press, 2002).

Lake, Peter, and Michael Questier (eds), *Conformity and Orthodoxy in the English Church, c. 1560–1660* (Woodbridge: Boydell Press, 2000).

Levack, Brian, *The Devil Within: Possession and Exorcism in the Christian West* (New Haven: Yale University Press, 2013).

Llewellyn, Nigel, '"[An] Impe entombed here doth lie": the Besford Triptych and Child Memorials in Post-Reformation England', in Gillian Avery and Kimberly Reynolds (eds), *Representations of Childhood Death* (Macmillan Press, 2000, London).

MacCulloch, Diarmaid, *Tudor Church Militant* (London: Allen Lane, 1999).

————— *The Boy King: Edward VI and the Protestant Reformation* (London: Palgrave, 2001).

————— *The Later reformation in England, 1547–1603* (London: Palgrave, 2nd edn, 2001).

————— *Reformation, Europe's House Divided 1490–1700* (London: Penguin, 2004).

Macfarlane, Allan, *Witchcraft in Tudor and Stuart England: A regional and comparative study* (London: Routledge, 1999 edn).

Maltby, Judith, *Prayer Book and People in Elizabethan and Early Stuart England* (Cambridge: Cambridge University Press, 1998).

Marsh, Christopher, *Popular Religion in Sixteenth-Century England: Holding their Peace* (Basingstoke: Macmillan, 1998).

Marshall, Peter (ed.), *The Impact of the English Reformation 1500–1640* (London: Arnold, 1997).

————— '"The map of God's word": geographies of the afterlife in Tudor and early Stuart England', in Bruce Gordon and Peter Marshall (eds), *The Place of the Dead, Death and Remembrance in Late Medieval and Early Modern Europe* (Cambridge University Press, 2000).

————— *Beliefs and the Dead in Reformation England* (Oxford University Press, 2002).

————— *Reformation England, 1480–1642* (London: Hodder Arnold, 2003).

Marshall, Peter, and Alexandra Walsham, *Angels in the Early Modern World* (Cambridge: Cambridge University Press, 2006).

Martin, Jessica and Alec Ryrie, *Private and Domestic Devotion in Early Modern Britain* (Farnham: Ashgate, 2012).

Maxwell Stuart, P.G., *Satan's Conspiracy, Magic and Witchcraft in Sixteenth-Century Scotland* (East Lothian: Tuckwell Press, 2001).

McGrath, Alister, *Reformation Thought, an Introduction* (Cambridge: Blackwell Press, 1999).

Mears, Natalie and Alec Ryrie (eds), *Worship and the Parish Church in Early Modern Britain* (Farnham: Ashgate, 2013).

Murphy, Terence R., '"Woful Childe of Parents Rage": Suicide of Children and Adolescents in Early Modern England, 1505–1710', *The Sixteenth Century Journal*, Vol. XVII (Issue 3) (Fall 1986) 259–70.

Naphy, William G. and Penny Roberts, *Fear in Early Modern Society* (Manchester and New York: Manchester University Press, 1997).

Newton, Hannah, *The Sick Child in Early Modern England* (Oxford: Oxford University Press, 2012).

Newton, John (ed.), *Early Modern Ghosts; Proceedings of the 'Early Modern Ghosts' conference held at St. John's College, Durham on 24th March 2001* (Durham: Centre for Seventeenth Century Studies, University of Durham, 2002).

——— (ed.), *Witchcraft and the Act of 1604* (Leiden, Boston: Brill, 2008).

O'Day, Rosemary, *Education and Society 1500–1800; The Social Foundations of Education in Early Modern Britain* (London: Longman, 1982).

Oldridge, Darren, *The Devil in Early Modern England* (Stroud: Sutton, 2000).

——— (ed.), *The Witchcraft Reader* (London and New York: Routledge, 2002).

Orme, Nicholas, *Education and Society in Medieval and Renaissance England* (London, Hambledon Press, 1989).

Purkiss, Diane, 'Sounds of Silence: Fairies and Incest in Scottish Witchcraft Stories', in Stuart Clark (ed.), *Languages of Witchcraft: Narrative, Ideology and Meaning in Early Modern Culture* (Hampshire and London: Macmillan, 2001).

Putnam Demos, John, *Entertaining Satan, witchcraft and the culture of early New England* (New York and Oxford: Oxford University Press, 1982).

Roper, Lyndal, *Oedipus and the Devil, witchcraft, sexuality and religion in early modern Europe* (London and New York: Routledge, 1994, 1995 edn).

——— '"Evil Imaginings and Fantasies": Child-witches and the end of the Witch-Craze', *Past and Present*, Vol. 167 (2000) 107–139.

——— *Witch Craze, Terror and Fantasy in Baroque Germany* (New Haven and London: Yale University Press, 2004).

Ryrie, Alec, *The Gospel and Henry VIII, Evangelicals in the Early English Reformation* (Cambridge: Cambridge University Press, 2003).

——— *Being Protestant in Reformation Britain* (Oxford: Oxford University Press, 2013).

Sangha, Laura, *Angels and Belief in England 1480–1700* (London: Pickering and Chatto, 2012).

Schofield, Roger, 'Did the Mothers Really Die? Three Centuries of Maternal Mortality in "The World we have Lost"', in Lloyd Bonfield, Richard M. Smith and Keith Wrightson (eds), *The World We Have Gained: Histories of Population and Social Structure* (Oxford: Blackwell, 1986).

Scott, James C., *Domination and the Arts of Resistance: Hidden Transcripts* (New Haven, London: Yale University Press, 1990).

Scribner, Bob and Trevor Roper (eds), *Popular Religion in Germany and Central Europe, 1400–1800* (Macmillan, London, 1996).

Sharpe, James, *Crime in Early Modern England, 1550–1750* (London: Longman, 1984).

——— 'Disruption in the well-ordered Household: Age, Authority and Possessed Young People', in Paul Griffiths, Adam Fox and Steve Hindle (eds), *The Experience of Authority in Early Modern England* (London: Macmillan, 1996).

——— *Instruments of Darkness: Witchcraft in England 1550–1750* (London: Hamish Hamilton, 1996).

——— *The Bewitching of Anne Gunter, a Horrible and True Story of Deceptions, Witchcraft, Murder, and the King of England* (New York: Routledge, 1999, 2001 edn).

Sharpe, Kevin, *Selling the Tudor Monarchy: Authority and Image in Sixteenth-Century England* (London: Yale University Press, 2008).

Sharpe, Kevin, and Peter Lake, *Culture and Politics in Early Stuart England* (Macmillan, 1994).

Shepard, Alexandra, *Meanings of Manhood in Early Modern England* (Oxford: Oxford University Press, 2003).

Simpson, Jacqueline, 'The Folklore of Infant Deaths: Burials, Ghosts and Changelings', in Gillian Avery and Kimberly Reynolds (eds), *Representations of Childhood Death* (London: Macmillan, 2000).

Somers, Margaret R., and Gloria D. Gibson, 'Reclaiming the Epistemological "Other": Narrative and the Social Constitution of Identity', in Craig Calhoun (ed.), *Social Theory and the Politics of Identity* (Oxford: Blackwell, 1994).

Sommerville, C. John, *The Discovery of Childhood in Puritan England* (Athens and London: The University of Georgia Press, 1992).

Stone, Lawrence, *The Family, Sex and Marriage in England, 1500–1800* (London: Penguin, 1977).

Thomas, Keith, *Religion and the Decline of Magic* (London: Penguin, 1971, 1991 edn).

——— 'Age and Authority in Early Modern England', in *Proceedings of the British Academy*, Volume LXII (1976) 205–48.

Todd, Margo, *Christian Humanism and the Puritan Social Order* (Cambridge: Cambridge University Press, 1987).

——— *The Culture of Scottish Protestantism* (New Haven, London: Yale University Press, 2002).

Toolan, Michael J., *Narrative, A Critical Linguistic Introduction* (London and New York: Routledge, 1988).

Trexter, Richard C. 'Ritual in Florence: Adolescence and Salvation in the Renaissance', in Charles Trinkhaus and Heiko A. Oberman (eds), *The Pursuit of Holiness in Late Medieval and Renaissance Religion* (Leiden: Brill, 1974).

Trinkhaus, Charles and Heiko A. Oberman (eds), *The Pursuit of Holiness in Late Medieval and Renaissance Religion* (Leiden: Brill, 1974).

Underwood, Lucy, *Childhood, Youth and Religious Dissent in Post Reformation England* (London: Palgrave, 2014).

Walker, D.P., *Unclean Spirits, Possession and Exorcism in France and England in the late Sixteenth and early Seventeenth Centuries* (London: Scolar Press, 1981).

Walsham, Alexandra, '"Out of the Mouths of Babes and Sucklings": Prophecy, Puritanism and Childhood in Elizabethan Suffolk', in Diana Wood (ed.), *The Church and Childhood, the Ecclesiastical History Society, Vol. 31* (Oxford: Blackwell, 1994) 285–300.

——— *Providence in Early Modern England* (Oxford: Oxford University Press, 1999).

——— 'Reformed folklore? Cautionary tales and oral tradition in early modern England', in Adam Fox and Daniel Woolf (eds), *The Spoken Word, Oral Culture in Britain 1500–1850* (Manchester and New York: Manchester University Press, 2002).

Warner, Marina, *From the Beast to the Blonde* (London: Chatto and Windus, 1994).

——— *No Go the Bogeyman, Scaring, Lulling, and Making Mock* (London: Chatto and Windus, 1998).

Watt, Tessa, *Cheap Print and Popular Piety, 1500–1640* (Cambridge: Cambridge University Press, 1991).

Willis, Jonathan, *Church Music and Protestantism in Post-Reformation England: Discourses, Sites and Identities* (Farnham: Ashgate, 2010).

Wood, Diana (ed.), *Studies in Church History, 31, The Church and Childhood, Papers Read at the 1993 Summer Meeting and the 1994 Winter Meeting of the Ecclesiastical History Society* (Oxford: Blackwell, 1994).

Electronic Sources

Early English Books Online, Chadwyck Healey, 2003–2015 [http://eebo.chad wyck.com]

Oxford Dictionary of National Biography, Oxford University Press, 2004–2015 [http://www.oxforddnb.com]

Index